Boys, Bodies, and Physical Education

Using visual ethnography, this book explores the many forms of pleasures that boys derive in and through the spaces and their bodies in physical education. Employing the works of Michel Foucault and Judith Butler, Gerdin examines how pleasure is connected to identity, schooling and power relations and demonstrates how discourses of sport, fitness, health and masculinity work together to produce a variety of pleasurable experiences. At the same time, the book provides a critique of such pleasurable experiences within physical education by illustrating how these pleasures can still, for some boys, quickly turn into displeasures and can be associated with exclusion, humiliation, bullying and homophobia.

Boys, Bodies, and Physical Education argues that pleasure can be seen as an educational and productive practice in physical education but also a constraint that both engenders and privileges some boys over others as well as (re)producing narrow and limited conceptions of masculinity and pleasures for *all* boys. This book works to problematise these pleasures and their articulations with gender, bodies and spaces.

Göran Gerdin is Senior Lecturer of Physical Education and Sport at Linnaeus University, Sweden.

Routledge Critical Studies in Gender and Sexuality in Education

Series Editors: Wayne Martino, Emma Renold, Goli Rezai-Rashti, Jessica Ringrose and Nelson Rodriguez

Boys, Bodies, and Physical Education

Problematizing Identity, Schooling, and Power Relations through a Pleasure Lens

Göran Gerdin

Routledge
Taylor & Francis Group

LONDON AND NEW YORK

First published 2017 by Routledge

2 Park Square, Milton Park, Abingdon, Oxfordshire OX14 4RN
52 Vanderbilt Avenue, New York, NY 10017

Routledge is an imprint of the Taylor & Francis Group, an informa business

First issued in paperback 2018

Library of Congress Cataloguing-in-Publication Data
A catalog record for this book has been requested.

ISBN: 978-1-138-64997-2 (hbk)
ISBN: 978-0-367-19521-2 (pbk)

Typeset in Sabon
by Apex CoVantage, LLC

I dedicate this book to my three children, Oskar, Charlie and Olivia, may your lives be filled with pleasures and happiness, surrounded by great friends and family!

Contents

Preface

School physical education (PE)[1] continues to be critiqued for making ene-
mies with young people and having a negative impact on their lifelong physical activity habits and health (e.g., Engström, 2008; Tinning, 2010). It is
in particular the competitive and at times aggressive nature of PE built on
dominant notions of sport and masculinity (e.g., Azzarito & Hill, 2013;
Hickey, 2008) that is said to marginalise both girls and boys. Yet in my
ongoing research with boys, I have found that the majority enjoy participating in PE and even regard this as their favourite school subject.

So if most boys seem to enjoy PE, (why) is there a need to change it?
My response to this question in this book is to use a pleasure lens to interrogate what it is that these boys find pleasurable and why. In other words,
how are these pleasures produced, and what power relations do they constitute? I will argue that, yes, in one sense PE is enjoyable for many boys
because they learn how to perform gender in a way that aligns with stereotypical ideas about masculinity, sport, fitness and health. Although they are
deriving pleasure from such performances, they can also be seen to become
restricted in their way of embodying masculinities that simultaneously alien-
ate those boys who are not able or willing to live up to these notions. In this
way, PE is not only failing to make this subject more inclusive for everyone
but also failing to teach and promote a diversity of embodied masculinities
and movement pleasures.

However, at this juncture of the book, given that I cannot speak for
everyone else, I will provide an account of how my own conceptualisations
of sport, PE, masculinity and being gendered have been shaped by external
forces and developed over time. I believe that this form of researcher reflexivity (Alvesson & Sköldberg, 2000) is of particular importance because in
the study reported on in this book, I can be considered as the main 'research
instrument' (Hammersley & Atkinson, 1983), and therefore it is vital for
the reader to know the origins of my understanding.

Throughout my childhood and teenage years, I was actively involved in
a range of sports, including table tennis, swimming, soccer, golf and tennis,
which enabled me to create a sense of self as closely connected with sport.
It was especially tennis that I excelled in and that was going to form an

important part of my identity. With this came various sorts of privileges; for instance, I was often away from school playing tournaments and was allowed time off during school hours for practice. In terms of PE, it meant getting the highest mark possible (even though I probably did not deserve it) merely because of my national ranking in the sport. However, in my home country, Sweden, tennis is not considered a 'real' man's sport the way, for instance, ice hockey and soccer are, which meant that my gendered identity was created to some extent in opposition to dominant discourses of masculinity.

Various sports stars played an important role when I was growing up, with many boys wanting to be like our favourite sports stars. Whereas the majority of ice hockey and soccer playing boys had stereotypically male sports heroes, one of my heroes was tennis player Stefan Edberg, who contrasted starkly with some of the strong, aggressive and powerful ice hockey and soccer players. Edberg's modest and gentle manner, both on and off the tennis court, was something I always tried to live up to (not that I always did). As identified by Carr and Weigand (2001), our behaviour in PE was shaped by the perception we had of our own sports stars. While I was trying to be like Edberg, modest and gentle, many others were playing rough and aggressive, as their sporting heroes did. This highlights how sporting heroes as role models were an important influence on our gendered patterns of attitudes and behaviour during PE (Carr & Weigand, 2001).

Nevertheless, I was one of the fortunate ones who always had an 'easy' time in PE and I guess was considered one of the 'sporty' ones. Through playing many different sports from an early age, I had learned a variety of sporting skills, which PE often privileged. Apart from PE and sport, I was also highly focused on the more academic side of schooling. For as long as I can remember, I have been 'blessed' with the ability to acquire new knowledge/information quickly and demonstrate this in exams or other forms of assessment. In terms of my own identity and peer group manoeuvring, this meant that I was often able to blend in with both the 'sporty' and the 'academic' boys. However, at the time, I had very little empathy for those less able in either domain when involved in either PE and sport or academic subjects. When doing PE, I would have little understanding of those 'less able' boys (and girls) and would often think that they did not try hard enough or that they did not like PE. Conversely, when studying for an exam or an assignment, I would talk about how some of the sporty ones never studied hard enough or that they just did not care about those sorts of things. This divide between PE and sport and academics seemed to be a prevalent discourse when I was growing up and connected to dominant discourses of gender. Being one of the 'cool' boys meant either being really good at sports, training hard, trying to be the best at all times (especially during PE) and winning awards/trophies or being 'naturally' smart at school, where you would get the highest marks without being seen to try. Studying hard was considered 'nerdy' for boys and something that 'girls do'. In addition, a lot of effort went into sorting out what was 'boyish' or 'girlish' and 'masculine' or 'feminine'. Deciding what boys do often involved pointing out what boys should not do; in this sense, I recognise that there is nothing inherent in the notion of boy and masculinity as it is defined in contrast "to what it is understood to be *not*" (Paris, Worth, & Allen, 2002, p. 12 emphasis in original). Reaffirming 'acceptable' male identities involves a continued repudiation of 'unacceptable' (abject) identities because by pointing to what you are not, you are simultaneously confirming your own gendered identity (Butler, 1990).

Another important part of gender identity in my childhood and teenage years revolved around the body. In the early years, it was important not to be overweight because this was considered 'incompatible' with being good at sports, which, for instance, meant you risked being picked last for team sports in PE and/or being called 'fat'. Indeed, sport is often identified as an important site for the construction of gender and the embodiment of unequal gender relations, where the body plays a central role in the formation of gender identity (Bordo, 1989). Throughout my teenage years, this turned into the quest for the right male body shape, or what Drummond (2003) calls the "archetypal male body" (p. 134). Through playing sports and going to the gym, many of us were constantly shaping and re-shaping our bodies to impress both each other and those we were attracted to. Having the right body shape was closely connected with both sporting performance and peer group status. I remember vividly how highly 'gendered moments', such as getting changed before and after class and having swimming lessons together with the girls, were important in terms of performing and embodying dominant notions of masculinity.

The body played an important role in and shaped our performances of gender and, more specifically, what types of performances of gender were possible. I recall how many of the boys who had developed a poor body image as a result of, for instance, being overweight or too skinny, often struggled with their bodies being on display during PE. As a result, these boys ended up disengaging themselves from PE in order to prevent further mockery and humiliation, and many, especially in the late teenage years, stayed away from PE completely. This shows how the pressure of living up to an ideal of embodied gendered identities can cause significant stress and anxiety for boys participating in PE (Martino & Pallotta-Chiarolli, 2003). By looking back at these memories of the importance of the body, I became interested in exploring embodied power relations that shape boys' performances of gender. Moreover, I wanted to recognise the spatiality of these performances because just as, for instance, the space of the indoor courts at my tennis club induce pleasurable experiences for me every time I walk in there, equally, the spaces of PE, such as the changing rooms or the swimming pool, would for other boys be remembered with feelings of anxiety and discontent. That is, how do both the body and space intersect with performances of gender in PE?

When I was deciding what subject to have as my second teaching subject,[2] I never thought I would pick PE, mainly because I could not see myself teaching PE. However, after some extra consideration and as a way of furthering my tennis coaching qualification, I decided to give PE a chance. Even then, I did not expect to teach PE but thought that I might only teach English (my first subject) alongside my tennis coaching. Despite this, early on in my PE studies, and by looking back at my own experiences of PE, I became increasingly interested in the shaping of identities and the creation of the self in and through PE. However, as noted by Dowling (2006), I quickly identified that gender identity, equality and equity were not recognised as important parts of the development of a professional PE identity. Courses and the overall programme seemed to be implicitly reinforcing gender essentialist thinking through various scientific discourses. In fact, it seemed as if gender talk within physical education teacher education (PETE) often evoked strong emotional reactions and negative feelings (Dowling, 2008). Gender was perceived not as an important factor in the learning process but rather as a biological fact, which made me concerned over how this lack of a theoretical understanding of gender might lead new PE teachers to reinforce essentialist discourses of gender.

The experience of gender in PETE, coupled with my own gendered experiences of school and PE, ultimately led to the development of this research topic. I am deeply interested in exploring boys' gendered experiences of schooling, and in particular PE, and how this shapes their understanding of themselves and others. In this sense, I think this study has been a way for me to gain a better understanding of my own gendered identity as shaped by dominant discourses in school and PE.

Throughout the course of this study, my focus kept changing as I delved deeper into the literature and the boys' representation and interpretations of their gendered and pleasurable experiences and understandings of PE. Indeed, I soon started fully recognising the messiness of researching both gender and pleasure, which at times left me seriously doubting both the focus and eventual completion of this study. However, I find the following quote by Foucault (1997) particularly pertinent for my study:

> If one is to challenge the domination of particular truths/a particular truth regime then they must do so by playing a certain game of truth, by showing its consequences, by pointing out that there are other reasonable options, by teaching people what they don't know about their own situation, their working conditions and their exploitation.
>
> (pp. 295–296)

In my study, I use a Foucauldian framework because it provides useful tools/concepts (e.g., discourse, power/knowledge relations, disciplinary power and technologies of self) for examining how boys talk about their experiences of the workings of dominant discourses in PE. By examining how they represent and negotiate certain social practices and social relations, we might better understand the different and competing logics by which such social practices and social relations are constructed, which in turn opens the potential for new understandings that can lead to social change. Accessing and responding to boys' experiences and understandings of PE will enable researchers and PE teachers to develop programmes that are both meaningful and enjoyable for all boys. It is through learning from boys' experiences and understandings of PE that researchers and teachers might better understand how boys navigate dominant discourses of gender and relations of power. The focus of this book is on exploring, through the boys' articulations, how a group of Year 10 boys (ages 14–15) in New Zealand represent and negotiate the workings of gendered discourses in PE.

Before I begin, I would like to point out that this book is a social construction, a socially enacted, co-created entity, and although it exists in a material form, it is my hope that it will be re-created and reinterpreted by everyone who takes time to read it. It is not a final statement about boys, gender, pleasures and PE but rather a starting point, a springboard for new thought and new work, in the field of PE research.

Overview of the Book

Chapter one outlines the motivations for and conceptual foundations of this book and introduces why researching boys, gender, pleasures and PE is of importance. I suggest that there is further need to examine how the normalisation of gender and performances of gender enables/restricts boys' participation in and enjoyment of PE. Chapter two explains how my theoretical framework, drawing on Michel Foucault and Judith Butler, has shaped my understanding of gender as a performance, discourses, power, bodies, space and pleasures. I also discuss relevant research pertaining to gender, bodies, spaces and pleasures in order to show their interconnections with performances of gender. I locate my own study in relation to this body of research and demonstrate gaps in the literature that, if addressed, may better our understanding of boys' performances of gender in PE. Chapter three outlines the methodological assumptions underpinning my study as well as particulars of the data collection and analysis procedures.

Chapter four draws attention to how the spaces of schooling and PE are implicated in boys' performances of gender by highlighting how spaces are made meaningful and come to matter as productive and pleasurable spaces shaped by discourses and relations of power. In chapter five, I examine how dis/pleasures are produced in and through the spaces of PE via the workings of discourses related to fitness/health, sport and masculinity. Chapter six explores how spaces and dis/pleasures are embodied through the boys' performances of gender by demonstrating how the discursive practices of PE materialise boys' bodies as productive and pleasurable.

In the concluding chapter, chapter seven, I argue for the critical engagement of pleasures in PE as both an educational and productive practice that might enable more boys to experience PE as an enjoyable and meaningful subject, and I also suggest that pleasure might, indeed, be the 'glue' that locks PE into 'traditional' forms and is thus connected to the (re) production of unequal power relations between boys. Towards the end of the chapter, I reflect on the research design/methods used, including their limitations and possibilities for future research. I suggest that combining participatory visual research approaches with Foucauldian theoretical frameworks can be fruitful in terms of enabling students to critically examine the gendered (dis)pleasures of learning in, through and about movement in PE.

Notes

1   In some countries, this school subject is now called 'Health and Physical Education', with the acronym HPE. For instance, in 1999, New Zealand introduced a new curriculum document, 'Health and Physical Education in the New Zealand Curriculum' (Ministry of Education, 1999), that combined the previously separate subjects of health, physical education and aspects of home economics. However, with a broad international audience in mind, the more familiar acronym 'PE' will be used throughout the book.

2   In Sweden, primary and secondary school teachers need to be qualified to teach two different subjects.

References

Alvesson, M., & Sköldberg, K. (2000). *Reflexive methodology: New vistas for qualitative research*. London, UK: Sage.

Azzarito, L., & Hill, J. (2013). Girls looking for a 'second home': Bodies, difference and places of inclusion. *Physical Education and Sport Pedagogy, 18*(4), 351–375.

Bordo, S. (1989). The body and the reproduction of femininity: A feminist appropriation of Foucault. In A. Jaggar & S. Bordo (Eds.), *Gender/body/knowledge: Feminist reconstructions of being and knowing* (pp. 13–33). New Brunswick, NJ: Rutgers University Press.

Butler, J. (1990). *Gender trouble: Feminism and the subversion of identity*. London and New York: Routledge.

Carr, S., & Weigand, D. (2001). Parental, peer, teacher and sporting hero influence on the goal orientations of children in physical education. *European Physical Education Review, 7*(3), 305–328.

Dowling, F. (2006). Physical education teacher educators' professional identities, continuing professional development and the issue of gender equality. *Physical Education and Sport Pedagogy, 11*(3), 247–263.

Dowling, F. (2008). Getting in touch with our feelings: The emotional geographies of gender relations in PETE. *Sport, Education and Society, 13*(3), 247–266.

Drummond, M. (2003). The meaning of boys' bodies in physical education. *The Journal of Men's Studies, 11*(2), 131–143.

Engström, L.-M. (2008). Who is physically active? Cultural capital and sports participation from adolescence to middle age: A 38-year follow-up study. *Physical Education and Sport Pedagogy, 13*(4), 319–343.

Foucault, M. (1997). *Ethics: Subjectivity and truth* (Trans. R. Hurley and others). New York: New Press.

Hammersley, M., & Atkinson, P. (1983). *Ethnography, principles in practice.* London and New York: Tavistock.

Hickey, C. (2008). Physical education, sport and hyper-masculinity in schools. *Sport, Education and Society, 13*(2), 147–161.

Martino, W., & Pallotta-Chiarolli, M. (2003). *So what's a boy? Addressing issues of masculinity and schooling.* Buckingham, UK: Open University Press.

Ministry of Education. (1999). *Health and physical education in the New Zealand curriculum.* Wellington, NZ: Learning Media.

Paris, A., Worth, H., & Allen, L. (2002). Introduction. In H. Worth, A. Paris, & L. Allen (Eds.), *Life of Brian: Masculinities, sexualities and health in New Zealand* (pp. 11–26). Dunedin, NZ: University of Otago Press.

Tinning, R. (2010). *Pedagogy and human movement: Theory, practice, research.* New York: Routledge.

Acknowledgements

This book has been completed with insight, support, practical assistance and guidance from many people:

First of all, I would like to acknowledge the enormous work and dedication of my three first significant academic mentors. They all three in different ways carried me on the journey of this project. Thank you to Associate Professor Louisa Allen for always being positive, supportive and encouraging and for believing in me from the first day we met and constantly challenging my ideas and way of thinking to take my work to unexpected levels. Thanks to Associate Professor Richard Pringle and Dr Alan Ovens for always providing insightful and productive feedback throughout all stages of this research. Thank you to both of you for helping me work on recent publications, including this book.

Thank you also to my colleagues and friends at both the University of Auckland and Linnaeus University for always showing an interest and willingness to engage with my teaching and research. Our student exchanges and teaching and research collaboration are things I hope to keep building on in the future.

Thank you to the late Emeritus Professor Lars-Magnus Engström for simply being the most approachable academic I ever had the pleasure to meet. The memories of our conservations about teaching, research and life in general on the benches outside GIH in Stockholm I will cherish forever.

Thank you, Wayne Martino, for your guidance and invaluable feedback when creating the proposal for this book as part of the series Routledge Critical Studies in Gender and Sexuality in Education.

Thanks to all the people who have supported me, especially my parents who have always been there for me and encouraged me in every aspect of my life. Thanks to my good friend Michael Bolander for sharing countless hours of discussing teaching and research while on tramping tracks, ski fields or winery visits. To my amazing father-, mother-, brothers- and sisters-in-law for always being there for me and my family when we need you the most. To my wonderful wife Hannah for being the best wife, mother and, above all, friend that I could ever have wished for. To my three children, Oskar, Charlie and Olivia, for constantly bringing me back to reality and reminding me what matters the most in this world: learning about the world through unstructured, socially oriented and fun-filled play.

Finally, thanks to all the boys and teachers who participated in this study; without all of you, this book would not have been possible!

Versions of chapters from this book were originally published elsewhere. The author and publishers wish to thank the following for permission to reproduce copyrighted material:

Emerald Group Publishing for material from Gerdin, G. (2013). Boys' visual representations and interpretations of physical education. In Norman K. Denzin (ed.) *40th Anniversary of Studies in Symbolic Interaction (Studies in Symbolic Interaction, Volume 40* (pp. 203–225). Bingley, UK: Emerald Group Publishing Limited.

Routledge, Taylor and Francis Group for material from Gerdin, G. (2015). 'It's not like you are less of a man just because you don't play rugby': Boys' problematisation of gender during secondary school PE lessons in New Zealand. *Sport, Education and Society.* doi:10.1080/1 3573322.2015.1112781

Routledge, Taylor and Francis Group for material from Gerdin, G. (2016). A 'culture of everyone doing it' and 'playing games': Discourses of pleasure in boys' physical education. *Asia-Pacific Journal of Health, Sport & Physical Education.* 7(1), 55–75. doi:10.1080/18 377122.2016.1145428

SAGE publications for material from Gerdin, G. (2016). The disciplinary and pleasurable spaces of boys' PE: The art of distributions. *European Physical Education Review.* 22(3), 315–335. doi:10.1177/1356336X15610352

Part I
Background

1 Boys Will Be Boys?

I walk across the sports fields, which I must have done over a hundred times by now. The fields are still muddy from all the winter rain. The mud keeps splashing up on my bag, and my shoes make a funny squeaking sound when walking through the mud. There is a sign saying 'Fields closed', but some of the boys are still out playing a game of touch rugby during the break. In the distance, I see the top rugby field, which is being prepared for the next First XV rugby game on the weekend. I approach one of the school gyms. The PE class I am following today has inside PE on the schedule. Boys start pouring in from all directions. There comes the teacher, Mr Whyte. "Oh, what a day. Just heard that Tyler (one of the Year 10 students) has been in a fight and is going to get suspended. If he could only stay out of trouble for another couple of months, he will have finished school and can go out and try and find a job. But doesn't look very likely now does it? Boys will be boys!" The boys keep pouring into the gym, and a group of them say to me, "Good morning, sir, we will make you proud today". The gym we are in is very basic, four walls and a roof, and is getting pretty run down and old. You can hear some birds flying in and out of the roof, and some birds' nests are scattered across the sides of the roof. The colours inside the gym are grey and dull, except for the lines on the floor, which have been painted recently. The boys are now getting changed into their PE gear. Once all the boys are ready, they all get into this warm-up/fitness regime that lasts for about 10–15 minutes. The boys then get into teams as picked by two team captains and start playing a game of 'dodgeball'. As the game goes on, the screams and the cheering grow louder and louder, to the point where it is eventually difficult to make out any individual words or comments. The game continues for the rest of the lesson. At the end of the lesson, the boys get changed back into their school uniforms, and the air in the gym is by now filled with sweat and odour. Just as the combination of this with the musky and mouldy smell of the worn-down gym starts getting unbearable, the first boy opens the gym door and walks outside, bringing some welcomed fresh air into the gym again.

Logbook entry 21/08/2010

The excerpt above comes from my personal logbook written while conducting a visual ethnography of PE at an all-boys[1] school I have chosen to call *Kea College*[2]. This chapter provides the reader with the necessary background information to put the study reported on in this book in context. In particular, it addresses the why question; that is, why do we need to study boys, bodies and PE, both in relation to existing literature and my own interest in this topic?

My research focuses on the processes by which boys[3] come to understand gendered aspects of their identities. I am particularly interested in examining the power/knowledge relations that operate alongside binary descriptors, such as boy/girl and masculine/feminine, which in turn enable or limit the possibilities of gendered identities. My interest is specifically related to how the boys' (i.e., the subjects of this study) performances of gender in PE enable or limit them to be physically active and how they perform gendered identities in and through PE; that is, their physically educated identities.

My ongoing goal is to encourage more teachers to recognise boys' diverse ways of performing gender and to further challenge the image of boys as a homogeneous group, aligned with stereotypical perceptions of activities and behaviours of which they are capable and in which they should be engaging. However, as pointed out by Richard Pringle (2010), that is not to say that the role of PE is to "create universal happiness [or] solve significant social issues" (p. 130) but that we, as physical educators, need to recognise the workings of gendered power relations so that more students experience movement and being physically active as something meaningful, enjoyable and pleasurable. Indeed, one of the primary aims throughout this research project was to try to gain some understanding of the ways that boys who participate in PE derive pleasures in and through their performances of gender.

As a PE teacher, I recognise the ever-increasing importance of health and physical activity as a core of well-being in our society. I am committed to enabling all people, regardless of age, gender, class or ethnicity, to experience the excitement of participating in a range of health and movement related contexts. By providing opportunities for young people to learn in, through and about movement, I believe that PE is uniquely located to foster a population of active and critical consumers of physical culture in our society (Macdonald & Tinning, 2003). Examining the processes through which boys come to understand themselves as 'physically educated' may give us the tools to intervene and construct a PE culture in which young people are less constrained by gender stereotypes and help them in their pursuit of pleasurable movement experiences.

Although generalisations cannot be made based on this study, it can still lead to a better understanding of boys, gender, pleasure and the workings of discourse and power/knowledge relations in my research setting, which may have important pedagogical implications for the teaching practices of PE that apply beyond this context. By drawing on Guba and Lincolns' (2005) notion of 'reader resonance', my book aims to 'persuade' the reader that although the findings presented are based on a particular time and place, they are important and worth paying attention to. This increased awareness may encourage physical educators across the globe to produce new ideas about how to (re)assure that (more) boys (and girls) experience PE as something both enjoyable and meaningful.

Certainly, some of the findings from my study presented in this book rehearse earlier studies, but I also believe that my visual and pleasure lens provides different insights into issues about gendered identities and bodies in PE. For instance, the use of participatory visual research methods enabled the boys to 'speak for themselves' and, thus, provided a more intimate representation of the boys' contextually embedded everyday experiences compared to previous studies. By engaging the boys in both the representation and interpretation of the visual material, I attempted to encourage meaning-making grounded in the boys' own specific context. My book will contribute to the existing body of literature through findings that are very much located in boys' lived experiences of PE and the meanings they make of it. When it comes to pleasure, for example, I highlight how dominant understandings of the social and peer group status attained by sporty boys, along with the added fitness/health benefits, represented experiences/outcomes that were desirable for many boys in my study. The fact that some boys perform dominant forms of masculinity in PE can in this way be related to their desire of (re)asserting privileged masculine identities, which involves having power or superiority over other boys who are not able or willing to live up to these masculine ideals. This exercise and experience of power can thus be seen as both productive and pleasurable. The Butlerian and Foucauldian perspective used in my book add to our understanding of how boys' pleasures constitute and are constituted by their performances of gender at the intersection of bodies and spaces. The pleasure and visual lens adds a different perspective and new insights to be gained.

Furthermore, based on the findings presented in this book, I will argue that it might be helpful to (re)conceptualise boys' performances of gender in PE by interpreting discursive practices related to fitness, health and sport not only as constrained and disciplined but also as engendering boys' agency/freedom and pleasure. My book adds to existing knowledge by demonstrating how both conforming to and disrupting discourses of PE can be both productive and pleasurable. I will also suggest that less pleasure (or even lack of pleasure) can be productive both in terms of learning outcomes and in the construction of alternative/more diverse masculinities in PE. In this sense, the enabling and restricting of certain (sporting) pleasures in boys' PE can be seen as a productive educational practice.

In my research, I take the position that PE as a subject area is a site of educational practice that constitutes, and is constituted by, multiple and competing discourses, including discourses of gender. That is, in PE, boys (and girls) can be seen to be under pressure to perform in particular gendered ways (Butler, 1990) as shaped by discourses (Foucault, 1972). As alluded to in the title of this chapter, is it that boys will *not* be boys unless they are made to be by their surrounding discourses and practices? Thus, in examining boys' performances of gender, it is also imperative to go beyond the interpersonal level to a more comprehensive theoretical framework that can be used to explore the effects of, and responses to, the institutionalisation of gender. For this purpose, I have particularly found Michel Foucault's theorising of the workings of discourse a useful way of analysing how historically and culturally located systems of power/knowledge relations construct subjects and their worlds. In my research, I employ Foucault's (1978, 1985, 1988, 1995, 2000) thinking around the workings of discourse and relations of power to both examine and challenge our understanding of gendered performances and pleasures in PE. I will return to discussing this theoretical lens later in the next chapter. First, I want to address the *why* question; that is, why do we need to study boys, gender, pleasures and PE?

Why Study Boys, Gender, Pleasures and Physical Education?

This research was generated by my own interest in boys' PE based on both personal and teaching experiences of the subject. As a student and more recently a teacher and teacher educator of PE, I have always been interested in why some boys seem to be more engaged in and to better enjoy their PE classes than others. For example, I have observed how one group of boys (in particular those often labelled as 'non-sporty') often show little or no engagement/enjoyment and at times even resistance/resentment towards the subject. In contrast, the majority of boys are seemingly both engaged in and enjoying their PE classes. In the twenty-first century, concerns about young people's diminishing physical activity levels and lifelong physical activity habits and health (e.g., Engström, 2008; Green, 2004; MacNamara et al., 2011) are becoming more prevalent and raise important questions for professionals working in PE and sport. Lack of, or limited participation in, PE and sporting activities at a young age may have consequences for boys' and girls' levels of physical activity across their lifespan (Kirk, 2002). However, debates about physical activity and health also raise important gender issues. Indeed, the normalisation of gender, which simultaneously includes and excludes performances of gender by privileging certain performances over others, continues to be a dominant process in PE (Gutierrez & García-López, 2012; Hay & MacDonald, 2010; Larsson, Fagrell, & Redelius, 2009), which is why it deserves further focused theoretical attention.

At every level, education is fundamentally concerned with the formation of human subjects. Central to the enterprise of PE, then, must be a concern with its ethical dimension; that is, the question of what kind of people we want our students to become and how our practices are contributing to this formation. In New Zealand (along with other countries such as Australia and Sweden), PE teachers are under obligations as stated by the curriculum documents to teach from a socially critical perspective (MacDonald & Kirk, 1999).

Despite clear messages from current PE curricula about the importance of adopting a socially critical perspective, dominant discourses of gender relating to physical activity, bodies and health are being (re)produced both within PETE programmes (e.g., Dowling, 2008) and the school subject itself (e.g., Larsson et al., 2009). These gendered discourses, for instance, include: the prevalence of (hyper)masculinised sports in PE (Kirk, 2010); notions of archetypal male bodies (Drummond, 2003); and the impact of the obesity epidemic on what are considered healthy or health hazardous masculinities and masculine bodies (Gard & Wright, 2005). These 'traditional' forms of PE, constituted by dominant discourses of gender, can also be seen to (re)produce existing unequal (gendered) power relations.

The privileging of certain performances of gender as related to physical activity, bodies and health in PE might lead to the alienation and exclusion of those students who are not able, or not willing, to adhere to these notions. In contrast to early research on gender and PE, which mainly highlighted girls' alienation and exclusion in PE (e.g., Bain, 1985; Ennis, 1999; Griffin, 1984, 1985, 1993; Hastie, 1998; Nilges, 1998; Satina, Solmon, Cothran, Loftus, & Stockin-Davidson, 1998), research over the last two to three decades has demonstrated that more boys than is commonly supposed experience PE negatively (Kirk, 2003; Pringle, 2007). These negative experiences, for instance, involve: the competitive, aggressive and sometimes violent nature of boys' PE (Hickey, 2008; Parker, 1996a, 1996b) and feeling embarrassed about having their bodies on display before/during/after class (Atkinson & Kehler, 2010; Drummond, 2003). Although many boys experience this, PE is also commonly quoted as a 'fun' or even the 'best' school subject (Pringle, 2010). In my view, this calls for further research that focuses on the normalisation of gender in boys' PE and how boys' performances of gender enable and limit boys' engagement and enjoyment of this subject.

Moreover, and partly related to the works of Raewyn Connell, Michael Kehler and others, my book will engage in discussions about ongoing concerns about boys' so-called 'failure' in education and some boys' turning away from physical education. In current debate, shaped by the obesity epidemic discourse and concerns about young people's lifelong physical activity habits, many scholars and people from the public seem to tap into a moral panic about some boys' failure in education and lack of participation in and enjoyment of physical education while simultaneously not acknowledging how the spaces of schooling and PE continue to act as significant sites for endorsing, confirming and enhancing dominant forms of masculinity for boys. So while my book focuses on the pleasures of participation in physical education, it is also concerned with understanding why some boys are not actually participating in and finding enjoyment from PE. For instance, are these boys' displeasures of PE related to the occurrence of bullying in the locker room or fear/anxieties about their bodies?

In relation to Connell's (e.g., Connell, 2005), Kehler's (e.g., Kehler & Atkinson, 2010) and others' (e.g., Martino, 1999, 2000; Martino & Pallotta-Chiarolli,

2003; O'Donoghue, 2007; Rawlings & Russell, 2012; Renold, 1997, 2004; Ringrose & Renold, 2010) studies on masculinity and bullying, my book will also address the issue of gendered bullying. However, the way bullying is often framed as consisting of a 'bully' and a 'victim'—each with specific attributes and performances—simplifies and reduces the complexity of such practices rather than attempting to deconstruct the gender/sexuality regulation framework involved (Rawlings & Russell, 2012). Indeed, bullying research and policy has been largely 'gender blind' (Ringrose & Renold, 2010), failing to note the socio-cultural context of bullying and ways in which exclusion and violence are often rooted in reinforcing 'rules' for heteronormative gender (Payne & Smith, 2013).

In this sense, my book importantly addresses the whole question of pleasure and ongoing investment in PE while also addressing the question of marginalisation and alienation for those boys who might not fit or live up to normative gender expectations. It offers nuanced analytical insights into issues of investment, participation and (dis)pleasures in PE as related to gender, bodies and spaces.

The book will examine, partly from this backdrop of a moral panic surrounding boys' failure in schooling and PE, the tendency to look at some boys as victims and the ongoing prevalence of gendered bullying and interrogate the complexities of power relations and the pleasures derived from investing in dominant forms of masculinity.

That is, my critical intention is not to simply explore the boys' experiences of (dis)pleasure but to also problematise them by revealing the discourses that they are constituted within and the associated power relations. For instance, because of the pleasures some boys derive from performances of gender that conform with dominant discourses of fitness, health, sport and masculinity, I argue that power-induced (gendered) pleasures might be the 'glue' that locks PE into 'traditional' forms and is thus connected to the legitimation/production of existing unequal (gendered) power relations.

Focusing on students' gendered and pleasurable experiences in PE may also be of particular importance because in recent times far-reaching shifts in educational policy, national assessment mode and curriculum initiatives, along with widespread social reform, have generated some interesting challenges for physical educators. In the context of what many social commentators refer to as new and uncertain times (Fernández-Balboa, 1997), it has been identified that there exists an uncertainty about the PE subject's educational purpose. It seems as if both teachers and students have difficulties in articulating what the students are supposed to learn in PE. Kirk (2010) argues that in many countries around the world, money is spent on PE and school sports with the intention of increasing the numbers of winning international sports performers, reducing the numbers of obese children and adults and ensuring the good behaviour and citizenship of all members of society. This 'intervention aspect' (Kirk, 2010) of many school PE programmes works to normalise, through discourses of sport and fitness/

health, students into adopting an active lifestyle, avoiding obesity and, in the process, becoming sporty and moral citizens. Kirk (2010) suggests that this form of 'sportification'[4] of PE may even lead to the demise of PE as a school subject.

I will now briefly discuss and identify PE as a (gendered) socio-cultural construct, which is of importance in terms of contextualising boys' performances of gender in this study.

Physical Education as a (Gendered) Socio-Cultural Construct

PE as a subject has been shaped by discourses of gender, masculinity and femininity and thus has been responsible for producing gendered subjects ever since its curriculum introduction during the nineteenth century (Kirk, 1992; Ross, 1990; Stothart, 1974; Wills, 1965). Connell (1983), for instance, highlights the historical importance of PE as a mechanism for the development of 'manliness' in young Victorian and Edwardian 'gentlemen'. Indeed, in the late 1800s, public schools across the UK regarded team games such as football and cricket "a powerful force in the education of the sons of the middle and upper classes" (McIntosh, 1968, p. 11). In New Zealand, the provision of 'physical training' mainly focused on producing a strong and fit military force, a force comprised of men (Stothart, 1974). Wright (1996) argues that it is also important to note that the games and drills boys were involved in varied depending on their social class and ethnicity, in that white middle- and upper-class boys were trained for leadership roles, whereas working class boys were trained to become obedient and disciplined. This highlights how gender in PE is also performed at the intersection of other social variables, such as social class and ethnicity (Wright, 1996). Outside of public schools and in most other Western countries, gymnastics, which is also permeated by strong gender associations, long formed the basis of school PE programmes. Whether it was Swedish (or Ling) gymnastics, educational gymnastics or German (or Olympic) gymnastics, all were practiced differently according to dominant notions of femininity and masculinity (Lines & Stidder, 2003). For example, when women performed Swedish gymnastics, their movements were required to be dainty, nimble and flexible, whereas men were required to be strong and powerful (Kirk, 2002). Burrows (2000) also argues that when females took part in Swedish gymnastics, focus was on developing good posture and improving the capacity to reproduce healthy children based on the biological determinism that young women needed to be prepared to fulfil their roles as reproducers and mothers. Dudley Wills, Superintendent of PE in New Zealand in the 1950s, reaffirmed this essentialist view when talking about girls' and boys' different needs in PE:

> Most adolescent boys want to be physically fit, to hold their own on the games field, to mix successfully with their peers and to give expression

to their expanding feelings of confidence and vitality. Most adolescent girls want to be attractive, to feel wanted and respected by their peer group and to succeed in activities shared with their companions.

(Wills, 1955, pp. 20–21)

Such talk about boys' and girls' different needs in PE added to a discourse of gender in which boys are positioned as strong, vigorous and competitive and girls as passive, preoccupied with their appearance and mostly concerned with interpersonal relationships (Burrows, 2000). As the work of Bradbury (1989), Chalmers (1991) and Mitchell (1992) has shown, these discourses of gender, based on the argument that boys and girls have different 'needs' in relation to PE, have resulted in gender-differentiated language, expectations and organisational practices. Kirk (2002) argues that the image legitimated and reinforced is of two homogeneous groups aligned with stereotypical perceptions of activities and behaviours of which they are capable and in which they should be engaging with no recognition of different needs among either girls or boys. Thus, PE has long been strongly associated with discourses of gender containing stereotypical views about the behaviours and activities that are believed appropriate for girls and boys and with notably singular images of femininity and masculinity (Kirk, 2002). In this sense, PE has played, and continues to play, a pivotal role in the development and social construction of masculinities and femininities, which makes it an important site for exploring performances of gender.

In New Zealand, the release of *Health and Physical Education in the New Zealand Curriculum* (Ministry of Education, 1999) provided some ways of rethinking PE practices that contribute to these dominant discourses of gender. For instance, the curriculum stated that health and PE programmes would "provide opportunities for students to critically analyse the ways in which some existing concepts of masculinity and femininity may have a detrimental effect on the health and the physical activity patterns of boys and girls, men and women" (p. 51) and that students "will critically analyse the impacts that conceptions of personal, cultural, and national identity have on people's well-being, for example, by examining social constructions of gender and the body [and] the changing roles of men and women in New Zealand society" (p. 28). However, published research exploring the effectiveness of these gender reform strategies is sparse, and in general, there has been little research examining gendered practices and experiences of teachers and students in school PE (Burrows, 2000). Since the 1991 publication of the *New Zealand Journal of Health, Physical Education and Recreation* monograph devoted to gender equity, there has been little sustained examination of what goes on in the name of PE for girls and boys in New Zealand schools (for notable exceptions see Fitzpatrick, 2013 and Petrie, 2004). In addition, in the updated 2007 *New Zealand Curriculum* (Ministry of Education, 2007), there is no mention of gender issues in either the core curriculum or the Health and PE curriculum. Instead, issues of identity are discussed in broader terms, such as students should "analyse the beliefs, attitudes, and practices that reinforce stereotypes and role expectations, identifying ways in which these shape people's choices at individual, group, and societal levels" (p. 7), with no explicit reference to gender. Burrows (2000) implies that one could be forgiven for thinking that gender is no longer an issue in NZ schools and PE. Kirk (2002) further claims:

> Many members of the general public and of the teaching profession do not recognise the gender dimensions of physical education and assume that the subject is unproblematically androgynous, or gender-neutral.
>
> (p. 25)

It is therefore important to revisit PE programmes in countries such as New Zealand and explore the gendered messages that shape student thinking within this context. As suggested by Burrows (2000), it is not only how the experiences of girls or women in school PE are influenced by discourses of gender but also the boys that need to be examined. Burrows (2000), in particular, argues that PE teachers need to encourage their students to not only learn how to do certain physical activities but become aware of the cultural expectations of gender that frame their experiences of physical activity and the possibilities/limits these expectations place on the range and nature of physical activities they engage in.

This book aims to contribute to current knowledge of boys' experiences and understandings of gendered discourses in PE and how the workings of these discourses shape boys' participation and enjoyment in this subject by asking: How can we understand that certain performances of gender are privileged within PE practice as a result of these discourses of gender in PE? In addition, how can we understand that the gendered discourses of PE are problematic but also produce pleasure? This book is therefore concerned with how, by means of the study of discourses of gender in PE, we can understand boys' performances of gender in relation to the (dis)pleasures underpinning the ideology of PE learning 'in, through and about movement' (Arnold, 1979). The importance of recognising pleasures in PE has been acknowledged internationally for a long time (e.g., Locke, 1996; Pringle, 2009; Tinning, 2000); however, both current and previous HPE curricula have been critiqued for marginalising movement pleasure in favour of 'dry' formal educational and instrumental/developmental objectives (Gard, 2008; Morgan, 2006; Pringle, 2010). Consequently, students' gendered and pleasurable experiences of PE as enabled/constrained by prevalent discourses of gender, sport, fitness and health, remain a critical issue that calls for further examination.

Notes

1   I acknowledge that the concept of an all-boys school may be an unfamiliar practice for some of the readers of this book. New Zealand, along with only a few

other countries in the world, maintains a range of both single-sex and coeducational schools. The single-sex schools are mainly well established, representing their links back to early colonial times, and located in larger towns and cities where there are several secondary schools. The school in this study is one of the older, more traditional all-boys schools and, in this respect, prides itself on providing a broad education that includes sport and physical activity (for a full discussion of research setting and participants, see chapter three).

2   Pseudonym used for the participating school.
3   The term 'boys' is used to refer to the male interviewees/subjects of this research in a colloquial rather than analytical sense. This descriptor was selected since it was used by the participants in this study to refer to both themselves and others (i.e., 'being one of the boys' and 'come on boys').
4   For an extended discussion of this model of PE and its continued popularity, see Gerdin & Pringle (2015).

References

Arnold, P. J. (1979). *Meaning in movement, sport and physical education*. London, UK: Heinemann.

Atkinson, M., & Kehler, M. (2010). Boys, gyms, locker rooms and heterotopia. In M. Kehler & M. Atkinson (Eds.), *Boys' bodies: Speaking the unspoken* (pp. 73–90). New York: Peter Lang.

Bain, L. (1985). The hidden curriculum re-examined. *Quest, 37*, 145–153.

Bradbury, H. (1989). *The hidden curriculum in physical education*. Dunedin, NZ: Dunedin College of Education.

Burrows, L. (2000). Old games in new rompers? Gender issues in New Zealand physical education. *Journal of Physical Education New Zealand, 33*(2), 30–41.

Butler, J. (1990). *Gender trouble: Feminism and the subversion of identity*. London and New York: Routledge.

Chalmers, S. (1991). Gender equity in physical education. *The International Bulletin of Physical Education and Sport, 61*(3), 4–10.

Connell, R. W. (1983). *Which way is up? Essays on sex, class and culture*. Sydney: Allen & Urwin.

Connell, R. W. (2005). *Masculinities* (2nd ed.). Cambridge, UK: Polity Press.

Dowling, F. (2008). Getting in touch with our feelings: The emotional geographies of gender relations in PETE. *Sport, Education and Society, 13*(3), 247–266.

Drummond, M. (2003). The meaning of boys' bodies in physical education. *The Journal of Men's Studies, 11*(2), 131–143.

Engström, L.-M. (2008). Who is physically active? Cultural capital and sports participation from adolescence to middle age: A 38-year follow-up study. *Physical Education and Sport Pedagogy, 13*(4), 319–343.

Ennis, C. D. (1999). Creating a culturally relevant curriculum for disengaged girls. *Sport, Education and Society, 4*, 31–49.

Fernandez-Balboa, J.-M. (1997). *Critical postmodernism in human movement, physical education and sport*. Albany, NY: SUNY Press.

Fitzpatrick, K. (2013). *Critical pedagogy, physical education and urban schooling*. New York: Peter Lang.

Foucault, M. (1972). *The archaeology of knowledge and discourse on language* (1st American ed.). New York: Pantheon Books.

Foucault, M. (1978). *The history of sexuality, volume 1*. Harmondsworth, UK: Penguin.

Foucault, M. (1985). *The use of pleasure: The history of sexuality, volume 2.* London, UK: Penguin Books.

Foucault, M. (1988). Technologies of the self. In L. H. Martin, H. Gutman & P. H. Hutton (Eds.), *Technologies of the self: A seminar with Michel Foucault* (pp. 16–49). Amherst, MA: University of Massachusetts Press.

Foucault, M. (1995). *Discipline and punish: The birth of the prison.* Westminster, MD: Vintage.

Foucault, M. (2000). *Power: Essential works of Foucault, 1954–1984, volume 3.* London, UK: Penguin.

Gard, M. (2008). When a boy's gotta dance: New masculinities, old pleasures. *Sport, Education and Society, 13*(2), 181–193.

Gard, M., & Wright, J. (2005). *The 'obesity epidemic': Science, ideology and morality.* London, UK: Routledge.

Gerdin, G., & Pringle, R. (2015). The politics of pleasure: An ethnographic examination exploring the dominance of the multi-activity sport-based physical education model. *Sport, Education and Society.* doi:10.1080/13573322.2015.1019448

Green, K. (2004). Physical education, lifelong participation and 'the couch potato society'. *Physical Education and Sport Pedagogy, 9*(1), 73–86.

Griffin, P. (1984). Girls' participation in a middle school team sports unit. *Journal of Teaching in Physical Education, 4,* 30–38.

Griffin, P. (1985). Teachers' perceptions of and responses to sex equity problems in a middle school physical education program. *Research Quarterly for Exercise and Sport, 56,* 103–110.

Griffin, P. (1993). Addressing social diversity and social justice in physical education. In J. Rink (Ed.), *Critical crossroads: Middle and secondary school physical education* (pp. 79–84). Reston, VA: National Association for Sport and Physical Education.

Guba, E. G., & Lincoln, Y. S. (2005). Paradigmatic controversies, contradictions, and emerging confluences. In N. K. Denzin & Y. S. Lincoln (Eds.), *Handbook of qualitative research* (pp. 191–216). Thousand Oaks, CA: Sage.

Gutierrez, D., & García-López, L. M. (2012). Gender differences in game behaviour in invasion games. *Physical Education and Sport Pedagogy, 17*(3), 289–301.

Hastie, P. A. (1998). The participation and perceptions of girls within a unit of sport education. *Journal of Teaching in Physical Education, 17,* 157–171.

Hay, P. J., & MacDonald, D. (2010). The gendering of abilities in senior PE. *Physical Education and Sport Pedagogy, 15*(3), 271–285.

Hickey, C. (2008). Physical education, sport and hyper-masculinity in schools. *Sport, Education and Society, 13*(2), 147–161.

Kehler, M., & Atkinson, M. (2010). *Boys' bodies: Speaking the unspoken.* New York: Peter Lang.

Kirk, D. (1992). *Defining physical education: The social construction of a school subject in postwar Britain.* London and Washington, DC: Falmer Press.

Kirk, D. (2002). Physical education: A gendered history. In D. Penney (Ed.), *Gender and physical education: Contemporary issues and future directions* (pp. 24–37). London, UK: Routledge.

Kirk, D. (2003). Student learning and the social construction of gender in sport and physical education. In S. Silverman & C. Ennis (Eds.), *Student learning in physical education: Applying research to enhance instruction* (pp. 67–81). Champaign, IL: Human Kinetics.

Kirk, D. (2010). *Physical education futures.* London, UK: Routledge.

Larsson, H., Fagrell, B., & Redelius, K. (2009). Queering physical education: Between benevolence towards girls and a tribute to masculinity. *Physical Education and Sport Pedagogy, 14*(1), 1–17.

Lines, G., & Stidder, G. (2003). Reflections on the mixed- and single-sex PE debate. In S. Hayes & G. Stidder (Eds.), *Equity and inclusion in physical education and sport: Contemporary issues for teachers, trainees and practitioners* (pp. 65–88). London, UK: Routledge.

Locke, L. (1996). Dr. Lewin's little liver patties: A parable about encouraging healthy lifestyles. *Quest, 48*, 422–431.

MacDonald, D., & Kirk, D. (1999). Pedagogy, the body and Christian identity. *Sport, Education and Society, 4*(2), 131–142.

MacDonald, D., & Tinning, R. (2003). Reflective practice goes public: Reflection, governmentality and postmodernity. In A. Laker (Ed.), *The future of physical education: Building a new pedagogy* (pp. 82–101). London and New York: Routledge.

MacNamara, A., Collins, D., Bailey, R., Toms, M., Ford, P., & Pearce, G. (2011). Promoting lifelong physical activity and high level performance: Realising an achievable aim for physical education. *Physical Education and Sport Pedagogy, 16*(3), 265–278.

Martino, W. (1999). 'Cool boys', 'party animals', 'squids' and 'poofters': Interrogating the dynamics and politics of adolescent masculinities in school. *The British Journal of the Sociology of Education, 20*(2), 239–263.

Martino, W. (2000). Policing masculinities: Investigating the role of homophobia and heteronormativity in the lives of adolescent boys at school. *The Journal of Men's Studies, 8*(2), 213–236.

Martino, W., & Pallotta-Chiarolli, M. (2003). *So what's a boy? Addressing issues of masculinity and schooling*. Buckingham, UK: Open University Press.

McIntosh, P. C. (1968). *Physical education in England since 1800* (Revised & enlarged ed.). London, UK: Bell.

Ministry of Education. (1999). *Health and physical education in the New Zealand curriculum*. Wellington, NZ: Learning Media.

Ministry of Education. (2007). *The New Zealand curriculum*. Wellington, NZ: Learning Media.

Mitchell, R. (1992). Gender difference is alive and well in the playground. *New Zealand Journal of Health, Physical Education and Recreation, 25*(4), 13–18.

Morgan, W. (2006). Philosophy and physical education. In D. Kirk, M. O'Sullivan, & D. MacDonald (Eds.), *The handbook of research in sport and physical education* (pp. 97–108). Thousand Oaks, CA: Sage.

Nilges, L. M. (1998). I thought only fairy tales had supernatural power: A radical feminist analysis of title ix in physical education. *Journal of Teaching in Physical Education, 17*(2), 172–194.

O'Donoghue, D. (2007). 'James always hangs out here': Making space for place in studying masculinities at school. *Visual Studies, 22*(1), 62–73.

Parker, A. (1996a). The construction of masculinity within boys' physical education. *Gender and Education, 8*(2), 141–158.

Parker, A. (1996b). Sporting masculinities: Gender relations and the body. In M. Mac an Ghaill (Ed.), *Understanding masculinities: Social relations and cultural arenas* (pp. 126–138). Buckingham, UK: Open University Press.

Payne, E., & Smith, M. (2013). LGBTQ kids, school safety, and missing the big picture: How the dominant bullying discourse prevents school professionals from thinking about systemic marginalization or . . . why we need to rethink LGBTQ bullying. *QED: A Journal of GLBTQ Worldmaking, 1*(1), 1–36.

Petrie, K. (2004). Social hierarchies in physical education: How they contribute to gender construction. *Journal of Physical Education New Zealand, 37*(1), 29–44.

Pringle, R. (2007). Sport, males and masculinities. In C. Collins & S. Jackson (Eds.), *Sport in Aotearoa/New Zealand society* (pp. 355–380). Melbourne: Thomson.

Pringle, R. (2009). Defamiliarizing heavy-contact sports: A critical examination of rugby, discipline, and pleasure. *Sociology of Sport Journal, 26*, 211–234.

Pringle, R. (2010). Finding pleasure in physical education: A critical examination of the educative value of positive movement affects. *Quest, 62*, 119–134.

Rawlings, V., & Russell, K. (2012). Gender control: (Re) framing bullying, harassment and gender regulation. *University of Sydney Papers in Human Movement, Health and Coach Education, 1*(1), 17–27.

Renold, E. (1997). 'All they've got on their brains is football': Sport, masculinity and the gendered practices of playground relations. *Sport, Education and Society, 2*(1), 5–23.

Renold, E. (2004). Other' boys: Negotiating non-hegemonic masculinities in the primary school. *Gender and Education, 16*(2), 247–266.

Ringrose, J., & Renold, E. (2010). Normative cruelties and gender deviants: The performative effects of bully discourses for boys and girls in schools. *British Educational Research Journal, 36*(4), 573–596.

Ross, B. (1990). Exercise and exersense: The role of formal exercise in physical education. *New Zealand Journal of Health, Physical Education and Recreation, 23*(2), 16–19.

Satina, B., Solmon, M. A., Cothran, D. J., Loftus, S. J., & Stockin-Davidson, K. (1998). Patriarchal consciousness: Middle school students' and teachers' perspectives of motivational practices. *Sport, Education and Society, 3*, 181–200.

Stothart, R. A. (1974). *The development of physical education in New Zealand.* Auckland, NZ: Heinemann Educational Books.

Tinning, R. (2000). Seeking a realistic contribution: Considering physical education within HPE in New Zealand and Australia. *Journal of Physical Education New Zealand, 33*(3), 8–21.

Wills, D. (1955). The school and the adolescent. *New Zealand Journal of Physical Education, 7*, 20–30.

Wills, D. (1965). *Physical education in New Zealand.* Wellington, NZ: Department of Education.

Wright, J. (1996). The construction of complementarity in physical education. *Gender and Education, 8*(1), 61–79.

2 Gender, Bodies, Spaces and (dis)Pleasures

Introduction

In this chapter, I will provide more detail on the theoretical framework and body of literature underpinning my study. This study is informed by post-structural theorising and in particular the works of Michel Foucault (1972, 1973, 1978, 1985, 1988, 1995, 2000) and Judith Butler (1990, 1993, 1997, 2004). Theories of these academics have recently become influential for researchers and scholars working in the field of gender and PE (Wright, 2006). Drawing in particular on pleasures as the productive effect of power (Foucault, 1985), along with Butler's (1990, 1993) concepts of performativity and materialisation in relation to gender, spaces and bodies, the research questions that guided this study were: (i) *How do boys' performances of gender in PE articulate with (dis)pleasures? (ii) How are spaces and bodies implicated in these performances?* In this chapter, I demonstrate the implications of the questions I ask and the assumptions underlying the methodologies I use to answer those questions. In particular, I discuss how Foucauldian and Butlerian thinking has shaped my understanding of gender, bodies, spaces and (dis)pleasures, which are at the core of the discussion in this book. The reader will need to be able to engage with these concepts to fully recognise the prime arguments progressed. I critically review relevant literature to show how my research is located in relation to the current body of knowledge.

Gender and PE: Moving Beyond Essentialist and Hegemonic Performances of Gender

In this section, I begin by introducing gender studies in PE broadly and highlight how poststructural theories have been used to draw attention to gender as socially constructed rather than 'natural'. Drawing largely on Connell's (1987) concept of 'hegemonic masculinity', this body of research has demonstrated how certain boys are privileged at the expense of marginalised others (Drummond, 2003; Hickey, 2008; Parker, 1996). I will critique how research on gender and PE has employed this concept, reinforcing certain 'types' of (hegemonic) masculinities as rigid/fixed (e.g., Demetriou, 2001;

Pringle, 2005), before in the following three sections turning my attention to studies that have instead drawn on the works of Michel Foucault (1978, 1985, 1988, 1995, 2000) and Judith Butler (1990, 1993) to examine how the workings of discourse and relations of power shape performances of gender in PE.

Gender as Natural and True—Constructing Binary and Homogenous Categories

One prevailing discourse supported in much of the research and writing about gender is the framing of boys and girls as binary opposites, inherently different both biologically and socially. Research based on this line of theorising reinforces the notion of gender as something *natural* and that there is a *true* gender that individuals belong to. Alton-Lee and Praat (2000) and Jones (1990) argue that this form of biological determinism has long dominated educational practice and policy in New Zealand schools. In particular, this has helped shape a gender-differentiated curriculum in which boys and girls are often encouraged to pursue different and distinct interests as a consequence of their biological differences. Indeed, the earliest empirical studies on gender and PE focused largely on determining whether or not biological sex differences influenced the type and quantity of physical activity girls and boys could do (e.g., Dyer, 1982;. Fry, 1988; Hall & Richardson, 1982). This research, largely based on Parson's sex-role theory, in particular focused on the sex discrimination experienced by girls (e.g., Celeste, 1978; Priest & Summerfield, 1994; Ray, 1979), based on the belief that schools and PE classes are pervaded by sex-based role expectations in society that reinforce girls' inferior status to boys (Ray, 1979). This focus on challenging unequal power relations between the sexes resulted in New Zealand in various training modules and teaching guidelines being developed, such as girls' "Breaking Through Kits" (New Zealand Association of Health Physical Education and Recreation, 1991). Internationally, it also led to the development of single-sex PE classes in order to improve girls' physical activity levels (Hannon & Ratliffe, 2007; Osborne, Bauer, & Sutliff, 2002; Taylor et al., 1999). However, these efforts also helped reinforce and construct girls and boys as *binary* and *homogenous* categories, ignoring the fluidity and diversity found within these categories (Jackson, 2009). In particular, this focus on improving girls' situations in PE led to boys' experiences remaining relatively unproblematised based on the commonly held (mis)belief that *all* boys enjoy PE (Kehler & Atkinson, 2010).

Gender and Performativity

Central to this book is the idea that 'gender' is constructed, performed and regulated but in a manner that is neither uniform nor universally generalisable to all boys/girls and men/women in society (Cornwall & Lindisfarne, 1994). Drawing on Foucault's (1972) and Deleuze's (1986) critique of an origin or an essence from which things are initiated, Butler (1990) suggests that gender is always a 'doing' but not a 'doing' by a subject who might be said to pre-exist the deed. That is, gender is not programmed into our genes or something that is singularly 'possessed' or something that one 'is', but something that is continually 'performed' through sustained social interaction and a series of repetitive acts (Butler, 1990). Informed by the work of Austin (1955), and by explicitly rejecting theatrical notions of performance, Butler (1990) uses the notion of *performativity* to claim that "the substantive effect of gender is performatively produced and compelled by the regulatory practices of gender coherence" (p. 24). In terms of this research, this means that there is no essence or origin of gender to be found but that gender is constantly (re)performed in multiple and socio-historic ways (Foucault, 1978). Therefore, I want to reaffirm that, based on my Foucauldian and Butlerian lens, my use of 'boys' is in no way meant to essentialise/ homogenise boys or their performances of gender. The use of the term 'boys' throughout this book is done in a way that recognises that there are both multiple ways of being a boy and describing such gendered subjects (i.e., young males or young masculinities). In this book, I explore how a group of students who are biologically determined as of the male sex do or perform gender. In using the term performativity, I take the position that gender comes into existence as boys perform, using the resources and strategies available in a given social setting. Hence, I choose to define gender as a multiple and socio-historic performance shaped by *discourses of gender*.

Discourses of Gender

One of the key assumptions of my study is that boys cannot perform gender in PE as they please but that they are shaped by their surrounding culture, society and social group, what Foucault (1972) calls the 'workings of discourse'. Foucault (1972) introduced the term 'discourse' to refer to a system of values and beliefs that produces particular social practices and social relations, which are then perceived as 'truths'. Discourse can further be seen as a way of speaking or a network of rules establishing what is meaningful, producing reality rather than reflecting it (Foucault, 1972). Indeed, Foucault (1972) rejects the idea of language as constituted by the world, as a reflection of a pre-existing reality. Instead, he sees language as constitutive, which is to say, it constitutes our thinking and shapes how we see things. Discourses are thus "practices that systematically form the objects of which they speak" (p. 49). In this sense, boys' performances of gender always take place within discourse because discourse is a prerequisite for something to become meaningful and thereby possible to understand. Nothing can be seen as outside discourse; everything is constituted by discourse (Butler, 1993; Foucault, 1980). The language available to boys to describe their experiences and understandings of PE is in this way also shaped by contextually specific discourses because language not only describes a 'thing' but simultaneously defines it: "Discourses are not about objects; they constitute them and in the practice of doing so conceal their own intervention" (Foucault, 1972, p. 49). The important thing here is that boys are never outside of discourse; they make sense of their experiences through discourses available to them.

In my study, I explore boys' performances of gender based on Foucault's (1978) proposition that human subjectivity is conceived as forged in the play of various power-knowledge formations. According to Foucault, the individual self is formed in the intersections of different power relations and discursive formations. As such, instead of a fixed or stable self, I acknowledge the fluidity of gender as well as its unstable and uncertain location and reject essentialist arguments that, for instance, limit masculinity as static and unchanging. Indeed, masculinity is no longer seen as a "monolithic and unitary entity" (Willott & Griffin, 1996, p. 79) but rather understood as containing many images and behaviours that may be competing, contradictory and mutually undermining, and "completely variant notions of masculinity can refer simultaneously or sequentially to the same individual" (Cornwall & Lindisfarne, 1994, p. 12). As noted by Cornwall and Lindisfarne (1994), notions of masculinity also vary over time and across different contexts and cultures. In other words, the "conception of what it is to be a man is culturally, historically and socially specific" (Paris, Worth, & Allen, 2002, p. 12). By adopting the position that gender is performative, I reject essentialist categories of masculinity and femininity because these can be seen to conceal gender's performative character (Butler, 1990). Although the terms masculinity and femininity are typically used in sociology to refer to the socially constructed gender assigned to the male and female sex (Paris et al., 2002), I draw on Foucauldian theorising to argue that masculinity and femininity are not fixed to the male or female body (Pascoe, 2007). Thus, I define masculinity and femininity as concepts that are detached from the biological body and part of discourses that shape performances of gender.

In this book, I examine how the workings of different discourses in PE consist of values, beliefs and meanings about gender, boys/girls and masculinity/femininity that shape boys' performances of gender. Discourses of PE can, for instance, involve values and beliefs about what the role and purpose (meaning) of PE should be, as determined by the curriculum, the school and the teacher(s). For example, Kirk (2010) contends that many PE students think they are supposed to learn the skills and rules of different kinds of sports. Conventional sport activities tend to dominate the subject in terms of both content and the use of language associated with competitive sport (Kirk, 2010). Indeed, as shown earlier, sport has long been regarded as a key social institution for turning boys into men (Bell, 2009; Chandler, 1996). Therefore, for a boy to resist the values associated with team sports or to show himself as unskilled or uninformed about a sport can bring into question his masculinity, his very identity as male (Wright, 2000). In this sense, discourses of PE can be seen to produce not only social practices and relations but also gendered meanings, subjects and subjectivities. Different types of gendered identities are produced or 'made available' to the students both in school in general (Skelton, 2001a) and in PE (Kirk, 2002). Davies and Harré (1990) use the concept 'subject positions', which can be understood as possible ways of being (Baxter, 2003); that is, different ways of being a boy in school and PE are made possible or impossible by the workings of discourse as a result of *power/knowledge relations*.

Power/Knowledge Relations

To examine how the discourses that shape boys' performances of gender in PE are constructed and maintained, I draw on Foucault's work on power/knowledge relations. Foucault (1980) argues that power is deeply integrated and implicated within knowledge because power is understood as producing knowledge. The notion of knowledge as a product of power plays an important role in discourses because it is in the ways in which discourses constrain what is considered as the 'truth' that knowledge and power are connected (Foucault, 1978). Power thus operates in and through discourses as the other face of knowledge, hence the term power/knowledge (Holstein & Gubrium, 2005). The mutual implication of power and knowledge is of particular importance to this book because power/knowledge relations can be seen as gendered (Paechter, 2000, 2007). Differing discourses produce different forms of knowledge or 'truths' about gender. Gendered truths that are produced by discourses of PE may, for instance, involve stereotypical notions of boys being 'sporty', 'fit' and 'healthy'. By drawing on Foucault's notions of discourse and power/knowledge relations, I recognise there is a complex relationship between performing particular forms of gender because some forms are more powerfully positioned than others. In this book, I explore how discourses of PE produce various gendered identities that in turn privilege certain performances of gender over others. That is, the meanings, subjects and subjectivities produced by discourses are not all equal due to the workings of *normalisation*.

Normalisation

Discourses of gender play an important role in the production of gendered identities (Bordo, 1993; Sparkes, 1997) because they reinforce particular images of male and female identities through techniques of 'normalisation' (Foucault, 1995). Foucault (1995) argues that it is through processes of normalisation that subjects are produced both as individuals and as different by constituting what and who is to be seen as 'normal' or 'deviant'. Performing gender involves both reaffirming acceptable notions of gender and rejecting what is considered unacceptable within a particular discourse, or what Butler (1993) calls the "constitutive outside" (p. 3). This constitutive outside comprises those gendered identities that are seen as unacceptable and unrecognisable, or 'abject' identities. Butler (1990) argues that individuals must reject those identities that are considered abnormal or 'abject' to reaffirm their own identity as 'normal' or 'culturally intelligible'. For instance, masculinity is often understood as opposed to femininity, which is why being a boy typically involves rejecting that which is considered feminine (i.e., being aggressive over passive and playing rugby instead of netball). Reaffirming male and female identities is also often linked to the pervasiveness of 'heteronormativity' (Warner, 1993), which is based on the assumption that everyone is heterosexual and that heterosexual desire is related to girls and boys being different and opposite. For instance, in PE, heteronormativity can be seen to determine the way in which boys (and girls) feel they can 'appropriately' engage in certain activities and still be viewed as 'normal' (Larsson, Fagrell, & Redelius, 2009). In addition, those boys who do not perform what is considered to be 'appropriate' masculinities, such as being outwardly (hyper)masculine and expressing a heterosexual desire, are positioned as the 'other' and denied the particular status that is attributed to the performance of heterosexual masculinities (Epstein, 1997). This highly rigid regulatory frame of reaffirming acceptable and simultaneously rejecting abject performances of gender helps (re)construct various discourses of gender (Foucault, 1995). Discourses of gender can in this sense be seen as responsible for producing unequal power relations both between and within the sexes.

Arguably, one of the most influential concepts that has contributed to our understanding of boys' social construction of gender within school and PE as both multiple and ordered hierarchically has been Connell's (1987) concept of 'hegemonic masculinity'.

Social Construction of Gender—Multiple and Hierarchically Ordered Masculinities

Connell (2002) describes hegemonic masculinity as the "most honoured or desired in a particular context" (p. 28). More specifically, he defines it as "the configuration of gender practices which embodies the currently accepted answer to the problem of the legitimacy of patriarchy, which guarantees (or is taken to guarantee) the dominant position of men and the subordination of women" (Connell, 1995, p. 77). Research on boys and gender in schools has used this notion to argue that school practices, with particular reference to PE, are an important site for reproducing an ideology of masculinity (e.g., Connell, 1990; Frosh, Phoenix, & Pattman, 2002; Haywood & Mac an Ghaill, 1996; Hickey & Fitzclarence, 1999; Mac an Ghaill, 1994; McKay, Messner, & Sabo, 2000; Messner, 1990, 1992; Schacht, 1996). For example, Hickey and Fitzclarence (1999) argue that PE acts as a site where "it is expected that young males will learn how to practice and embrace dominant cultural understandings of masculinity" (p. 53). The presence of hegemonic masculinity can be seen to put pressure on all males, whether or not they conform to these notions (Frosh et al., 2002). However, Connell

(1995) stresses that very few males, if any, are in fact hegemonically masculine but that all males do benefit, to different extents, from this sort of definition of masculinity and refers to this as the "patriarchal dividend" (p. 41). Some males do not benefit much (or at all) from hegemonic masculinities, such as 'gay' males. Coupled with the recognition that not all males get to share equally in the performance of hegemonic masculinity (Messner & Sabo, 1990), studies have shown how hierarchies of masculinities contribute to unjustified treatment of not only girls but also boys in schools and PE (Fernandez-Balboa, 1993; Light & Kirk, 2000; Renold, 2004; Wetherell & Edley, 1999).

Most researchers who have examined how masculinities operate within these settings have shown how they simultaneously support and privilege certain forms of hegemonic masculinities while marginalising others (Bramham, 2003; Connell, 2008; Dalley-Trim, 2007; Davison, 2000; Drummond, 2003; Hickey, 2008; Millington, Vertinsky, Boyle, & Wilson, 2008; Parker, 1996). In his seminal study, Parker (1996) elucidates how schools and PE are influential in shaping boys' gendered identities and in determining hierarchical peer group positions that favour boys who perform behaviours associated with hegemonic forms of masculinity. Thus, various masculinities do not occupy equal status but are organised hierarchically and regulated through various techniques of normalisation in relation to hegemonic masculinities prevailing in the school (Haywood & Mac an Ghaill, 1996; Mac an Ghaill, 1994). Hickey (2008), for instance, demonstrates how, through the differentiation of 'insiders' and 'outsiders', individuals who perform alternative masculinities are subjected to oppression and violence by those who perform hegemonic masculinities. Similarly, Millington et al. (2008) show how boys who embody 'Chinese' masculinities (equated with 'small', 'effeminate' and 'weak' bodies) are victims of obvious, as well as concealed, forms of domination that normalise and support 'White' hegemonic masculinities, which also extend to the broader school environment and community. From this perspective, school and PE classes can be seen as sites of masculinising practices through which boys learn, embrace and embody, or are damaged by, particular codes of hegemonic masculinity (Connell, 2000; Kehler, 2007; Kehler & Martino, 2007).

While recognising that boys perform multiple and hierarchically ordered masculinities, I believe that the way in which Connell's concept has been employed in previous studies promotes a problematic understanding of boys' performances of gender (Seidler, 2006; Thorpe, 2010).

Firstly, the concept of hegemonic masculinity is as difficult and complex to understand as the idea of masculinity (Donaldson, 1993). For instance, despite Connell's (2005) insistence that his terms should not be regarded as "fixed character types but configurations of practice generated in particular situations in a changing structure of relationships" (p. 81), his terminology has been used as if it is a type (Hearn, 2004; Skelton, 2001b). Hegemonic masculinity–inspired studies on gender and PE have in this way reinforced the idea that there are certain immutable values/attributes connected with these forms of masculinity (Pringle, 2007), such as 'Chinese' or 'White' masculinities (Millington et al., 2008).

Secondly, the concept is often used to refer to actual individuals or groups of boys (Beasley, 2008), such as 'sporty' boys (Kenway, 1997). This type of analysis leads to an understanding of boys' performances of gender as determined by pre-existing notions of (hegemonic) masculinity 'possessed' by individuals or groups of boys or even 'institutions', such as high school rugby (Light & Kirk, 2000). Rather than further reinforcing masculinities as 'fixed', 'types' or 'possessed', through a Foucauldian lens, I am interested in how masculinities are (re)performed by boys in multiple and socio-historic ways, as shaped by the workings of discourse (Foucault, 1978).

Finally, Connell's concept has often been used in a way that assumes that hegemonic masculinity somehow 'guarantees' male privilege over females (Flood, 2008). Indeed, since this concept was developed by second-wave feminism in the 1960s, some argue that it is not as useful for understanding the multiple and fluid nature of gendered identities in the twenty-first century (e.g., Seidler, 2006; Thorpe, 2010), in particular because boys (and girls) grow up within very different gender relations than previous generations (Seidler, 2006).

Wright (2006) suggests that Foucault's work on discourses and relations of power has been particularly well suited to this type of research because it has helped analyse and deconstruct the way that masculinities/femininities and gender relations are produced in PE. In view of this, I turn attention to research that has drawn on Foucauldian theories to tease out what I would argue are the central tenets responsible for producing masculinities and gender relations in PE and are therefore of significance to this book: bodies, space and pleasure.

Bodies—Disciplined, Productive and Pleasurable

The role the body plays can be seen as crucial because the body is integral to how masculinities are perceived, performed and lived—"the very 'stuff' of subjectivity" (Grosz, 1994, p. ix). Moreover, the centrality of the body to PE practices (Berg & Lahelma, 2010; Paechter, 2003), such as the process of getting changed and the visibility of the body during PE classes (Kirk, 2010; O'Donovan & Kirk, 2007; Wellard, 2009), means that PE classes are important sites for understanding, seeing and hearing how gender is negotiated and renegotiated through the bodily practices of boys and girls (Azzarito, 2009). In this section, I examine research that has drawn on Foucauldian analyses of the body in response to criticisms of the natural body, to demonstrate the discursively constructed gendered body in PE and highlight that boys' bodies should be seen as not only passive, disciplined and docile but also productive and pleasurable. Drawing on recent critique that research focusing on the material body has received (Larsson, 2012; Larsson & Quennerstedt, 2012),

I then introduce how my book aims to extend current knowledge of boys' bodies in PE by exploring the "materialisation" (Butler, 1993, p. 9) of pleasurable (gendered) bodies in boys' PE.

Disciplinary Power and the Body

According to Foucault (1995), it is in our institutions such as prisons and schools, which he calls 'disciplines' or 'disciplinary blocks', that various discourses and power/knowledge relations are developed as an effect of power being exercised. Using his concept of power as relational, presupposing that there are multiple forms of power, Foucault (1995) is particularly interested in what he calls 'disciplinary power', by which he refers to the control, judgement and normalisation of subjects in such a way that they were "destined to a certain mode of living or dying" (p. 94). He in particular explores the position of the body as a site of the subject's social production and suggests that bodies are subjugated to certain forms of 'disciplinary power'. Foucault (1995) claims that the body is a crucial site of disciplinary, normalising practices and the workings of power: "The body is invested with relations of power . . . power exercised on the body . . . rather than possessed" (p. 26). Foucault (1995) further argues that disciplinary power is a form of power that focuses on the control and discipline of bodies and that is mainly achieved "by means of surveillance" (p. 104). Hence, disciplinary power defines:

> how one may have a hold over others' bodies, not only so that they may do what one wishes, but so that they may operate as one wishes, with the techniques, the speed and the efficiency that one determines. Thus discipline produces subjected and practised bodies, "docile" bodies.
>
> (Foucault, 1995, p. 138)

Schools can be seen as disciplinary institutions that are centred around regimes of measured, corrective and continuous corporal training, designed to facilitate the controlled manufacturing of suitably docile and gendered bodies. A Foucauldian examination of the role that boys' bodies play in performances of gender is therefore of particular importance because it can be used to examine dominant discourses of the masculine body and mechanisms of power that help shape these performances. Through the workings of normalisation, which regulate and reproduce images of the normal versus the abnormal masculine and feminine body, a hierarchy of ideal bodies is created (Andrews, 2000). In this book, I take the position that practices that discipline and normalise the body in PE, such as the promotion of specific sports or fitness regimes, create a hierarchy of ideal gendered bodies. Throughout, I attempt to highlight how dominant discourses of gendered bodies and certain PE practices 'teach' boys to inhabit and experience their bodies in different ways.

Foucault's focus on the body, as opposed to the individual, when it comes to the workings of power, highlights his anti-essentialist stance because the individual, according to Foucault, "was already the effect of the workings of power and not some inner essence" (Markula & Pringle, 2006, p. 40). Foucault's analysis of the human body is an attempt to show that the 'body' is a contingent effect of power rather than a given fact of nature and "conceives the body as 'the inscribed surface of events' and as 'totally imprinted by history'" (Shilling, 2012, p. 203).

Sporty, Fit and Healthy—The Disciplining and Normalisation of Boys' Bodies in PE

Foucault's arguments against the notion of the body as a natural construct have been used by PE researchers to examine how boys' and girls' bodies, as social or discursive bodies, are shaped by discourses and disciplinary power (Azzarito, 2009; Azzarito & Solmon, 2006; Kirk, 1997; Oliver & Lalik, 2004; Wright, 2004; Wright & Harwood, 2009). This body of research highlights how discourses of sport, fitness and health circulating in schools and PE function to discipline and normalise the body by promoting the ideal gendered body (Burrows, 2000, 2005; Wright, 1996, 2004). Wright (2004), for instance, demonstrates how the disciplinary sites of boys' PE and the particular regimes of 'truths' related to sport and fitness it draws on to legitimate its existence and to define what it does normalises boys' bodies as sporty and fit bodies. A particularly dominant health discourse in contemporary PE is related to the so-called 'obesity epidemic' because, as noted by Tinning (2010), physical educators are increasingly regarding themselves, or being regarded by others, as playing a key role in fighting this epidemic (e.g., Irwin, Symons, & Kerr, 2003; NASPE, 2002; Thomas, 2004). This obesity epidemic, although not without its critics (e.g., Gard & Wright, 2001, 2005; Pringle & Pringle, 2012), has had significant implications for discourses related to healthy masculine and feminine bodies, which position certain body types and habits as health hazardous or obesity prone (Burrows, 2005).

PE practices that serve to discipline and normalise the body, such as the promotion of specific sports and fitness practices or the fighting of the obesity epidemic, create not only ideal gendered bodies but also a hierarchy of gendered bodies (high status and low status) (Azzarito, 2009). Understood through Foucault's (1995) principle of the "panopticon" (p. 208), boys and girls then police and discipline themselves through techniques of (self-)surveillance to achieve or maintain a specific shape, size and muscularity to perform ideals of masculinity and/or ideals of femininity (Azzarito, 2009; Kirk, 1997; Rave, Perez, & Poyatos, 2007). That is, the production of gendered ideal docile bodies does not function by external regulation and supervision, but rather boys and girls are engaged in self-regulation and self-control (Grosz, 1995). Privileged masculinities, which serve as high status markers among boys in the school culture, are particularly associated with size, muscularity and athletic physicality (Connell, 2005; Gorely, Holroyd, & Kirk, 2003; Kirk & Tinning, 1994; Klomsten, Marsh, & Skaalvik, 2005; Martino & Pallotta-Chiarolli, 2003; Renold, 2004; Tinning & Glasby, 2002). Based on these findings, I wanted to further explore how such notions of masculine body ideals shape boys' performances of gender in PE.

While there is an ongoing and understood privileged status accorded to certain masculine bodies, other bodies, such as those associated with physical weakness, are being subordinated (Andrews, 2000; Azzarito & Solmon, 2009; Wellard, 2009). The fear of not living up to these masculine body ideals may lead to anxieties about the body, negative body images and low self-esteem (Grogan & Richards, 2002; Salisbury & Jackson, 1997), which all have implications for boys' masculine identities (Drummond, 2003). Kehler and Atkinson (2010), therefore, argue that the centrality of the male body and ongoing negotiation of masculine identities among boys can no longer remain silent. The study of boys' bodies can be seen as a highly sensitive topic because it draws attention to the effects of power at the most intimate level of the self (Grosz, 1994). By recognising the corporeal nature of gendered identities, what Grosz (1994) calls "embodied subjectivity" or "physical corporeality" (p. 22), my study seeks to explore the construction and performances of masculinities in PE as inextricably linked to the lived experiences of the boys' bodies (Foucault, 1995). That is, if corporeality is "the material condition of subjectivity" (Grosz, 1995, p. 103), then it is vital to understand not only how boys present their bodies or bodily attributes (the discursive body) but boys' embodied performances of gender in PE.

From Passive, Disciplined and Docile to Active, Productive and Pleasurable Bodies

Research employing Foucault's approach to the body has been criticised for directing attention to how social practices are inscribed on the human body as merely a passive object (Turner, 2008). However, Foucault also asserted that at points where power is exercised, there is also the potential for resistance: "Where there is power, there is resistance, and yet, or rather consequently, this resistance is never in a position of exteriority in relation to power" (Foucault, 1978, p. 95). That is, this book also takes the view argued by Foucault (1978) that power relations within discourses are made up of a constant interaction between power and resistance. Thus, when we think about power and how it is configured within different discourses, we also have to think about resistance and to trace its points and pathways (Foucault, 1978). An important aspect of power as Foucault views it, which is in direct contrast with Marxist theorising, is that it originates from interactions between individuals and groups at the lower levels of society. Because power is universally present in society, it cannot be understood as being imposed from above. Foucault (1980, p. 99) argues that we must have an "ascending analysis" of power and encourages researchers to analyse the workings of power at the micro-levels of society. The Foucauldian approach was chosen for this study because it provides a useful framework for uncovering dominant discourses in small aspects of education practice, such as the practices of PE, that are not only unchallenged but unseen: "It enables us to uncover the hidden workings of gendered power/knowledge relations, and therefore to challenge them" (Paechter, 2001, p. 47). By employing Foucault's (1978) notion that power and resistance are inseparable, locally acting and constantly shifting, I am particularly interested in exploring how power operates and how boys come to accept what can be seen as oppressive power relations. The aim of using this approach can be viewed as making "visible the ways in which power and knowledge operate to privilege certain practices and forms of subjectivity and to examine their effects on the lives of individuals and groups" (Wright, 2006, p. 345).

Foucault's theorising of power and resistance also serves to emphasise the role of the individual in the way that discourses are both constructed and deconstructed. Foucault's (1983a) notion of discourses as a social practice therefore also stresses the importance of the practices of subjectivity, how subjects simultaneously shape and are shaped by discourses. In other words, the way boys perform gender in PE has an impact on discourses of gender in PE; thus, they are simultaneously constructed by and responsible for reconstructing these discourses. In my study, Foucault's notions of discourse and power/knowledge relations are used to explore how boys' performances of gender both influence and are influenced by discourses of PE. This book focuses on boys as both objects and subjects of power relations; that is, they are subjected to power, but to what extent are they active subjects within power relations (Azzarito & Solmon, 2006; Markula, 2003)?

One of the main criticisms levelled at Foucault is that in his theorising of power/knowledge relations, he did not fully address the role of the individual within those power relations. However, throughout his entire career, he maintained that his primary concern was always going to be to examine the relationship of the self to power and truth, but it was not until his later years that he started doing so. Indeed, Foucault's understandings about the self-shifted over the years, and in his later work, he noted that he may have concentrated "too much on the technology of domination and power" (Foucault, 1988, p. 19). Particularly at the end of *Discipline and Punish*, Foucault (1995) argues that the disciplinary techniques employed never completely work, that the disciplines never fully succeed in turning individuals into docile bodies and instead they often ended up as recidivists. According to both Foucault (1972) and Butler (1990), individuals are not passively and inevitably shaped by discourses and relations of power/knowledge. Individuals can create themselves in more autonomous ways through problematising power relations and discourses. Individuals also have a certain degree of 'agency' in which they can reflexively and critically examine their conditions of possible subjectivities and in which they can both reinforce and subvert these (Davies, 2006). In my study, I was therefore interested in whether the boys recognised the workings of gendered discourses in PE and how their performances of gender conform to/disrupt these discourses and how they might act on this critical awareness.

Foucault (1985) further argues that we as subjects are perpetually engaged in processes whereby we define and produce our own ethical self-understanding. In this book, I draw on Foucault's (1985) framework for understanding the process of forming oneself as an 'ethical subject' because Foucault (1983b) argues that "the struggle against the forms of subjection—against the submission of subjectivity" (p. 213) is an ethical technique of self. Although Foucault analysed the technologies of self through the sexual ethics of the ancient Greeks and Romans, his 'teleology of the self' is, according to Markula and Pringle (2006), still relevant today among those individuals who seek to "recreate an identity within the . . . apparatus of domination" (p. 143). Foucault (1985) suggests that this process is dependent on the "modes of subjectivation" (p. 28) or styles of self-constitution, which he divided into four modes: the ethical substance, mode of subjection, ethical work and telos. The 'ethical substance' is concerned with determining an aspect of the self (e.g., an aspect of one's identity, set of behaviours or emotions) that needs to be problematised (Foucault, 1983b). After identifying the ethical substance, the next stage involves addressing the question of why change is needed, the 'mode of subjection'. Foucault (1983a) argued that through critically reflecting on the mode of subjection, the individual can then determine strategies for performing 'ethical work' or 'practices of self' to create new ways of performing and being. Furthermore, ethical work, according to Foucault (1985), is not necessarily an isolated practice but contributes, in association with other practices, to a "mode of being characteristic of the ethical subject" (p. 28), which he called the 'telos'.

Foucault's (1985) thinking around the four 'modes of subjectivation' as a way of resisting and transforming dominant discourse of gender was something I wanted to explore further in this study, to highlight boys as active agents in negotiations of their own and others' performances of gender. By building on the work of, for instance, Markula (2003); Markula and Pringle (2006) and Pringle and Hickey (2010), I was interested in examining whether some boys question and problematise their own performances of gender in PE and through practices of self are able to perform gender differently and construct alternative masculinities. Butler (1990) asserts that because gender is performative, "constituting the identity it is purported to be" (p. 25), there are possibilities for disruptions, for doing gender differently and even for radically redoing gender (Butler, 2004). This would importantly highlight how performances of gender are not only multiple and fluid but also change over time as the boys problematise and become critically aware of dominant discourses of gender. This might also provide educational opportunities to address these issues as part of the PE curriculum.

That is, although PE can be seen as responsible for reproducing gender stereotypes, it can also be seen as an important site for change. This is based on my belief that PE can and should act as a site where gender stereotypes are critiqued and resisted by providing both boys and girls with the opportunity to problematise dominant discourses around, for example, physical ability, bodies, health and gender.

Sport and PE researchers have employed Foucault's (1988) concept of "technologies of self" (p. 19) to illustrate that individuals are not simply a product of discourse and disciplinary power but that they are also able to critically reflect on their own involvement in sport and PE in a manner that can possibly produce resilient and challenging, rather than just passive, disciplined and docile bodies (Azzarito, Solmon, & Harrison, 2006; Chapman, 1997; Guthrie & Castelnuovo, 2001; Johns & Johns, 2000; Jones & Aitchison, 2007; Markula, 2003; Markula & Pringle, 2006; Pringle & Hickey, 2010; Thorpe, 2008; Wright, O'Flynn, & Macdonald, 2006). Azzarito, Solmon and Harrison (2006), for instance, identify how girls both conform to and disrupt dominant discourses of female bodies in PE. In contrast to previous studies on girls, their study shows how girls both enjoy and value their PE. As active agents, they choose to participate in or resist physical activities through their negotiations of gender relations (Azzarito et al., 2006). Wright et al. (2006) similarly highlight how one of the participating girls in their study actively problematises the pressure on women to achieve ever smaller body sizes, although they also conclude that despite this critical awareness, this girl is not completely free from the desire to achieve the 'ideal' female body. Drawing on these findings, I was interested in examining how boys, through their performances of gender, conform to and/or disrupt dominant discourses of the gendered body in PE and how these embodied performances of gender shape their pleasurable (and less pleasurable) experiences of PE.

In taking heed of Foucault's (1978) argument that discourses and related disciplinary technologies are not only disciplinary but also productive, I explored boys' bodies as productive and pleasurable bodies. Indeed, Foucault (1995) elaborates on his power/body relations further by claiming that "the body becomes a useful force only if it is both a productive body and subjected body" (p. 26). Viewing power as productive means that power constantly flows in all kinds of differ rent directions in which we are all to some extent taking part, even in relation to ourselves (Foucault, 1980). Markula and Pringle (2006), for instance, explain how disciplinary techniques relate closely to the production of docile but productive bodies within a fitness centre. The production of docile and productive bodies also links to discourses of pleasure insofar as we come to understand through dominant fitness and health discourses that participation in these kinds of activities is desirable (Markula & Pringle, 2006). Within a Foucauldian framework, power and pleasure do not cancel each other out. Bordo (1993) and Markula (1995) demonstrate how women who conform to disciplinary

regimes of the female body, such as diet, exercise and aerobic fitness practices, not only experience pain and frustration but also pleasure and power.
Drawing on the works of Bordo (1993), Markula (1995) and Markula and
Pringle (2006), my study examined how the discursive practices of PE not
only constrain and discipline the materialisation of boys' bodies but also at
the same time enable bodily pleasures.

From the Material Body to the Materialisation of Bodies

Drawing on Foucault's work, Butler's (1993) concept of 'materialisation'
suggests that the relation between bodies and discourse is inseparable
because "there is no reference to a pure body which is not at the same time
a further formation of that body" (p. 10). In particular, Butler critiques
distinctions between sex and gender for failing to recognise that male and
female bodies are also produced through discourses of gender. To distin-
guish between biological bodies and gender is to imply sex and bodies somehow exist outside of discourse. For Butler, the body is also performative,
meaning that just like gender, "it has no ontological status apart from the
various acts which constitute its reality" (Butler, 1990, p. 136). One of Butler's (1990) central arguments is that gender is not a reflection of an inner
female or male core but rather a performance, a "repeated stylization of the
body" (p. 45) that, by its repetition, asserts that there is such a core. The
ways in which we move, talk and comport ourselves thus function to "produce the appearance of substance, of a natural sort of being" (Butler, 1990,
p. 45). From this perspective, boys' performances of gender in PE might be
understood as embodied practices (Davis, 1997).

According to Shilling (2012), Foucault's epistemological view of the body
means that it disappears as a material or biological phenomenon, or what
he calls Foucault's "vanishing body" (p. 82). Ignoring the material or biological nature of bodies leads to what is sometimes referred to as 'discursive essentialism' (Shilling, 2012) or 'discourse determinism' (Turner, 2008).
Flintoff and Scraton (2008) argue that poststructural thinking has been useful to demonstrate the multiplicity and fluidity of gender in PE, but they
critique the same framework for not fully recognising the role of the material body. They further argue that a focus on the materiality of the body is
important because how bodies move and look matters in terms of ability
and status in the subject.

The critique of Foucauldian analyses of the body for denying the biological or material nature of bodies (Shilling, 2012; Turner, 2008) has in the
recent decade led to a number of body studies in PE focusing on the materiality of the body (Brown, 2006; Ennis, 2006; Fisette, 2011; Tinning, 2004;
Wellard, Pickard, & Bailey, 2007).

However, Larsson (2012) recently criticised previous body literature in
PE for using concepts such as the 'material body', which he argues is a sign
of ambivalence towards poststructural readings of the body when in fact
"there is nothing more material than a socially constructed body" (p. 4).

In fact, the claim that poststructural theorising disregards the materiality of the body can be seen as a misunderstanding (Larsson, 2012). The discursive body is about the material body and how bodies materialise through discursive practice. That is, "it is about how bodies matter, not what the material body 'is' in an objectified sense" (Larsson, 2012, p. 7).

This understanding of the body in PE can be seen as made up of a dualism between the discursively constructed gender and the materiality of the body. This dualism can be understood as based on the belief that the discursive can be separated from the material as "exclusive types of 'thing[s]' " (Grosz, 1994, p. vii). A similar dualistic way of thinking is evident in the work of Evans, Davies and Rich (2009), as they argue that discursive analyses fail to take account of the body as both material and productive. Their way of conceptualising the relationship between the discursive and the material also reinforces, rather than dissolves, the prevailing dualism of the material and the discursive (Larsson, 2012). In particular, this form of dualistic thinking can be seen as problematic because it ranks these two binaries in a way that ends up privileging one term over the other (Grosz, 1994). Arguably, based on the recent work on the body in PE quoted above, it seems that currently it is the material body that is ranked higher or privileged over the discursive body.

Conceptualising the body as discursively constructed does not equal ignoring its material aspects (Larsson, 2012; Rose, 1998). Indeed, the poststructural works of both Foucault and Butler recognise the materiality of the body. Foucault (1996) talks about the materiality of the body (i.e., nervous system, digestive apparatus, respiratory system, etc.), although this is not restricted to what is said and thought but also includes how discursive practices make the body matter (Larsson, 2012). This also serves as a reply to Turner's (2008) critique that Foucauldian analysis somehow leads to the "reduction of bodies to cultural texts" (p. 15), in which he argues, for instance, that "dance has an immediacy which cannot be captured by discourses analysis" (p. 15). Foucault further elaborates on this by saying that his discourse analysis was not aimed at "trying to seek beneath discourse for how human beings think, but rather to take discourse in its manifest existence as a practice that obeys certain definite rules" (Foucault, 1969, p. 23). He went on to describe these practices as creating what he called a "virtual materiality" (p. 23). Foucault was less interested in positivist accounts of what a 'thing' (i.e., the body) is than in analyses of the ways in which, and the means by which, we identify ourselves and come to matter. Similarly, Butler (1993) explains that "we all have bodies that live and die, eat and sleep, feel pain and pleasure" (p. xi) but that what these bodily experiences mean or how they come to matter is discursively constructed. Butler (1993) uses this term to suggest that intelligibility and materialisation are inseparable processes: "the notion of matter, not as site or surface, but as a process of materialization that stabilizes over time to produce the effect of boundary, fixity, and surface we call matter" (p. 9).

Although Butler's concepts of performativity and materialisation have been criticised by some, such as Barad (2007), for reinforcing "matter as a passive product of discursive practices rather than as an active agent participating in the very process of materialization" (p. 151), I still find Butler's thinking around the materialisation of bodies useful in terms of exploring how boys' bodies materialise through discursive practices of PE.

Butler's theorising of how bodies come to matter, understood through the concept of materialisation, can be used to critique previous studies on boys, bodies and PE. For instance, in Kehler and Atkinson's (2010) study, the focus was on boys' understanding "of the physical body as a signifier and marker of masculinity" (p. 161). The aim of their study implies that boys' bodies, as signified, somehow are seen as pre-existing the signifier and that it is possible and/or even fruitful to identify and discuss boys' bodies as separate from the socio-cultural contexts that simultaneously constitute and are constituted by those bodies. However, poststructural theorising rejects the idea of a split between signifier and signified; rather, they are constituted simultaneously (Butler, 1993). For Butler (1993), the sign is not an abstract representation of something else but something very much material and performative, something that performs what it represents. In terms of boys' bodies, this means that 'bodies that matter' are bodies that mean something, not a (fictional) 'material' body outside of discourse (Larsson, 2012). In my study, I did not want to be restricted to what is said and thought about the body but also to explore how certain discursive practices make the body matter (Butler, 1990; Foucault, 1996; Larsson, 2012) as a productive/pleasurable masculine body within the specific socio-cultural context of boys' PE in New Zealand.

Larsson (2012) further argues that this analytical framework is important for PE researchers because it can be used to go from focusing on bodily functions and appearances to how certain (discursive) practices in PE (i.e., competitive sport, fitness testing, fighting obesity) have shaped these bodily functions and appearances. In other words, Butler's concept of materialisation can be used to draw attention to the processes of materialisation that produce boys' bodies as perceivable masculine subjects and objects. In my study, this means that rather than focusing on the boys' bodies as objects (i.e., big, strong, muscular), I explore the practices that simultaneously form the boys as masculine subjects (i.e., sporty boy) and objects of truths (i.e., fit and healthy body). Particularly salient is the degree to which bodily (embodied) practices (Davis, 1997), or the materialisation of bodies, are encumbered with gendered knowledge related to masculine identities. Boys do not just have bodies, but they learn how to think about and experience their bodies in different (gendered) ways (McLaren, 1991). Hence, focus should be on boys' experiences and understandings of appropriate (gendered) ways of using their bodies (Gard, 2008). That is, how do PE practices engender boys' bodies, and how do boys' bodies materialise? Why do certain bodies matter in PE and through what discursive practices?

Previous studies have identified how gendered, sexualised and racialised bodies come to matter in PE (Azzarito, 2009; Azzarito & Solmon, 2006; Clarke, 2006; Fitzpatrick, 2013; Larsson et al., 2009; Larsson, Redelius, & Fagrell,

2011; Sykes, 2011). For instance, it has been demonstrated how the heteronormative character of discourses and practices associated with PE help produce particular gendered identities and bodies (Larsson et al., 2009). Heteronormative assumptions related to particular masculine and feminine ideals are embodied in and through the discursive practices of PE, which simultaneously enable/limit gendered identities and bodies (Larsson et al., 2011). The emphasis on the physical body in PE has also been shown to be a prime site for the manifestation of heterosexism and homophobia in both the teaching and content of PE (Clarke, 2004, 2006), evidenced, for instance, by single-sex classes/changing rooms (Sykes, 2011). In this book, I am interested in boys' bodies not only as inscribed with gendered knowledge related to, for instance, heteronormativity or heterosexism/homophobia but also as pleasurable bodies that contribute to boys' participation in and enjoyment of PE. I aim to extend current knowledge of how bodies materialise and come to matter by exploring the materialisation of pleasurable bodies in boys' PE.

In this book, I am also particularly interested in Grosz's (1994) critique of the dualistic fixing of bodies as nature/material and/or culture/discursive. By using the terms 'materialise' and 'matter', which place bodies instead at the juncture between the material and discursive (Grosz, 1994), I want to examine how the simultaneous and relational nature of boys' bodies as at once material and discursive shapes their experiences and understandings of PE, the self, their bodies and pleasure. That is, by drawing on the relational turn in social sciences, my work focuses on the "relational constructedness of things" (Massey, 2005, p. 10).

Indeed, researchers investigating gender and bodies have recently started considering how gender and the body also intersect with space. In the next section I will examine how space can be seen as implicated in the production of gendered identities, bodies and power relations but also pleasure.

Spaces

A growing number of studies on gender, schooling and PE are now concerned with discussing performances of gender both in terms of embodiment and spatiality (Allen, 2013; Atkinson & Kehler, 2010; Azzarito & Hill, 2013; Azzarito & Sterling, 2010; Clarke, 2004; Jamieson, Fisher, Gilding, Taylor, & Trevitt, 2000; McGregor, 2004; O'Donoghue, 2006, 2007; Paechter, 2004). The issue of embodiment and spatiality is also critical to Foucault's (1995) work because he argues that it is arbitrary to dissociate "the practice of social relations [from] spatial distributions. . . . If they are separated they become impossible to understand. Each can only be understood through the other" (p. 18). That is, the discursive practices of PE within which boys (and girls) perform gender take place through/via not only bodies but also the spaces of schooling and PE (Azzarito & Hill, 2013). In this section, I focus on the 'spatial turn' (Morgan, 2000) in the social sciences and examine how researchers, based on the critique of space as a 'backdrop' or 'site' for performances of gender (O'Donoghue, 2007), have highlighted space as a social production (Massey, 1994) that is thus implicated in the production of gendered identities and unequal power relations. In particular, I propose that a spatial analysis of boys' performances of gender can benefit from combining a Foucauldian analysis of space with Butler's notion of performativity to explore the performative spaces (Gregson & Rose, 2000) of boys' PE. I suggest that there exists a gap in current literature focusing on how space, from a Foucauldian perspective, contributes to pleasure in PE.

From Backdrops or Sites to Social Production—Masculinising Spaces

Although Gieryn (1999) argues that most sociological inquires have a space dimension to them, even if not overtly recognised or acknowledged, most studies to date that have examined boys' performances of gender in schools and PE (e.g., Drummond, 2003; Haywood & Mac an Ghaill, 1996; Hickey, 2008; Kehler, 2004; Mac an Ghaill, 1994; Martino & Pallotta-Chiarolli, 2003; Parker, 1996; Skelton, 2001a) have not specifically considered how spaces are implicated in these performances. For instance, both Connell (1995, 1996, 2000) and Parker (1996), in their work on schooling, PE and masculinities, use the notion of 'site' in their theorising of masculinities, in which this term is mainly used to describe the material context/location where boys perform masculinities.

This way of studying boys and masculinities in school and PE fails to recognise that spaces can also be seen to be implicated in the construction and performance of masculinities. Viewing spaces as absolute and passive has in turn contributed to an inattention to the power of particular spaces as implicated in the gendering processes in schools (Jamieson et al., 2000). O'Donoghue (2007) and Armstrong (2007) argue that the designation and provision of spaces for particular activities can be seen as responsible for constructing and reproducing stereotypical differences and power relations in the wider society.

Indeed, spaces embody specific values, beliefs and traditions. Stereotypical notions of what boys should be doing and what they like doing are also, for instance, materialised by the design and provision of PE spaces as 'sporting places' (Kirk, 2010). The use of space in PE can be seen as the materialisation of dominant discourses of sport, fitness and health. These discourses are based on what Crawford (1980) calls a form of 'healthism', which privileges individualistic notions of health and the assumption that sport equals fitness equals health. Indeed, Kehler (2014) argues, "In many schools, sport, masculinity, and health are often conflated, over-lapping and often times interchangeable. One term often means the other, although it is not articulated as such" (p. 63). There is therefore a need to further examine how spaces are implicated in boys' performances of gender in schools and PE because spaces can be seen as enabling and/or restricting certain forms of masculinities and male identities through social relations of power.

Based on the recent 'spatial turn' (Morgan, 2000) in the social sciences, and partly in response to space being seen as a 'backdrop' or 'site' for performances of gender in previous research (O'Donoghue, 2007), space has been seen to be implicated in the production of gendered identities and unequal power relations. More specifically, space has recently been explored in relation to boys' and girls' experiences in both formal and informal schooling and PE contexts (Atkinson & Kehler, 2010; Azzarito, 2009; Azzarito & Harrison, 2008; Azzarito & Hill, 2013; Azzarito & Sterling, 2010; Datta, 2008; Dunk & Bartol, 2005; Enright & O'Sullivan, 2012; Nast & Pile, 1998; O'Donoghue, 2007; O'Donovan & Kirk, 2007; Van Hoven & Meijering, 2005; Wellard, 2009). These studies demonstrate how boys' and girls' performances of masculinities and femininities are enabled and/or constrained by power structures that exist or are embedded in material contexts/locations, such as gyms, parks, schoolyards/playgrounds, basketball courts and PE classrooms/changing rooms. For instance, O'Donoghue's (2007) work provides important insights into how boys' embodied performances of gender are played out in particular schooling spaces such as the schoolyard, the entrance hall, corridors and toilets. He particularly illustrates how one of the boys in this study (James) intimidates and bullies the other students in one of the corners of the schoolyard that is located away from the surveilling gaze of the teachers.

Although most studies show how boys occupy and dominate both official and unofficial schooling and PE spaces at the cost of girls (e.g., Bramham, 2003; Pronger, 1999; Vertinsky, 2004), other studies highlight spaces of exclusion for boys. For instance, Atkinson and Kehler (2010) draw on Foucault's (1967) notion of 'heterotopia' to illustrate how the PE changing rooms as a "ritually heterotopic scapeland" (p. 78) become a cultural setting of fear in which boys who do not possess particular ideal-type embodiments of masculinity are placed on display, monitored by conforming boys and critiqued for their deficiencies. They argue that the changing rooms are places where boys' masculine identities and bodies are enforced and monitored among themselves in largely hidden, anxiety-producing and ritual ways that have no ostensible (or inherent) link to the pedagogy of PE itself (Atkinson & Kehler, 2010).

While I recognise the importance of these findings as drawing attention to the spatiality of boys' performances of gender, the way space is conceptualised in these studies (e.g., Bramham, 2003; Datta, 2008; Dunk & Bartol, 2005; van Hoven and Meijering, 2005) reinforces the rigid and fixed nature of both spaces and masculinities. For instance, O'Donoghue's (2007) study focuses on the boys' performances of gender in already existing spaces (i.e., schoolyards, corridors and toilets), whereas Atkinson and Kehler (2010) mix Foucault's work with that of the Gramsci-inspired concept of hegemony to imply that these masculinities are somehow 'embedded' in the changing rooms and used by dominant males to exert their power over subordinates. The focus on pre-existing spaces and masculinities overlooks how space constitutes and is constituted by the (re)production of discourse and relations of power (Blunt & Rose, 1994). My book aims to draw more closely on Foucauldian thinking to explore how boys' performances of gender articulate with space as shaped by the workings of discourse. Based on a Foucauldian and Butlerian framework, I argue that it is not the spaces per se that determine various actions, but it is the repeated use of these spaces, as shaped by discourses of masculinity and power relations, that render these as 'bullying' and 'heterotopic scapeland' spaces.

The Disciplinary Use of Space in Schools and PE

Spaces constitute and are constituted by power/knowledge relations (Blunt & Rose, 1994). The construction and organisation of spaces in PE can be seen as a product of power/knowledge relations inherent in discourses (Foucault, 1980). Discourses have produced knowledge or truths about what spaces are needed in PE. Viewing power as universally present, Foucault (1973) claims that analysing knowledge in spatial terms makes it possible to "capture the process by which knowledge functions as a form of power" (p. 177). In this way, Foucault links the spatial with his rejection of abstract theories of power. Foucault (1982) argues that "space is fundamental in any exercise of power" (p. 20), and indeed, he later claims that "a whole history remains to be written of spaces—which would at the same time be a history of powers" (Foucault, 1984, p. 149). According to Foucault:

> The great obsession of the 19th century was . . . history . . . with its themes of development and suspension, of crisis and cycle . . . with its great preponderance of dead men. . . . The present epoch will perhaps be above all the epoch of space. . . . We are at a moment . . . when our experience of the world is less that of a long life development through time, than that of a network that connects points and intersects with its own skein.
>
> (Foucault, 1967, p. 22)

In this book, I will examine the spaces of PE as an exercise of power and relate my notion of space to Foucault's idea of disciplinary power. Foucault (1995) argues that to enable effective disciplinary practices, the spaces accommodating such practices are needed. In this sense, disciplinary practices are aimed at turning individuals into docile, useful and productive bodies by distribution of individuals in space (Foucault, 1995).

I will now look more closely at research that draws on Foucauldian analyses of space to examine how spaces are implicated in the production of gendered identities and bodies.

Foucault's theorising of space has been used by researchers to highlight how the construction and production of space can be seen as implicated in the disciplining of individuals, identities and bodies, as shaped by discourse and disciplinary power (e.g., Bale, 1993; Gore, 1998; Markula & Pringle, 2006; Pringle, 2009; Spielvogel, 2002; Thomson, 2004; Vertinsky, 2004; Webb & Macdonald, 2007; Webb, McCaughtry, & MacDonald, 2004; Wright, 2000). Schools have been identified as particularly important arenas for the study of disciplinary use of space because both activities and students are highly structured by both space (i.e., allocation of space for both lessons and breaks) and time (i.e., the use of timetables) (McGregor, 2004). Various people then draw on this configuration of space and time to maintain certain power relations, such as between teachers and students and different subjects (Gordon & Lahelma, 1996). In this sense, individuals within schools are positioned differently within a 'power-geometry' (Massey, 1993). Educational discourses and relations of power are in this way inscribed in the spaces of schooling as the 'concretisations of power', evidenced by the majority of secondary schools in Western countries being similarly designed and constructed (Markus, 1993). For instance, most secondary schools in New Zealand have one or more rugby fields, with the best field often exclusively reserved for the school's top rugby team, the 'First XV'. What are notably missing are spaces for other recreational activities, such as skateboarding, BMXing, dance and yoga. That is, in this book, I want to explore how the spaces of school and PE enable and restrict certain performances of gender and pleasures.

It could be argued that PE is also, to some extent, both determined by and the producer of space (Eichberg, 1990). Markula and Pringle (2006) demonstrate how a fitness centre, through the allocation and production of spaces in this way, is involved in the production and disciplining of fit, healthy and docile bodies as shaped by discourses of fitness/health. Using rugby as an example, Pringle (2009) further illustrates how:

> Foucault (1977) detailed how "discipline proceeds from the distribution of individuals in space" (p. 141) and how it [discipline] employed technologies related to enclosure (e.g., rugby team drills within bounded areas), partitioning (e.g., team positions), function (e.g., the specific role of each position), and rank (e.g., coach, captain, forward leader, reserve).
>
> (p. 220)

Indeed, instructions in PE lessons are also often about the spatial organisation of students, such as requiring students to form groups and assigning activities in different parts of the classroom (Gore, 1998). Webb and Macdonald (2007) point out how the teaching of PE often also takes place in open spaces like fields and multipurpose outdoor shelters (with no walls), which means that the classes are highly visible. Drawing on Foucault's observation that individuals who are being watched or who feel that they are being watched, evidenced in PE by phrases such as "I am watching you" (Wright, 2000, p. 156), Webb et al. (2004) conclude that surveillance as a technique of power in PE is internalised by the students who then regulate their behaviours and identities according to dominant discourses within society, such as sport, fitness, health and gender.

This book also explores how the disciplinary use of space in boys' PE is implicated in the production of gendered identities and bodies, as shaped by discourses and relations of power. It adds to this body of knowledge by extending this exploration to include how, through their performances of gender, boys capitalise on the spaces of PE. This serves to highlight not only the disciplinary but also the productive and pleasurable spaces of boys' PE. Indeed, Foucauldian analyses of space have been critiqued by scholars who claim that Foucault mainly explored the exercise of power as being mapped onto space (Lefebvre, 1991; Smith & Katz, 1993; Soja, 1989; Spivak, 1988). Soja (1989), for instance, calls this Foucault's "deflected emphasis on spatiality", which he argues "fails to recognize how social agents produce and resist space and sociospatial relations" (p. 63). Acknowledging this critique of Foucault's theorising of space as not addressing the role of the individual in the production of space, I now turn to research drawing on Butler's notion of performativity to examine space (Gregson & Rose, 2000).

The Performative Spaces of PE

This study draws on Gregson and Rose's (2000) extension of Butler's notions of performativity and materialisation to involve the spaces of PE. In particular, I view spaces, just as bodies, as non-rigid and non-fixed and instead as both performative and the materialisation of discourses (Butler, 1993). That is, in my understanding of space as performative and as the materialisation of discourse, I also conceptualise spaces in progressive ways so that spaces are seen more as dynamic, contested and multiply constructed than fixed and historically bounded entities (Massey, 1994). By combining Butler's notion of performativity with Foucault's linking of power and space, I wanted to explore how boys (re)perform the spaces of PE and how these 'performative spaces' (Gregson & Rose, 2000) in turn shape/produce boys' gendered identities and bodies.

By bringing together Foucault's perspective on space and Butler's theory of performativity, it is possible to interrogate space and gender in PE simultaneously because the spaces of PE can be seen as the materialisation of "discourses around sport, health, fitness and gender" (Hunter, 2004, p. 190). Understood through Butler's concept of materialisation, discourses are viewed as having material effects that cannot be separated from the construction of identity and social reality. As such, discourse and materiality, such as bodies and spaces, are inextricably linked (Grosz, 1994). In contrast to many of the studies on schooling, PE, masculinities and spaces discussed above, this book aims to demonstrate that boys' performances of gender do not merely take place in already existing material contexts/locations, such as the playground (Oliver, Hamzeh, & McCaughtry, 2009), the schoolyard

(O'Donoghue, 2007) or the locker room (Atkinson & Kehler, 2010), but that specific performances bring these spaces into being. Although spaces (just as bodies) undeniably exist, spaces are made meaningful and come to matter through boys' performances of gender. However, since these performances are themselves the effect of workings of discourse, these spaces also need to be regarded as performative of discourse and power relations (Gregson & Rose, 2000). In my study, I draw on Gregson and Rose's (2000) work to explore the "performative spaces" (p. 442) of boys' PE.

The notion of performative space has mainly been used by poststructuralist and feminist geographers to explore the intersections of space with gender, sexuality and ethnicity (e.g., Bell, Binnie, Cream, & Valentine, 1994; Kirby, 1996; Rose, 1997). These researchers have highlighted how gendered, sexualised and racialised discourses and power relations inscribed in spaces shape individuals. The use of performativity in spatial analyses has been critiqued by some (e.g., Nelson, 1999) based on the assumption of an abstracted subject that is incapable of reflection, negotiation or agency. This could be seen as a misreading of Butler, who holds that agency is related to the issue of repetition or 'iteration'. In other words, agency is to not repeat a certain performance or to perform in a different way (Butler, 1990). I believe that this way of discussing agency is valid in relation to both spaces and gender; that is, to be able to not repeat a certain performance but perform differently is to remake or even undo spaces (Crang, 2005) or gender (Butler, 2004). Indeed, studies have shown how the (re)performing of spaces includes boys' resistant use of schooling spaces expressed through smokers' haunts (Willis, 1977), the unstable, performative space of the car-boot sale (Gregson & Rose, 2000), the transforming of the heteronormative space of the street into a 'gay space' during 'pride marches' (Valentine, 2001) and high school students' renegotiation of 'bike sheds', 'sports fields' and 'locker rooms' as sexualised spaces (Allen, 2013). In relation to the space of the 'car-boot sale', Gregson and Rose (2000), for instance, argue that "the space of the car-boot sale is produced through the citation in performance of particular subject positions, and that – precisely because of this – that it, this space, is citational, and itself iterative, unstable, performative" (p. 447). That is, the performance of gender in space not only shifts with each performance, but each performance also changes the space in which it is performed (Gregson & Rose, 2000). Massey (1994) argues that space is a relational becoming, "a moment in the intersection of configured social relations" (p. 265), both producing and a product of interconnecting social practices. In investigating how boys' performances of gender intersect with bodies, spaces and pleasures, my intention was to explore how, through their performances of gender, boys (re)perform the spaces of PE.

Just as Grosz (1992) describes individuals, identities, bodies and cities as mutually constitutive, so, too, can boys' performances of gender, their bodies and the spaces of school and PE. Schools and PE shape the individuals, identities and bodies within them, and concurrently, these individuals, identities and bodies affect the nature of the space of the school and PE. That is, there is a complex interrelationship between individuals, identities, bodies and spaces in the way in which they reciprocally produce each other (Grosz, 1992). For instance, it has been noted by Thorpe (2010) and Stoddart (2011) how mountainous sport spaces are usually associated with dominant notions of masculinity and femininity. Stoddart's (2011) study is particularly interesting because he draws attention to the ways in which the physical environment of skiing inscribes skiers' bodies. Using a 'gender-environment nexus' (Nightingale, 2006), Stoddart (2011) demonstrates how gendered embodiment, power, and ski resorts are inextricably linked. More specifically, he argues:

> The co-construction of gender and landscape through skiing is accomplished through the circulation of discourses in ski magazines and websites, as well as through skiers' talk. It is also accomplished through the embodied performances of skiers within the physical spaces of ski hills and backcountry terrain.
>
> (p. 120)

I agree with Stoddart's claim about the co-constructed nature of gender, bodies and space but also extend his research by considering the co-construction of not just gendered, but also pleasurable, bodies and spaces in PE. Indeed, my interest in challenging and resisting dominant discourses of gender also led to a focus on pleasure in this study. This was also partly based on Foucault's assertion that power and pleasure are not inherently opposed, while simultaneously acknowledging that pleasures are not somehow divorced from power. Indeed, he regards pleasure as the productive effect of power. I am particularly interested in how, from a Foucauldian perspective, power, as articulated in and through the spaces of PE, produces pleasure(s) at the intersection with boys' performances of gender. In the next section, I will examine how pleasure has been theorised and researched to date in PE.

Pleasure (and (dis)Pleasure) in Physical Education

Pleasure is often a key feature of PE. No doubt, a lot of students find pleasure in and through PE, whereas others do not. Pleasure is seldom considered to be of explicit educational value in the subject, a situation that Pringle (2010) finds unsatisfying. Indeed, it is easy to sympathise with a wish to legitimise the educational value of PE through pleasure as a complement to the range of instrumental values that currently dominate. However, because pleasure is integral to power (Foucault, 1980; Gerdin & Pringle, 2015), this is not entirely straightforward. Following Foucault (1997), pleasure can be dangerous because power—both the exercise of power and the subjection to dominating social norms—might induce pleasure (Foucault, 1980).

Although Foucault's concept of power has been aptly utilised in post-structural qualitative PE research in recent years (e.g., Gore, 1998; Kirk,

1997; Webb & Macdonald, 2007; Webb et al., 2004; Wright, 1997, 2000), power as producing pleasure is noticeably absent in this body of research. In order to examine and extend current knowledge of boys' performances of gender in PE, this study draws on Foucault's (1980) work on power and pleasure, in which he highlights pleasure as the productive effect of power; that is, power not only produces things, knowledge and discourse but also induces pleasure (Foucault, 1980). I propose a focus on pleasure as constituting boys' gendered subjectivities because the exercise and experience of power related to certain performances of gender can be seen as intensely pleasurable (Foucault, 1980). In this section, I draw attention to the absence of pleasure in research on gender and PE, drawing on Foucauldian perspectives of pleasures as discursively constructed, as compared to psychological models that have attempted to establish motivation for participation and enjoyment based on notions of satisfying needs, positive affects and flow states, mainly to increase physical activity levels. I suggest that examining pleasure from a Foucauldian perspective can better our understanding of how boys' pleasures constitute and are constituted by their performances of gender at the intersection of bodies and spaces.

Pleasure and PE—The Satisfying of Needs, Positive Affects and Flow States

In recent years, a number of PE researchers have examined the role of pleasure in satisfying needs and as a factor in motivation, mainly to improve boys' and girls' involvement and levels of physical activity against the backdrop of unhealthy activity and obesity levels (Cox, Smith, & Williams, 2008; Haerens, Kirk, Cardon, De Bourdeaudhuij, & Vansteenkiste, 2010; Lim & Wang, 2009; Rutten, Boen, & Seghers, 2012; Standage, Duda, & Ntoumanis, 2003, 2005; Wang, Chatzisarantis, Spray, & Biddle, 2002; Zhang, Solmon, & Gu, 2012; Zhang, Solmon, Kosma, Carson, & Gu, 2011). Drawing largely on psychological models, such as 'self-determination theory' (Ryan & Deci, 2000), these studies explore how teachers' beliefs and actions can enhance motivation in PE, based on the assumption that students who find PE 'inherently enjoyable' will transfer this learning to being physically active outside of school and into adulthood, thus potentially facilitating public health (Cox et al., 2008; Haerens et al., 2010; Rutten et al., 2012). In order to improve boys' and girls' participation and enjoyment in PE and foster intrinsically motivated students, it is argued that teachers need to create a 'need-supportive environment' (Liukkonen, Barkoukis, Watt, & Jaakkola, 2010; Ommundsen & Kvalø, 2007), which helps satisfy three basic, or 'innate', psychological needs: autonomy, competence and relatedness (Deci & Ryan, 2002; Shen, Li, Sun, & Rukavina, 2010; Standage et al., 2005; Zhang et al., 2011).

Creating a need-supportive environment leading to intrinsically motivated students is also purported to result in 'positive affects' such as pleasure, desire, fun and enjoyment (Ferrer-Caja & Weiss, 2000; Ntoumanis,

2001; Standage et al., 2003; Zembylas, 2007). Pleasure is seen as both a positive affective response and a motivating factor in determining participation (Bailey et al., 2009; MacPhail, Gorley, & Kirk, 2003; Wankel, 1985). Indeed, attempts are being made to clarify the process of affective development through biochemical, physiological and psychological models. Suggested explanations include links to raised core body temperature as a consequence of activity (Koltyn, 1997), increased endorphin production (Hoffman, 1997), changes in the production of serotonin (Chaouloff, 1997), influence on neurotransmitters (Dishman, 1995) and generation of a 'feel-good factor' through mastery of new tasks (Fox, 1997).

Other researchers draw on Csikszentmihalyi's (1990) theory of 'flow' in relation to motivation, enjoyment, pleasure and continued participation in PE (Cervelló, Moreno, Alonso, & Iglesias, 2006; González-Cutre, Sicilia, Moreno, & Fernández-Balboa, 2009), although most of the research on flow in physical activity focuses on pleasurable moments in sport (e.g., Atkinson, 2008; Bale, 2004; Jackson, 1996). Csikszentmihalyi's theory suggests that people are in a flow state when they become so involved in what they are doing that they lose all sense of what is happening around them; nothing else seems to matter. Experiencing flow in PE may therefore not only enhance students' enjoyment but also increase the students' motivation to participate in physical activity both in school and outside of school (Kimiecik, 2000; Ntoumanis, 2005). González-Cutre et al. (2009) suggest that to facilitate flow, or an "optimal psychological state" (p. 426), PE teachers should know the ability level of each student so as to plan, as much as possible, activities suited to their characteristics.

Although I am also interested in the production of pleasure as a way of improving young people's engagement and enjoyment of PE, I want to do so from a poststructural framework, in which pleasure does not stem from satisfying innate needs, nor is it the result of physiological/psychological affects and flow states, but instead the productive effect of power. That is, I draw on a Foucauldian understanding of needs, desires and pleasures as discursively constructed, in which discourses of, for instance, sport, fitness, health and gender shape students' understandings and experiences of the self and PE.

Pleasure and Desire

My interest in challenging and resisting dominant discourses of gender also led to a focus on pleasure in this book. This was also partly based on Foucault's assertion that power and pleasure are not inherently opposed, while simultaneously acknowledging that pleasures are not somehow divorced from power. Indeed, he regards pleasure as the productive effect of power. In the first volume of *History of Sexuality* (Foucault, 1978), he draws attention to the pleasure associated with exercising power. For instance, pleasure can be attributed to the effect of various disciplinary regimes, such as dieting and exercise. Viewing power as productive means that disciplinary power also induces pleasure. Foucault draws on Nietzsche (1969), who understands pleasure as the increased feeling of power that accompanies an activity, a feeling that signals an enhancement of our capacity to act. In this sense, disciplinary power not only renders subjects more docile, but it also enhances their capacities; it is productive. In my work, I take the view that pleasures bound to gender are double-edged. They can be used to reinforce problematic power relations, but they can also be a source of their subversion or rearticulation (Butler, 1990).

According to Foucault (1978), pleasure is more likely to move individuals to change than is the idea of the desiring subject. He asked, in an interview, "Why do we see ourselves as subjects of desire as opposed to agents of pleasure?" and argued that pleasure is less bound up with bio-power than desire. He claims that "pleasure has no passport; this is not because it is unbounded or ahistorical but because it is less bound within the modern regime of sexuality than its counterpart, desire-sex" (Davidson, 2001, p. 213). Foucault (1978) claims that "the rallying point for the counterattack against the deployment of sexuality ought not to be sex-desire, but bodies and pleasure" (p. 157). In this sense, pleasure can be seen as less discursively determined than desire. However, pleasure is hard to define, and in fact Foucault himself once said: "Acts are not very important, and pleasure—nobody knows what it is!" (Foucault, 1983b, p. 234).

In everyday talk, pleasure is often used interchangeably with fun, enjoyment, happiness, satisfaction, etc. Pleasure can be experienced in many different, and at times competing, ways, such as taking part in strict exercise regimes or receiving/inflicting pain (Pringle, 2009) while in pain and struggling to complete a marathon (Kretchmar, 2005), adhering to various diet and fitness regimes (Bordo, 1993), conforming to or refusing ideal gendered bodies (Azzarito & Solmon, 2006) and helping others (Kretchmar, 2005). In fact, Shilling (2002) argues that providing a definition of pleasure is not important or even possible. Although agreeing on a definition of pleasure might be difficult or not even necessary, I believe it is important to discuss how we understand the production of pleasure.

From a bio-medical view, pleasure is seen as a physiological response to a given set of stimuli (Aho, 1998), which means that pleasure is an essential quality that we all possess and experience in similar ways, in and through our bodies (Coveney & Bunton, 2003). However, my understanding of pleasure is informed by a Foucauldian perspective, which asserts that there are no preexisting, inherent pleasurable feelings; rather pleasure is interpreted by people in relation to the discourses circulating in a given socio-cultural context (Foucault, 1978). Similar to his analysis of power, Foucault's (1985) interest was not in the origins, essential nature or meanings of pleasure but in "the ontology of force that linked together acts, pleasures, and desires" (p. 43).

The connection between pleasures and desire is also important to consider because some suggest that what we find pleasurable is dependent on what we desire (Aho, 1998). In this sense, pleasure can be seen as the satisfaction of a desire that is intrinsic or an inherent feeling that we all possess. However, desire, like pleasure, can be viewed as discursively constructed and constituted by the workings of discourse and relations of power. In this respect, Turner (2008) argues that Foucault avoids the pitfall of treating desire as a unified phenomenon because he treats desire as the product of certain socio-historic discourses. Rand (2008) argues in this regard that what we come to think of as 'social norms' function in such a way to regulate our desires. She writes: "Norms solicit our desires. They create, meet, and frustrate our needs with an intensity that is often challenging to explain and, as a result, crucial to explain" (p. 571).

The relationship between desire and pleasure is also an important one for Foucault. It would seem that, in desire, Foucault saw the limits, the constraints and the regulatory power dispersed through discourses of expertise that constructed certain kinds of desire as normal and productive and, therefore, desirable (Turner, 1997). His contention is that desire, although popularly taken to be a natural drive or instinct, is rather produced through the regulations of desires in ways that are construed as benefitting the welfare of the population as a whole. Rose (1999) refers to the 'technology of desire', which he explains is a mechanism that induces in us desires that we work to satisfy. That is, while in most conventional philosophy and social theory, power is seen to repress desire, Foucault treats power as constructive and productive; desire is brought about by power/knowledge. Indeed, Foucault (1980) argues that power should not necessarily be seen as negative but above all as productive: "It traverses and produces things, it induces pleasure, forms of knowledge, produces discourse" (p. 119). He also importantly highlights the corporeal element of power and pleasure by stating that "nothing is more material, physical, corporal than the exercise of power", and if "power is strong this is because, as we are beginning to realize, it produces effects at the level of desire—and also at the level of knowledge" (Foucault, 1980, pp. 58–59). For example, dominant understandings of the social and peer group status attained by 'sporty' boys might represent experiences/outcomes that are desirable for many boys in school and in PE. It is in this sense that Foucault (1980) suggests "power is not simply oppressive; we are caught in its networks precisely because some aspects of the exercise and experience of power are profoundly pleasurable" (p. 34).

PE and Instrumental Goals versus Movement Pleasures

Viewing pleasure as discursively constructed means that specific discourses shape, limit and constrain the way that people come to experience pleasure and make sense of it in their own lives. For instance, discourses of sport, fitness and health tend to focus on instrumental goals, such as rewards, recognition, achievement, accomplishment and social networking (Atkinson, 2008; Booth, 2009; Paul, 2006; Pringle, 2009; Wright & Dewar, 1997). Booth, for instance, draws attention to how New Zealand's Push Play, Sport and Recreation New Zealand's (SPARC) programme, at first seems to be encouraging pleasure but then involves instrumental goals evidenced by slogans such as, "the buzz of sport and recreation is not the positive affect of physical movement but the affect of achievement [better health]" (2009, p. 146). Indeed, Pringle points out how the New Zealand Curriculum (Ministry of Education, 2007), along with the curricula of other countries such as the US, also largely justifies the teaching of PE on instrumental goals related to the production of "healthy, socially well-adjusted and productive citizens" (2009, p. 122).

The most notable translation of these instrumental goals related to health, and in particular concerns over the obesity epidemic, into PE practice has been the use of fitness testing. Wrench and Garrett (2008), for instance, explore pleasure (and pain) as part of fitness testing in PE and illustrate how discursive practices of 'healthism' (Crawford, 1980) are clearly evident in their participants' statements. In particular, they highlight how the participants feel that they are 'responsible' for their own health by monitoring and testing their fitness and bodies. However, a number of critical PE scholars question this focus on instrumental goals in PE and instead argue for a shift towards (movement) pleasures (Booth, 2009; Gard & Wright, 2001; Locke, 1996; Morgan, 2006; Pringle, 2010). Morgan (2006) argues that justifications for PE should relate directly to what can be gained from being physically educated. That is, rather than a focus on producing fit and healthy bodies, emphasis should be on how being fit and healthy enables pleasurable and meaningful experiences.

The ideological aspect of actively promoting movement pleasures in PE is, according to Twietmeyer (2012), nothing to be 'afraid of'. Indeed, the New Zealand Curriculum (Ministry of Education, 2007) encourages its teachers to provide students with positive movement experiences so they can "gain an understanding that movement is integral to human expression and that it can contribute to people's pleasure and enhance their lives" (p. 23). Rintala (2009) argues that it is the responsibility of PE teachers to make sure that the students move in as many different ways as possible so that they eventually get to experience the same satisfaction and pleasure that the PE teachers themselves have experienced. Reid (1997) particularly points towards the fundamental part that games and sport should play in PE because games and sport are considered as "intrinsically good things" (Morgan, 2006, p. 102) or as possessing "intrinsic elements or internal goods" (Rintala, 2009, p. 284). For instance, nearly a decade ago, Wright (2004) called for more research that explores pleasure based on the idea that certain activities will lead to pleasurable experiences. Referring to Kretchmar's (1994) list of 'prime intrinsic values' (satisfactory, pleasant, enjoyable, agreeable) and drawing on Arnold (1996), Wright (2004) argues that children should learn how to value certain activities for 'their own sake'. Indeed, Kretchmar (1994) also commented on the pleasures of PE as related to intrinsic values and stated that "experiences that are pleasurable would need no further justification" (p. 127).

However, I would argue that pleasurable experiences do need to be interrogated because pleasures can be seen as the effect of the workings of discourse and relations of power. It is important to note here that Foucault, as an anti-essentialist, does not view pleasures as inherently 'good' or 'bad' because he is more interested in the power effects of these pleasures. That is, he is interested in how the same pleasures are experienced and made sense of differently by different people. Accordingly, in my work, I am not interested in boys' engagement with 'good' or 'bad' pleasures (Lee & George, 2008; Turner, 2008; Twietmeyer, 2012) but how pleasures articulate with and/or produce relations of power that (reciprocally) shape boys' performances of gender.

In addition, I find the idea of engaging in activities 'for their own sake' problematic because it implies that engagement in the activity then leads to positive outcomes/pleasures that somehow are inherent in the activity itself. Pringle (2010) warns us against the idea that certain physical activities "automatically result in experiences of pleasure" (p. 129) because pleasure is culturally contingent. He further argues that pleasure can therefore not be the foundation of PE because pleasures "are constructed subjectively, are not necessarily rational, and exist in multiple and competing forms" (Pringle, 2010, p. 132). Drawing on Tinning's (2002) 'modest pedagogy', Pringle encourages PE teachers to be careful in their advocating for pleasure as their focus. Indeed, much of what a child learns in PE is generated through an adult PE teacher's formulations of how he or she thinks it 'should' be experienced. These formulations are based upon past, positive experiences, which are in turn reflected upon favourably (and with pleasure) (Wellard, 2012). In this way, Pringle (2010) believes that the call to legitimate the educational value of pleasure in PE is primarily a reflection of physical educators' subjective and favourable experiences of games and sport. That is, similar to games and sport, pleasures should not be pursued for their own sake. For instance, nobody is programmed at birth to enjoy playing football or doing ballet (Gard, 2008). There are no innate or intrinsic feelings, understandings or experiences of pleasure; instead, they are discursively constructed. Activities in PE can therefore be seen as constituting and constituted by the workings of contextually specific socio-historic discourses that shape students' experiences of *any* activity in different and unique ways. That is why my study set out to explore how pleasures experienced through the boys' engagement with different activities in PE are produced through the workings of discourse and relations of power, with particular respect to performances of gender.

Boys, Gender and (dis)Pleasures

What we want and what we strive for are, in a Foucauldian perspective, discursively constructed. I believe that exploring the constructions of pleasure and of desire can reveal the discursive practices/formations circulating in boys' PE that shape boys' ideas about their gendered selves and bodies. In particular, Foucault's theories of power and pleasure, and their connection to the construction of the self, may help us better understand the workings of discourse and relations of power in the making of boys' masculine selves. Foucault's theorising is useful for demonstrating how discursive practices in boys' PE are not only constraining but also enabling of boys' enjoyment in this subject. The intent of this book is to explore pleasure in its many forms as an effect of the workings of discourse and relations of power. More specifically, my aim in this book is not to merely highlight the discursive construction of pleasures in boys' PE but to problematise these pleasures and their articulations with boys' performances of gender. In order to do so, I also use the term (dis)pleasures.

I have used the term '(dis)pleasures' throughout this book in recognition that pleasures are multiple, fluid and assessed differently by different people and even by the same people over time. That is, what is first seen/interpreted as displeasure might turn into pleasure, or that which is displeasurable might over time become pleasurable. For instance, the displeasurable experience of having to do the beep-test can, after some time, turn into the pleasurable experience of being able to demonstrate a fit and able body or the long-term outcome of better fitness and health. Ultimately, pleasures and (dis)pleasures, just as gender and masculinities/femininities, are messy/tricky concepts, which is why there is a need to interrogate the (gendered) pleasures and (dis)pleasures of PE. An analysis of the (gendered) pleasures and (dis)pleasures of PE can help us better understand what contributes to (or inhibits) ongoing participation in and enjoyment of PE.

So how can we understand that certain performances of gender are privileged in PE? In addition, how can we understand that the discursive practices of PE are not only disciplining and constraining but also productive and a source of pleasures? As pointed out by Jackson (1996), while theorising about gender, sexuality and subjectivity is getting ever more sophisticated, there is no satisfactory way of answering the fundamental question, 'How did I get this way?' Booth (2009), Gard (2008) and Pringle (2010) argue that if critical PE scholars want to change the social influence associated with dominated discourses of masculinity, there is a need to examine the discourses of PE pleasure.

In order to better our understanding of pleasure, we need to know more about how different students understand and experience certain activities in PE, ranging from the positive to the negative. For instance, how do certain PE practices related to sports, competition, fitness testing and skill learning enable and restrict students' pleasurable experiences? Gard and Meyenn

(2000) remind us that discourses of competitive sports not only involve pain and violence but also bodily pleasures. Although the traditional male sport of rugby has typically been implicated in the production of unequal gender power relations, it can also be seen as a site for the production of pleasure related to skill development, physical contact/intimacy and affirming/challenging gendered identities (Pringle, 2009). Indeed, the interviewees in Pringle's (2009) study spoke about rugby as a way of being socially accepted and as a source of pleasure, about which one of the boys (Tom) said:

> Well, rugby was really my saving; it gave me something to be proud of. . . . In my senior class at primary school I wasn't really accepted in the "cool" group in our year . . . and intellectually I was just average. But my saving grace at school and with my headmaster was that I was a very good rugby player and so I would get respect by performing in the sport arena. And so I just loved, totally loved, rugby.
>
> (p. 219)

However, Gard's (2001, 2003, 2008) and Risner's (2007) research on boys and dance has also highlighted how discourses of masculinity work to restrict boys' pleasures. Using an example from his study of boys and dancing, Gard (2003) talks about Alex, who outwardly hates dancing and constructs himself as a desirable boy by using technologies of bodily pleasures. Gard argues that there is a correlation between the absence of pleasure and the notion that "boys don't dance" (p. 109). Similarly, Risner (2007) asserts that this "boy code" restricts pleasure since "the power of narrowly defined masculinity and its 'boy code' continues to police the behaviours of young men, regardless of the joy and pleasure they experience while dancing" (p. 145). So while finding pleasure in engaging in traditional masculine sports, such as rugby, reaffirms privileged masculinities, outwardly finding pleasure in non-traditional masculine physical activities, such as dance, would possibly give evidence of subjugated masculinities. What boys find pleasurable (or not) shapes their gendered identities (physically educated identities). In my research, I am therefore interested in examining how discourses of masculinity circulating within the context of boys' PE might restrict as well as enable pleasure when boys attempt to construct themselves according to discourses of desirable boys. Although the likes of Kretchmar (2001) and Siedentop (1994) have explored the complexities associated with producing meaningful movement pleasures within PE, we know little about how this intersects with the social construction of gender and boys' performances of masculinities. My study contributes to this knowledge through findings that are very much located in boys' lived experiences of PE and the meanings they make of it.

In the next chapter, I discuss the methods in more detail and reflect on ethical considerations in this study and in the field of visual ethnography more broadly.

References

Aho, J. A. (1998). *The things of the world: A social phenomenology.* London, UK: Praeger.

Allen, L. (2013). Behind the bike sheds: Sexual geographies of schooling. *British Journal of Sociology of Education, 34*(1), 56–75.

Alton-Lee, A., & Praat, A. (2000). *Explaining and addressing gender differences in the New Zealand compulsory school sector: A literature review.* Wellington, NZ: Ministry of Education.

Andrews, D. L. (2000). Posting up: French post-structuralism and the critical analysis of contemporary sporting culture. In J. Coakley & E. Dunning (Eds.), *Handbook of Sport Studies* (pp. 106–137). Thousand Oaks, CA: Sage.

Armstrong, F. (2007). Disability, education and space: Some critical reflections. In K. N. Gulson & C. Symes (Eds.), *Spatial theories of education: Policy and geography matters* (pp. 95–110). New York: Routledge.

Arnold, P. J. (1996). Olympism, sport and education. *Quest, 48,* 93–101.

Atkinson, M. (2008). Triathlon, suffering, and exciting significance. *Leisure Studies, 27*(2), 165–180.

Atkinson, M., & Kehler, M. (2010). Boys, gyms, locker rooms and heterotopia. In M. Kehler & M. Atkinson (Eds.), *Boys' bodies: Speaking the unspoken* (pp. 73–90). New York: Peter Lang.

Austin, J. L. (Ed.). (1955). *How to do things with words.* Cambridge, MA: Harvard University Press.

Azzarito, L. (2009). The panopticon of physical education: Pretty, active and ideally white. *Physical Education and Sport Pedagogy, 14,* 19–40.

Azzarito, L., & Harrison, L. (2008). 'White men can't jump': Race, gender and natural athleticism. *International Review for the Sociology of Sport, 43,* 347–364.

Azzarito, L., & Hill, J. (2013). Girls looking for a 'second home': Bodies, difference and places of inclusion. *Physical Education and Sport Pedagogy, 18*(4), 351–375.

Azzarito, L., & Solmon, M. A. (2006). A feminist poststructuralist view on student bodies in physical education: Sites of compliance, resistance, and transformation. *Journal of Teaching in Physical Education, 25*(2), 200–225.

Azzarito, L., Solmon, M. A., & Harrison, L. (2006). '. . . If I had a choice, I would. . . .': A feminist poststructuralist perspective on girls in physical education. *Research Quarterly for Exercise and Sport, 77*(2), 222–239.

Azzarito, L., & Solmon, M. A. (2009). An investigation of students' embodied discourses in physical education: A gender project. *Journal of Teaching in Physical Education, 28,* 173–191.

Azzarito, L., & Sterling, J. (2010). 'What it was in my eyes': Picturing youths' embodiment in 'real' spaces. *Qualitative Research in Sport and Exercise, 2*(2), 209–228.

Bailey, R., Armour, K., Kirk, D., Jess, M., Pickup, I., Sandford, R., & BERA Physical Education and Sport Pedagogy Special Interest Group. (2009). The educational benefits claimed for physical education and school sport: An academic review. *Research Papers in Education, 24*(1), 1–27.

Bale, J. (1993). The spatial development of the modern stadium. *International Review for the Sociology of Sport, 28*(2/3), 121–134.

Bale, J. (2004). *Running cultures: Racing in time and space.* London, UK: Routledge.

Barad, K. (2007). *Meeting the universe halfway: Quantum physics and the entanglement of matter and meaning.* Durham, NC: Duke University Press.

Baxter, J. (2003). *Positioning gender in discourse.* Basingstoke, UK: Palgrave.

Beasley, C. (2008). Rethinking hegemonic masculinity in a globalizing world. *Men and Masculinities, 11*(1), 86–103.

Bell, B. (2009). *Sport studies.* Exeter, UK: Learning Matters.

Bell, D., Binnie, J., Cream, J., & Valentine, G. (1994). All hyped up and no place to go. *Gender, Place and Culture, 1,* 31–48.

Berg, P., & Lahelma, E. (2010). Gendering processes in the field of physical education. *Gender and Education, 22*(1), 31–46.

Blunt, A., & Rose, G. (1994). *Writing women and space: Colonial and postcolonial geographies.* London, UK: Guildford Press.

Booth, D. (2009). Politics and pleasure: The philosophy of physical education revisited. *Quest, 61*(2), 133–153.

Bordo, S. (1993). *Weight, feminism, western culture, and the body.* Berkeley, CA: University of California Press.

Bramham, P. (2003). Boys, masculinities and PE. *Sport, Education and Society, 8*(1), 57–71.

Brown, D. (2006). Pierre Bourdieu's 'Masculine Domination' thesis and the gendered body in sport and physical culture. *Sociology of Sport Journal, 23,* 162–188.

Burrows, L. (2000). Old games in new rompers? Gender issues in New Zealand physical education. *Journal of Physical Education New Zealand, 33*(2), 30–41.

Burrows, L. (2005). Do the 'right' thing: Chewing the fat in physical education. *Journal of Physical Education New Zealand, 33*(1), 7–16.

Butler, J. (1990). *Gender trouble: Feminism and the subversion of identity.* London and New York: Routledge.

Butler, J. (1993). *Bodies that matter: On the discursive limits of 'sex'.* New York: Routledge.

Butler, J. (1997). *Excitable speech: A politics of the performative.* New York: Routledge.

Butler, J. (2004). *Undoing gender.* New York: Routledge.

Celeste, U. (1978). Gym and gender: The educational value of performing experiences. Washington, DC: ERIC Clearinghouse.

Cervelló, E., Moreno, J. A., Alonso, N., & Iglesias, D. (2006). Goal orientations, motivational climate and dispositional flow of high school students engaging in extracurricular involvement in physical activity. *Perceptual and Motor Skills, 102,* 87–92.

Chandler, T. J. L. (1996). The structuring of manliness and the development of rugby football at the public schools and Oxbridge, 1830–1880. In J. Nauright & T. Chandler (Eds.), *Making men: Rugby and masculine identity* (pp. 13–31). London, UK: Frank Cass.

Chaouloff, F. (1997). The serotonin hypothesis. In W. P. Morgan (Ed.), *Physical activity and mental health* (pp. 179–198). Washington, DC: Taylor and Francis.

Chapman, G. E. (1997). Making weight: Lightweight rowing, technologies of power, and technologies of the self. *Sociology of Sport Journal, 14,* 205–223.

Clarke, G. (2004). Threatening space: (Physical) Education and homophobic body work. In J. Evans, B. Davies, & J. Wright (Eds.), *Body knowledge and control: Studies in the sociology of physical education and health* (pp. 191–205). New York: Routledge.

Clarke, G. (2006). Sexuality and physical education. In D. Kirk, D. Macdonald, & M. O'Sullivan (Eds.), *The handbook of physical education* (pp. 723–739). London, UK: Routledge.

Connell, R. W. (1987). *Gender and power.* Cambridge, UK: Polity Press.

Connell, R. W. (1990). An iron man: The body and some contradictions of hegemonic masculinity. In M. Messner & D. Sabo (Eds.), *Sport, men and the gender order: Critical feminist perspectives* (pp. 83–95). Champaign, IL: Human Kinetics.

Connell, R. W. (1995). *Masculinities.* Sydney: Allen & Unwin.

Connell, R. W. (1996). Teaching the boys: new research on masculinity, and gender strategies for schools. *Teachers College Record, 98,* 206–235.

Connell, R. W. (2000). *The men and the boys.* Cambridge, UK: Polity Press.

Connell, R. W. (2002). Masculinities and globalisation. In H. Worth, A. Paris, & L. Allen (Eds.), *The life of Brian: Masculinities, sexualities and health in New Zealand* (pp. 27–42). Dunedin, NZ: University of Otago Press.

Connell, R. W. (2005). *Masculinities* (2nd ed.). Cambridge: Polity Press.

Connell, R. W. (2008). Masculinity construction and sports in boys' education: A framework for thinking about the issue. *Sport, Education and Society, 13*(2), 131–145.

Cornwall, A., & Lindisfarne, N. (1994). *Dislocating masculinity: Comparative ethnographies.* London, UK: Routledge.

Coveney, J., & Bunton, R. (2003). In pursuit of the study of pleasure: Implications for health research and practice. *Health, 7*(2), 161–179.

Cox, A. E., Smith, A. L., & Williams, L. (2008). Change in physical education motivation and physical activity behavior during middle school. *The Journal of Adolescent Health, 43*(5), 506–513.

Crang, M. (2005). Time: Space. In P. Cloke & R. Johnston (Eds.), *Space of geographical thought: Deconstructing human geography's binaries* (pp. 199–220). London, UK: Sage.

Crawford, R. (1980). Healthism and the medicalization of everyday life. *International Journal of Health Services, 10*, 365–388.

Csikszentmihalyi, M. (1990). *Flow: The psychology of optimal experience.* New York: Harper & Row.

Dalley-Trim, L. (2007). 'The boys' presenHegemonic masculinity: A performance of multiple acts. *Gender and Education, 19*(2), 199–217.

Datta, A. (2008). Spatialising performance: Masculinities and femininities in a 'fragmented' field. *Gender, Place & Culture: A Journal of Feminist Geography, 15*(2), 189–204.

Davidson, A. (2001). Appendix: Foucault, psychoanalysis, and pleasure. In A. Davidson (Ed.), *The emergence of sexuality: Historical epistemology and the formation of concepts* (pp. 209–216). Cambridge, MA: Harvard University Press.

Davies, B. (2006). Subjectification: The relevance of Butler's analysis for education. *British Journal of Sociology of Education, 27*(4), 425–438.

Davies, B., & Harré, R. (1990). Positioning: The discursive production of selves. *Journal for the Theory of Social Behaviour, 20*(1), 43–63.

Davis, K. (1997). *Embodied practices: Feminist perspectives on the body.* London, UK: Sage.

Davison, K. G. (2000). Boys' bodies in school: Physical education. *The Journal of Men's Studies, 8*(2), 255–266.

Deci, E. L., & Ryan, R. M. (2002). Self-determination research: Reflections and future directions. In E. L. Deci & R. M. Ryan (Eds.), *Handbook of self-determination research* (pp. 431–441). Rochester, NY: University of Rochester Press.

Deleuze, G. (1986). *Foucault.* Paris: Editions de Minuit.

Demetriou, D. (2001). Connell's concept of hegemonic masculinity: A critique. *Theory and Society, 30*(3), 337–361.

Dishman, R. (1995). Physical activity and public health: Mental health. *Quest, 47*, 362–385.

Donaldson, M. (1993). What is hegemonic masculinity? *Theory and Society, 22*(5), 643–657.

Drummond, M. (2003). The meaning of boys' bodies in physical education. *The Journal of Men's Studies, 11*(2), 131–143.

Dunk, T., & Bartol, D. (2005). The logic and limitations of male working-class culture in a resource hinterland. In B. Van Hoven & K. Horschelmann (Eds.), *Spaces of masculinities* (pp. 31–44). London, UK: Routledge.

Dyer, K. F. (1982). *Challenging the men: The social biology of female sporting achievement.* St Lucia, Australia: University of Queensland Press.

Eichberg, H. (1990). Race-track and labyrinth: The space of physical culture in Berlin. *The Journal of Sport History, 17*(2), 245–260.

Ennis, C. D. (2006). Curriculum: Forming and reshaping the vision of physical education in a high need, low demand world of schools. *Quest, 58,* 41–59.

Enright, E., & O'Sullivan, M. (2012). 'Producing different knowledge and producing knowledge differently': Rethinking physical education research and practice through participatory visual methods. *Sport, Education and Society, 17*(1), 35–55.

Epstein, D. (1997). Boyz' own stories: Masculinities and sexualities in schools. *Gender and Education, 9*(1), 105–115.

Evans, J., Davies, B., & Rich, E. (2009). The body made flesh: Embodied learning and the corporeal device. *British Journal of Sociology of Education, 30*(4), 391–406.

Fernandez-Balboa, J.-M. (1993). Socio-cultural characteristics of the hidden curriculum in physical education. *Quest, 45*(2), 230–254.

Ferrer-Caja, E., & Weiss, M. R. (2000). Predictors of intrinsic motivation among adolescent students in physical education. *Research Quarterly for Exercise and Sport, 71,* 267–279.

Fisette, J. L. (2011). Exploring how girls navigate their embodied identities in physical education. *Physical Education and Sport Pedagogy, 16*(2), 179–196.

Fitzpatrick, K. (2013). *Critical pedagogy, physical education and urban schooling.* New York: Peter Lang.

Flintoff, A., & Scraton, S. (2008). The challenges of intersectionality: Researching difference in physical education. *International Studies in Sociology of Education, 18*(2), 73–85.

Flood, M. (2008). Men, sex, and homosociality: How bonds between men shape their sexual relations with women. *Men and Masculinities, 10*(3), 339–359.

Foucault, M. (1967). Of other spaces. *Diacritics, 16*(1986), 22–27.

Foucault, M. (1969). [Interview by J.J. Brochier]. *Magazine Littkraire, 29,* 23–25.

Foucault, M. (1972). *The archaeology of knowledge and discourse on language* (1st American ed.). New York: Pantheon Books.

Foucault, M. (1973). *The birth of the clinic: An archaeology of medical perception.* London, UK: Tavistock.

Foucault, M. (1977). *Discipline and punish: The birth of the prison.* London: Penguin Books.

Foucault, M. (1978). *The history of sexuality, volume one.* Harmondsworth, UK: Penguin.

Foucault, M. (1980). *Power/knowledge: Selected interviews and other writings, 1972–1977.* New York: Pantheon.

Foucault, M. (1982). Space, Knowledge, and Power: Interview with P. Rabinow. *Skyline* March 16–20.

Foucault, M. (1983a). Afterword: The subject and power. In H. L. Dreyfus & P. Rabinow (Eds.), *Michel Foucault: Beyond structuralism and hermeneutics* (2nd ed., pp. 208–226). Chicago, IL: University of Chicago Press.

Foucault, M. (1983b). On the genealogy of ethics: An overview of work in progress. In H. L. Dreyfus & P. Rabinow (Eds.), *Michel Foucault: Beyond structuralism and hermeneutics* (2nd ed., pp. 229–252). Chicago, IL: University of Chicago Press.

Foucault, M. (1984). *The Foucault reader.* (Edited by P. Rabinow). New York: Pantheon.

Foucault, M. (1985). *The use of pleasure: The history of sexuality, volume 2.* London, UK: Penguin Books.

Foucault, M. (1988). Technologies of the self. In L. H. Martin, H. Gutman, & P. H. Hutton (Eds.), *Technologies of the self: A seminar with Michel Foucault* (pp. 16–49). Amherst, MA: University of Massachusetts Press.

Foucault, M. (1995). *Discipline and punish: The birth of the prison*. Westminster, MD: Vintage.

Foucault, M. (1996). Nietzsche, genealogy, history. In L. Cahoone (Ed.), *From modernism to postmodernism: An anthology* (pp. 360–378). Cambridge, MA: Blackwell.

Foucault, M. (1997). *Ethics: Subjectivity and truth* (Trans. R. Hurley and others). New York: New Press.

Foucault, M. (2000). *Power: Essential works of Foucault, 1954–1984, volume 3*. London, UK: Penguin.

Fox, K. (1997). *The physical self: From motivation to well-being*. Champaign, IL: Human Kinetics.

Frosh, S., Phoenix, A., & Pattman, R. (2002). *Young masculinities: Understanding boys in contemporary society*. Hampshire and New York: Palgrave.

Fry, R. (1988). The curriculum and girls' secondary schooling 1880–1925. In S. Middleton (Ed.), *Women and education in Aotearoa* (pp. 31–45). Wellington, NZ: Allen.

Gard, M. (2001). Dancing around the 'problem' of boys and dance. *Discourse: Studies in the Cultural Politics of Education, 22*(2), 213–225.

Gard, M. (2003). Moving and belonging: Dance, sport and sexuality. *Sex Education, 3*(2), 105–118.

Gard, M. (2008). When a boy's gotta dance: New masculinities, old pleasures. *Sport, Education and Society, 13*(2), 181–193.

Gard, M., & Meyenn, R. (2000). Boys, bodies, pleasure and pain: Interrogating contact sports in schools. *Sport, Education and Society, 5*(1), 19–34.

Gard, M., & Wright, J. (2001). Managing uncertainty: Obesity discourses and physical education in a risk society. *Studies in Philosophy and Education, 20*(6), 535–549.

Gard, M., & Wright, J. (2005). *The 'obesity epidemic': Science, ideology and morality*. London, UK: Routledge.

Gerdin, G., & Pringle, R. (2015). The politics of pleasure: An ethnographic examination exploring the dominance of the multi-activity sport-based physical education model. *Sport, Education and Society*. doi:http://dx.doi.org/10.1080/135733 22.2015.1019448

Gieryn, T. (1999). *Cultural boundaries of science: Credibility on the line*. Chicago, IL: University of Chicago Press.

González-Cutre, D., Sicilia, A., Moreno, J. A., & Fernández-Balboa, J. M. (2009). Dispositional flow in physical education: Relationships with motivational climate, social goals, and perceived competence. *Journal of Teaching in Physical Education, 28*, 422–440.

Gordon, T., & Lahelma, E. (1996). 'School is like an Ants' Nest': Spatiality and embodiment in schools. *Gender and Education, 8*(3), 301–310.

Gore, J. M. (1998). Disciplining bodies: On the continuity of power relations in pedagogy. In T. Popkewitz & M. Brennan (Eds.), *Foucault's challenge: Discourse, knowledge and power in education* (pp. 231–251). New York: Teachers College Press.

Gorely, T., Holroyd, R., & Kirk, D. (2003). Muscularity, the habitus and the social construction of gender: Towards a gender-relevant physical education. *British Journal of Sociology of Education, 24*(4), 429–448.

Gregson, N., & Rose, G. (2000). Taking butler elsewhere: Performativities, spatialities and subjectivities. *Environment and Planning D: Society and Space, 18*, 422–452.

Grogan, S., & Richards, H. (2002). Body image: Focus groups with boys and men. *Men and Masculinities, 4*(3), 219–232.

Grosz, E. (1992). Bodies-cities. In B. Colomina (Ed.), *Sexuality and space* (pp. 241–253). New York: Princeton Architectural Press.

Grosz, E. (1994). *Volatile bodies: Toward a corporeal feminism*. Bloomington, IN: Indiana University Press.

Grosz, E. (1995). *Space, time, and perversion: Essays on the politics of bodies*. New York: Routledge.

Guthrie, S. R., & Castelnuovo, S. (2001). Disability management among women with physical impairments: The contributions of physical activity. *Sociology of Sport Journal, 18*, 5–20.

Haerens, L., Kirk, D., Cardon, G., De Bourdeaudhuij, I., & Vansteenkiste, M. (2010). Motivational profiles for secondary school physical education and its relationship to the adoption of a physically active lifestyle among university students. *European Physical Education Review, 16*(2), 117–139.

Hall, M., & Richardson, D. (1982). *Fair ball*. Ontario, Canada: Canadian Advisory Council on the Status of Women.

Hannon, J., & Ratliffe, T. (2007). Opportunities to participate and teacher interactions in coed versus single-gender physical education settings. *Physical Educator, 64*(1), 11–20.

Haywood, C., & Mac an Ghaill, M. (1996). Schooling masculinities. In M. Mac an Ghaill (Ed.), *Understanding masculinities* (pp. 50–60). Buckingham, UK: Open University Press.

Hearn, J. (2004). From hegemonic masculinity to the hegemony of men. *Feminist Theory, 5*(1), 49–72.

Hickey, C. (2008). Physical education, sport and hyper-masculinity in schools. *Sport, Education and Society, 13*(2), 147–161.

Hickey, C., & Fitzclarence, L. (1999). Educating boys in sport and physical education: Using narrative methods to develop pedagogies of responsibility. *Sport, Education and Society, 4*(1), 51–62.

Hoffman, P. (1997). The endorphin hypothesis. In W. P. Morgan (Ed.), *Physical activity and mental health* (pp. 163–177). Washington, DC: Taylor and Francis.

Holstein, J. A., & Gubrium, J. F. (2005). Interpretive practice and social action. In N. K. Denzin & Y. S. Lincoln (Eds.), *Handbook of qualitative research* (pp. 483–506). Thousand Oaks, CA: Sage.

Hunter, L. (2004). Bourdieu and the social space of the PE class: Reproduction of Doxa through practice. *Sport, Education and Society, 9*(2), 175–192.

Irwin, C. C., Symons, C. W., & Kerr, D. L. (2003). The dilemmas of obesity how can physical educators help? *Journal of Physical Education, Recreation & Dance, 74*(6), 33–39.

Jackson, J. (2009). 'Dangerous presumptions': How single-sex schooling reifies false notions of sex, gender, and sexuality. *Gender and Education, 22*(2), 227–238.

Jackson, S. (1996). Heterosexuality as a problem for feminist theory. In L. Adkins & V. Merchant (Eds.), *Sexualising the social: Power and the organisation of sexuality* (pp. 15–34). London, UK: Macmillan.

Jackson, S. A. (1996). Toward a conceptual understanding of the flow experience in elite athletes. *Research Quarterly for Exercise and Sport, 67*, 76–90.

Jamieson, P., Fisher, K., Gilding, T., Taylor, P., & Trevitt, C. (2000). Place and space in the design of new learning environments. *Higher Education Research and Development, 19*(2), 221–237.

Johns, D. P., & Johns, J. S. (2000). Surveillance, subjectivism and technologies of power: An analysis of the discursive power of high performance sport. *International Review for the Sociology of Sport, 35*(2), 219–234.

Jones, A. (1990). Politics, policy and pedagogy: Discourses on education for women and girls. In A. Jones, G. McCulloch, J. Marshall, G. Hingangaroa Smith, & L. Tuhiwai Smith (Eds.), *Myths and realities: Schooling in New Zealand* (pp. 88–122). Palmerston North, NZ: Dunmore.

Jones, A., & Aitchison, C. C. (2007). Triathlon as space for women's technologies of the self. In C. C. Aitchison (Ed.), *Sport and gender identities: Masculinities, femininities and sexualities* (pp. 53–73). Oxon, UK: Routledge.

Kehler, M. (2004). Masculinities and resistance: High school boys (un)doing boy. *Taboo, 8*(1), 97–113.

Kehler, M. (2007). Hallway fears and high school friendships: The complications of young men (re)negotiating heterosexualised identities. *Discourse: Studies in the Cultural Politics of Education, 28*, 259–277.

Kehler, M. (2014). When boys talk about their bodies: How boys learn 'that person's useless'. In S. Barnard Flory, A. Tischler, & S. Sanders (Eds.), *Sociocultural issues in physical education: Case studies for teachers* (pp. 55–70). London, UK: Rowman & Littlefield.

Kehler, M., & Atkinson, M. (2010). *Boys' bodies: Speaking the unspoken.* New York: Peter Lang.

Kehler, M., & Martino, W. (2007). Questioning masculinities: Interrogating boys' capacities for self-problematization in schools. *Canadian Journal of Education, 30*, 90–112.

Kenway, J. (1997). Boys' education, masculinity and gender reform: Some introductory remarks. *Curriculum Perspectives, 17*(1), 57–61.

Kimiecik, J. C. (2000). Learn to love exercise. *Psychology Today, 33*, 20–22.

Kirby, K. (1996). Cartographic vision and the limits of politics. In N. Duncan (Ed.), *BodySpace: Destabilizing geographies of gender and sexuality* (pp. 1–17). London, UK: Routledge.

Kirk, D. (1997). Schooling bodies in new times: The reform of school physical education in high modernity. In J.-M. Fernandez-Balboa (Ed.), *Critical postmodernism in human movement, physical education and sport* (pp. 39–64). Albany, NY: State University of New York Press.

Kirk, D. (2002). Physical education: A gendered history. In D. Penney (Ed.), *Gender and physical education: Contemporary issues and future directions* (pp. 24–37). London, UK: Routledge.

Kirk, D. (2010). *Physical education futures.* London, UK: Routledge.

Kirk, D., & Tinning, R. (1994). Embodied self-identity, healthy lifestyles and school. *Sociology of Health and Illness, 16*, 600–625.

Klomsten, A. T., Marsh, H. W., & Skaalvik, E. M. (2005). Adolescents' perceptions of masculine and feminine values in sport and physical education: A study of gender differences. *Sex Roles, 52*(9/10), 625–636.

Koltyn, K. F. (1997). The thermogenic hypothesis. In W. P. Morgan (Ed.), *Physical activity and mental health* (pp. 213–226). Washington, DC: Taylor and Francis.

Kretchmar, R. S. (1994). *Practical philosophy of sport.* Champaign, IL: Human Kinetics.

Kretchmar, R. S. (2001). Duty, habit, and meaning: Different faces of adherence. *Quest, 53*, 318–325.

Kretchmar, R. S. (2005). *Practical philosophy of sport and physical activity.* Champaign, IL: Human Kinetics.

Larsson, H. (2012). Materialising bodies: There is nothing more material than a socially constructed body. *Sport, Education and Society.* doi:10.1080/1357332 2.2012.722550

Larsson, H., Fagrell, B., & Redelius, K. (2009). Queering physical education: Between benevolence towards girls and a tribute to masculinity. *Physical Education and Sport Pedagogy, 14*(1), 1–17.

Larsson, H., & Quennerstedt, M. (2012). Understanding movement: A sociocultural approach to exploring moving humans. *Quest, 64*(4), 283–298.

Larsson, H., Redelius, K., & Fagrell, B. (2011). Moving (in) the heterosexual matrix: On heteronormativity in secondary school physical education. *Physical Education and Sport Pedagogy, 16*(1), 67–81.

Lee, P., & George, R. P. (2008). *Body-self dualism in contemporary ethics and politics*. New York: Cambridge University Press.

Lefebvre, H. (1991). *The production of space*. Oxford, UK: Basil Blackwell.

Light, R., & Kirk, D. (2000). High school rugby, the body and the reproduction of hegemonic masculinity. *Sport, Education and Society, 5*(2), 163–176.

Lim, B. S. C., & Wang, C. K. J. (2009). Perceived autonomy support, behavioural regulations in physical education and physical activity intention. *Psychology of Sport and Exercise, 10*(1), 52–60.

Liukkonen, J., Barkoukis, V., Watt, A., & Jaakkola, T. (2010). Motivational climate and students' emotional experiences and effort in physical education. *The Journal of Educational Research, 103*, 295–308.

Locke, L. (1996). Dr. Lewin's little liver patties: A parable about encouraging healthy lifestyles. *Quest, 48*, 422–431.

Mac an Ghaill, M. (1994). *The making of men: Masculinities, sexualities and schooling*. Buckingham, UK: Open University Press.

MacPhail, A., Gorley, T., & Kirk, D. (2003). Young people's socialisation into sport: A case study of an athletics club. *Sport, Education and Society, 8*(2), 251–267.

Markula, P. (1995). Firm but shapely, fit but sexy, strong but thin: The postmodern aerobicizing female bodies. *Sociology of Sport Journal, 12*(4), 424–453.

Markula, P. (2003). The technologies of the self: Sport, feminism, and Foucault. *Sociology of Sport Journal, 20*, 87–107.

Markula, P., & Pringle, R. (2006). *Foucault, sport and exercise: Power, knowledge and transforming the self*. New York: Routledge.

Markus, T. A. (1993). *Buildings and power: Freedom and control in the origin of modern building types*. London, UK: Routledge.

Martino, W., & Pallotta-Chiarolli, M. (2003). *So what's a boy? Addressing issues of masculinity and schooling*. Buckingham, UK: Open University Press.

Massey, D. (1993). Power-geometry and a progressive sense of place. In J. Bird, B. Curtis, T. Putnam, G. Robertson, & L. Tickner (Eds.), *Mapping the future: Local cultures, global change* (pp. 60–70). New York: Routledge.

Massey, D. (1994). *Space, place and gender*. Cambridge, UK: Polity Press.

Massey, D. (2005). *For space*. London, UK: Sage.

McGregor, J. (2004). Spatiality and the place of the material in schools. *Pedagogy, Culture and Society, 12*(3), 347–372.

McKay, J., Messner, M., & Sabo, D. (2000). *Masculinities, gender relations and sport*. Thousand Oaks, CA: Sage.

McLaren, P. (1991). Schooling the postmodern body: Critical pedagogy and the politics of enfleshment. In H. Giroux (Ed.), *Postmodernism, feminism and cultural politics* (pp. 144–173). Albany, NY: State University of New York Press.

Messner, M. (1990). Boyhood, organized sports, and the construction of masculinities. *Journal of Contemporary Ethnography, 18*(4), 416–444.

Messner, M. (1992). *Power at play: Sports and the problem of masculinity*. Boston, MA: Beacon Press.

Messner, M., & Sabo, D. (1990). Introduction: Toward a critical feminist reappraisal of sport, men, and the gender order. In M. Messner & D. Sabo (Eds.), *Sport, men, and the gender order: Critical feminist perspectives* (pp. 1–15). Champaign, IL: Human Kinetics.

Millington, B., Vertinsky, P., Boyle, E., & Wilson, B. (2008). Making Chinese-Canadian masculinities in Vancouver's physical education curriculum. *Sport, Education and Society, 13*(2), 195–214.

Ministry of Education. (2007). *The New Zealand curriculum*. Wellington, NZ: Learning Media.

Morgan, J. (2000). Critical pedagogy: The spaces that make the difference. *Pedagogy, Culture and Society, 8*(3), 273–288.

Morgan, W. (2006). Philosophy and physical education. In D. Kirk, M. O'Sullivan, & D. MacDonald (Eds.), *The handbook of research in sport and physical education* (pp. 97–108). Thousand Oaks, CA: Sage.

Nast, H., & Pile, S. (1998). *Places through the body*. London, UK: Routledge.

National Association for Physical Education (NASPE). (2002). *Active start: A statement of physical activity guidelines for children, birth to five years*. Reston, VA: American Alliance for Health, Physical Education, Recreation and Dance (AAHPERD).

Nelson, L. (1999). Bodies (and spaces) do matter: The limits of performativity. *Gender, Place & Culture: A Journal of Feminist Geography, 6*(4), 331–353.

New Zealand Association of Health Physical Education and Recreation. (1991). *Breaking through: A resource to promote equity for girls in physical education*. Wellington, NZ: New Zealand Association of Health Physical Education and Recreation.

Nietzsche, F. (1969). *On the genealogy of morals*. New York: Vintage Books.

Nightingale, A. (2006). The nature of gender: Work, gender, and environment. *Environment and Planning D: Society and Space, 24*, 165–185.

Ntoumanis, N. (2001). A self-determination approach to the understanding of motivation in physical education. *British Journal of Educational Psychology, 71*, 225–242.

Ntoumanis, N. (2005). A prospective study of participation in optional school physical education using a self-determination theory framework. *Journal of Educational Psychology, 97*, 444–453.

O'Donoghue, D. (2006). Situating place and space in the making of masculinities in schools. *Journal of Curriculum and Pedagogy, 3*(1), 15–33.

O'Donoghue, D. (2007). 'James always hangs out here': Making space for place in studying masculinities at school. *Visual Studies, 22*(1), 62–73.

O'Donovan, T. M., & Kirk, D. (2007). Managing classroom entry: An ecological analysis of ritual interaction and negotiation in the changing room. *Sport, Education and Society, 12*(4), 399–413.

Oliver, K. L., Hamzeh, M., & McCaughtry, N. (2009). Girly girls can play games/las ninas pueden jugar tambien: Co-creating a curriculum of possibilities with fifth-grade girls. *Journal of teaching in physical education, 28*(1), 90–110.

Oliver, K. L., & Lalik, R. (2004). Critical inquiry on the body in girls' physical education classes: A critical poststructural perspective. *Journal of Teaching in Physical Education, 23*(2), 162–195.

Ommundsen, Y., & Kvalø, E. S. (2007). Autonomy-mastery, supportive or performance focused? Different teacher behaviours and pupils' outcomes in physical education. *Scandinavian Journal of Educational Research, 51*(4), 385–413.

Osborne, K., Bauer, A., & Sutliff, M. (2002). Middle school students' perceptions of coed versus non-coed physical education. *Physical Educator, 59*(2), 83–89.

Paechter, C. (2000). *Changing school subjects: Power, gender and curriculum*. Buckingham, UK: Open University Press.

Paechter, C. (2001). Using poststructuralist ideas in gender theory and research. In B. Francis & C. Skelton (Eds.), *Investigating Gender: Contemporary perspectives in education* (pp. 41–51). Buckingham: Open University Press.

Paechter, C. (2003). Power, bodies and identity: How different forms of physical education construct varying masculinities and femininities in secondary schools. *Sex Education: Sexuality, Society and Learning, 3*(1), 47–59.

Paechter, C. (2004). Metaphors of space in educational theory and practice. *Pedagogy, Culture and Society, 12*(3), 449–466.

Paechter, C. (2007). *Being boys, being girls: Learning masculinities and femininities.* Maidenhead, UK: Open University Press.

Paris, A., Worth, H., & Allen, L. (2002). Introduction. In H. Worth, A. Paris, & L. Allen (Eds.), *Life of Brian: Masculinities, sexualities and health in New Zealand* (pp. 11–26). Dunedin, NZ: University of Otago Press.

Parker, A. (1996). The construction of masculinity within boys' physical education. *Gender and Education, 8*(2), 141–158.

Pascoe, C. J. (2007). *Dude, you're a fag: Masculinity and sexuality in high school.* Los Angeles, CA: University of California Press.

Paul, A. (2006). Body wisdom: The way of karate. *South Atlantic Quarterly, 105*(2), 397–407.

Priest, L., & Summerfield, L. M. (1994). *Promoting gender equity in middle and secondary school sports programs: ERIC digest.* Washington, DC: ERIC Clearinghouse on Teaching and Teacher Education.

Pringle, R. (2005). Masculinities, sport and power: A critical comparison of Gramscian and Foucauldian inspired theoretical tools. *Journal of Sport and Social Issues, 29*(3), 256–278.

Pringle, R. (2007). Sport, males and masculinities. In C. Collins & S. Jackson (Eds.), *Sport in Aotearoa/New Zealand society* (pp. 355–380). Melbourne: Thomson.

Pringle, R. (2009). Defamiliarizing heavy-contact sports: A critical examination of rugby, discipline, and pleasure. *Sociology of Sport Journal, 26*, 211–234.

Pringle, R. (2010). Finding pleasure in physical education: A critical examination of the educative value of positive movement affects. *Quest, 62*(2), 119–134.

Pringle, R., & Hickey, C. (2010). Negotiating masculinities via the moral problematization of sport. *Sociology of Sport Journal, 27*(2), 115–138.

Pringle, R., & Pringle, D. (2012). Competing obesity discourses and critical challenges for health and physical educators. *Sport, Education and Society, 17*(2), 143–161.

Pronger, B. (1999). Outta my end zone: Sport and the territorial anus. *Sociology of Sport, 23*(4), 373–389.

Rand, E. (2008). I wanted black skates: Gender, cash, pleasure, and the politics of criticism. *Criticism, 50*(4), 555–580.

Rave, J. M. G., Perez, L. M. R., & Poyatos, M. C. (2007). The social construction of gender in Spanish physical education students. *Sport, Education and Society, 12*(2), 141–158.

Ray, M. (1979). *Sex-role stereotyping is taught in public schools.* Washington, DC: ERIC Clearinghouse.

Reid, A. (1997). Value pluralism and physical education. *European Physical Education Review, 3*(1), 6–20.

Renold, E. (2004). Other' boys: Negotiating non-hegemonic masculinities in the primary school. *Gender and Education, 16*(2), 247–266.

Rintala, J. (2009). It's all about the -ing. *Quest, 61*(3), 279–288.

Risner, D. (2007). Rehearsing masculinity: Challenging the 'boy code' in dance education. *Research in Dance Education, 8*(2), 139–153.

Rose, G. (1997). Situating knowledges: Positionality, reflexivities and other tactics. *Progress in Human Geography, 21*(3), 305–320.

Rose, N. (1998). *Inventing ourselves: Psychology, power and personhood.* Cambridge, UK: Cambridge University Press.

Rose, N. (1999). *Powers of freedom: Reframing political thought.* Cambridge, UK: Cambridge University Press.

Rutten, C., Boen, F., & Seghers, J. (2012). How school social and physical environments relate to autonomous motivation in physical education: The mediating role of need satisfaction. *Journal of Teaching in Physical Education, 31*, 216–230.

Ryan, R. M., & Deci, E. L. (2000). Self-determination theory and the facilitation of intrinsic motivation, social development, and wellbeing. *American Psychologist, 55*, 68–78.

Salisbury, J., & Jackson, D. (1997). *Challenging macho values: Practical ways of working with adolescent boys*. London, UK: Falmer Press.

Schacht, S. (1996). Misogyny on and off the 'pitch': The gendered world of male rugby players. *Gender & Society, 10*(5), 550–565.

Seidler, V. J. (2006). *Transforming masculinities: Men, cultures, bodies, power, sex and love*. New York: Routledge.

Shen, B., Li, W., Sun, H., & Rukavina, R. B. (2010). The influence of inadequate teacher to student social support on amotivation of physical education students. *Journal of Teaching in Physical Education, 29*, 417–432.

Shilling, C. (2002). The two traditions in the sociology of emotions. In J. Barbalet (Ed.), *Emotions and sociology* (pp. 10–32). Oxford, UK: Blackwell.

Shilling, C. (2012). *The body & social theory* (3rd ed.). London, UK: Sage.

Siedentop, D. (1994). *Sport education: Quality P.E. through positive sport experiences*. Champaign, IL: Human Kinetics.

Skelton, C. (2001a). *Schooling the boys: Masculinities and primary education*. Buckingham, UK: Open University Press.

Skelton, C. (2001b). Typical boys? Theorizing masculinity in educational settings. In B. Francis & C. Skelton (Eds.), *Investigating gender: Contemporary perspectives in education* (pp. 164–176). Buckingham & Philadelphia: Open University Press.

Smith, N., & Katz, C. (1993). Grounding metaphor: Towards a spatialized politics. In M. Keith & S. Pile (Eds.), *Place and the politics of identity* (pp. 67–83). New York: Routledge.

Soja, E. (1989). *Postmodern geographies*. New York: Verso.

Sparkes, A. (1997). Reflections on the socially constructed self. In K. R. Fox (Ed.), *The physical self: From motivation to well-being* (pp. 83–110). Champaign, IL: Human Kinetics.

Spielvogel, L. G. (2002). The discipline of space in a Japanese fitness club. *Sociology of Sport Journal, 19*(2), 189–205.

Spivak, G. (1988). *In other worlds: Essays in cultural politics*. New York: Routledge.

Standage, M., Duda, J. L., & Ntoumanis, N. (2003). A model of contextual motivation in physical education: Using constructs from self-determination and achievement goal theories to predict physical activity intentions. *Journal of Educational Psychology, 95*(1), 97–110.

Standage, M., Duda, J. L., & Ntoumanis, N. (2005). A test of self-determination theory in school physical education. *British Journal of Educational Psychology, 75*, 411–433.

Stoddart, M. (2011). Constructing masculinized sportscapes: Skiing, gender and nature in British Columbia, Canada. *International Review for the Sociology of Sport, 46*(1), 108–124.

Sykes, H. (2011). *Queer bodies: Sexualities, genders & fatness in physical education*. New York: Peter Lang.

Taylor, W., Yancey, A., Leslie, J., Murray, N., Cummings, S., & Sharkey, S. (1999). Physical activity among African American and Latino middle school girls: Consistent beliefs, expectations, and experiences across two sites. *Women and Health, 30*, 67–82.

Thomas, K. (2004). Riding to the rescue while holding on by a thread: Physical activity in the schools. *Quest, 56*(1), 150–170.

Thomson, S. (2004). Just another classroom? Observations of primary school playgrounds. In P. Vertinsky & J. Bale (Eds.), *Sites of sport: Space, place, experience* (pp. 73–84). London, UK: Routledge.

Thorpe, H. (2008). Foucault, technologies of self, and the media: Discourses of femininity in snowboarding culture. *Journal of Sport and Social Issues, 32*(2), 199–229.

Thorpe, H. (2010). Masculinities in the snowboarding field Bourdieu, gender reflexivity, and physical culture: A case of. *Journal of Sport and Social Issues, 34*(2), 176–214.

Tinning, R. (2002). Toward a 'modest pedagogy': Reflections on the problematics of critical pedagogy. *Quest, 55*(3), 224–240.

Tinning, R. (2004). Rethinking the preparation of HPE teachers: Ruminations on knowledge, identity, and ways of thinking. *Asia-Pacific Journal of Teacher Education, 32*(3), 241–253.

Tinning, R. (2010). *Pedagogy and human movement: Theory, practice, research.* New York: Routledge.

Tinning, R., & Glasby, T. (2002). Pedagogical work and the 'cult of the body': Considering the role of HPE in the context of the 'new public health'. *Sport, Education and Society, 7*(2), 109–119.

Turner, B. S. (1997). From governmentality to risk: Some reflections on Foucault's contribution to medical sociology. In A. Petersen & R. Bunton (Eds.), *Foucault, health, and medicine* (pp. xi–xxi). London, UK: Routledge.

Turner, B. S. (2008). *The body and society* (3rd ed.). London, UK: Sage.

Twietmeyer, G. (2012). The merits and demerits of pleasure in kinesiology. *Quest, 64*(3), 177–186.

Valentine, G. (2001). *Social geographies: Space and society.* Harlow, UK: Pearson Education.

Van Hoven, B., & Meijering, L. (2005). Transient masculinities. In B. Van Hoven & K. Horschelmann (Eds.), *Spaces of masculinities* (pp. 75–85). London, UK: Routledge.

Vertinsky, P. (2004). Locating a 'sense of place': Space, place and gender in the gymnasium. In P. Vertinsky & J. Bale (Eds.), *Sites of sport: Space, place, experience* (pp. 8–24). London, UK: Routledge.

Wang, C. K. J., Chatzisarantis, N. L. D., Spray, C. M., & Biddle, S. J. H. (2002). Achievement goal profiles in school physical education: Differences in self-determination, sport ability beliefs, and physical activity. *The British Journal of Educational Psychology, 72*, 433–445.

Wankel, L. M. (1985). Personal and situational factors affecting exercise involvement: The importance of enjoyment. *Research Quarterly for Exercise and Sport, 56*(3), 275–282.

Warner, M. (1993). *Fear of a queer planet: Queer politics and social theory.* Minneapolis, MN: University of Minnesota Press.

Webb, L., & Macdonald, D. (2007). Dualing with gender: Teachers' work, careers and leadership in physical education. *Gender and Education, 19*(4), 491–512.

Webb, L., McCaughtry, N., & MacDonald, D. (2004). Surveillance as a technique of power in physical education. *Sport, Education and Society, 9*(2), 207–222.

Wellard, I. (2009). *Sport, masculinities and the body.* New York: Routledge.

Wellard, I. (2012). Body-reflexive pleasures: Exploring bodily experiences within the context of sport and physical activity. *Sport, Education and Society, 17*(1), 21–33.

Wellard, I., Pickard, A., & Bailey, R. (2007). 'A shock of electricity just sort of goes through my body': Physical activity and embodied reflexive practices in young female ballet dancers. *Gender and Education, 19*(1), 79–91.

Wetherell, M., & Edley, N. (1999). Negotiating hegemonic masculinity: Imaginary positions and psycho-discursive practices. *Feminism and Psychology, 9*, 333–356.

Willis, P. E. (1977). *Learning to labour: How working class kids get working class jobs.* Farnborough, UK: Saxon House.

Willott, S., & Griffin, G. (1996). Men, masculinity and the challenge of long-term unemployment. In M. Mac an Ghaill (Ed.), *Understanding masculinities: Social relations and cultural arenas* (pp. 77–92). Buckingham, UK: Open University Press.

Wrench, A., & Garrett, R. (2008). Pleasure and pain: Experiences of fitness testing. *European Physical Education Review, 14*(3), 325–346.

Wright, J. (1996). The construction of complementarity in physical education. *Gender and Education, 8*(1), 61–79.

Wright, J. (1997). The construction of gendered contexts in single sex and coeducational physical education lessons. *Sport, Education and Society, 2*(1), 55–72.

Wright, J. (2000). Reconstructing gender in sport and physical education. In C. Hickey, L. Fitzclarence, & R. Matthews (Eds.), *Where the boys are: Masculinity, sport and education* (pp. 13–26). Geelong: Deakin University Press.

Wright, J. (2004). Post-structural methodologies: The body, schooling and health. In J. Evans, B. Davies & J. Wright (Eds.), *Body knowledge and control: Studies in the sociology of physical education and health* (pp. 19–31). London, UK: Routledge.

Wright, J. (2006). Physical education research from postmodern, poststructural and postcolonial perspectives. In D. Kirk, D. Macdonald, & M. O'Sullivan (Eds.), *The handbook of physical education* (pp. 59–75). London, UK: Sage.

Wright, J., & Dewar, A. (1997). On pleasure and pain: Women speak out about physical activity. In G. Clarke & B. Humberstone (Eds.), *Researching women and sport* (pp. 80–95). London, UK: Macmillan Press.

Wright, J., & Harwood, V. (2009). *Biopolitics and the 'obesity epidemic': Governing bodies*. New York: Routledge.

Wright, J., O'Flynn, G., & Macdonald, D. (2006). Being fit and looking healthy: Young women's and men's constructions of health and fitness. *Sex Roles, 54*(9), 707–716.

Zembylas, M. (2007). The specters of bodies and affects in the classroom: A rhizo-ethological approach. *Pedagogy, Culture and Society, 15*(1), 19–35.

Zhang, T., Solmon, M., & Gu, X. (2012). The role of teachers' support in predicting students' motivation and achievement outcomes in physical education. *Journal of Teaching in Physical Education, 31*, 329–343.

Zhang, T., Solmon, M., Kosma, M., Carson, R., & Gu, X. (2011). Need support, need satisfaction, intrinsic motivation, and physical activity participation among middle school students. *Journal of Teaching in Physical Education, 30*(1), 51–68.

3 Boys' Visual Representations and Interpretations of PE

This book draws on findings from a year-long visual ethnography (Pink, 2007) of boys' PE at a single-sex secondary school in Auckland, New Zealand, involving observations, video recordings, focus groups and individual interviews. In this chapter, I explain why visual ethnography is a particularly powerful methodological approach to address the questions at the centre of this study. In devising an appropriate research method, my priority was to choose a method that would allow the participating boys to represent and interpret their own experiences, thus letting them 'speak for themselves'. This chapter also introduces the research setting and the participants and explains the key methods employed. In particular, I address the practicalities of conducting ethnographic research and the process of data generation through observations, video recordings, focus groups and individual interviews. I describe the research literature that shaped my choice of these methods and the process of generating data. I explain my approach to each of these in turn, along with limitations, ethical implications and the problems I encountered along the way. Following that is a discussion of thematic analysis and discourse analysis, the methods I used to analyse the data in order to draw attention to findings I consider most pertinent to answering my research questions.

Seen through a Foucauldian poststructural lens, there is no clear window into the 'inner life' of an individual because every glimpse into someone's life-world is influenced by factors such as the language, gender, social class, race and ethnicity of the observer. All observations are socially situated in the world as lived and interpreted by both the observer and the observed (Denzin & Lincoln, 2005). In recognition of this, I acknowledge that there are no objective observations, only subjective ones. A 'God's-eye view' of the world is impossible since we cannot see the world outside of our place in it. Social reality is mind-dependent; there can be no data that is free from interpretation (Sparkes, 1992). When conducting this study, it was equally important to attempt to interpret and understand how the boys (re)construct social reality and also make explicit relevant aspects of my own background and how these might have affected data generation and interpretations/analyses. This includes, for instance, beliefs, values, race, socio-economic status, politics, relationship with participants and, more importantly, my own gendered identity (which I have attempted to present in the preface to this book). However, in accordance with Denzin and Lincoln (2005), I also recognise that it is impossible to give full explanations of one's actions and intentions, and all I can offer are accounts or stories about what I have done and why, which is the prime focus of this chapter.

Ethnography

Methodological decisions need to consider "what information most appropriately will answer specific research questions, and which strategies are most effective for obtaining it" (LeCompte & Preissle, 1993, p. 30). My ontological and epistemological assumptions meant I adopted an approach in which getting close to my research participants and understanding their world was important. This is sometimes referred to as an 'ideographic' (qualitative) approach (Sparkes, 1992). Denzin and Lincoln (2005) argue that researchers using qualitative research designs often do not have a distinct set of methods or practices that are specific to the particular approach they are employing. Instead, they use a range of approaches, methods and techniques, all of which "can provide important insights and knowledge" (Grossberg, Nelson, & Treichler, 1992, p. 12). One such approach is 'ethnography', which, according to Delamont (2003), involves "spending long periods watching people, coupled with talking to them about what they are doing, thinking and saying, designed to see how they understand their world" (p. 218). Ethnography is currently a common approach in educational research; however, in PE research, ethnographies are not as common, and since Wang's (1977) seminal ethnographic work, most recent ethnographic studies in PE have mainly focused on girls' experiences (e.g., Azzarito, Solmon, & Harrison, 2006; Hills, 2007), which is why my study set out to do an ethnography of boys' performances of gender in PE.

Within an ethnographic approach, documenting multiple perspectives of realities in a given study is seen as crucial to understanding why people think and act in different ways. As a PE teacher, I have spent many hours with both boys and girls in the PE classroom, but when teaching a class of 20–30 students, you only really get a 'snapshot' of what life is like for these students. With this study, I really wanted to get an in-depth view of what it is like to be a boy in PE. To gain this in-depth understanding, I needed to spend an extended period of time with a group of boys in order to learn about their way of life in PE. This is why I decided to employ an ethnographic approach over other qualitative approaches. Spending extended periods of time with the boys in their naturalistic environment, in this case PE classes, was vital to allow the necessary "detailed investigation [interpretive work]", without which a "coherent, theoretical picture of the natures and varieties of student experiences" could not be developed (Erickson & Shultz, 1992, p. 479) By employing a multiple-method approach, which centres around valuing and respecting student voices (Kehily, 2002), I endeavoured to achieve an under-standing of the students at a deeper level through skilful observations of richly described contexts.

Throughout my ethnographic work, and informed by Foucauldian post-structuralism, I particularly wanted to reinforce understandings of the importance of gender in relation to PE, performances of gendered selves and relations of power. I also wanted to actively involve the students them-selves (Prosser & Burke, 2008) and endeavour to bridge the gap between the researcher and the researched because, through a poststructural lens, reality is a co-construction. I will now discuss how I accomplished this by employ-ing (participatory) visual research methods.

Visual Ethnography

I adopted visual research methods to explore how the boys themselves expe-rienced and made sense of their experience in PE. Azzarito (2010) contends that visual research methods can be used to further the study of students' gendered experiences in this setting because it "might allow them to express their ways of seeing the world they inhabit in their everyday lives" (Prosser & Burke, 2008, p. 411). Visual research, according to Pink (2007), provides a "context where ethnographers/authors can create or represent continuities between [these] diverse worlds, voices or experiences, and describe or imply points in the research at which they meet or collide" (p. 144). The intention of using visual methods in my research is not to somehow reveal the 'truth' about boys' performances of gender in PE but rather to highlight how repre-sentations and interpretations of the visual allow for the creation of multiple truths and multiple meanings (Eisner, 2005; Pink, 2001). Via a Foucauldian poststructural lens, which centres around the contested nature of truth and meaning, I wanted to use visual representations and interpretations to hope-fully challenge stereotypes and generalisations of boys' behaviour and expe-riences (Togman, 2011; Whyte, 1997). Through a research process based on visual research methods, I aimed to encourage the boys to creatively make sense of themselves and to reflect on the ways they create meaning, identities and the self (Gauntlett & Holzwarth, 2006), as constrained by the discourses of PE.

Visual research methods are relatively rare in education and mainly used for pedagogical reasons (e.g., Mitchell & Weber, 1998; Weber & Mitchell, 1995), not in the study of sociology of education (Allen, 2009). Prosser (1998) suggests that this could possibly be explained by the overall low status of visual-based research compared to word-based research. However, another reason for the low prevalence of research using visual methods in educational research may be the issue of getting access to a school and obtaining ethics approval. Indeed, many of the schools approached were initially interested in my research but later declined due to the video aspect, which can be seen as a further indication that videoing and issues of gender are perceived as 'high risk' (Allen, 2008). It also took several months for my study to receive ethical approval, which resulted in a number of stipulations that limited the freedom of the videoing. These regulations centred around camera usage and gaining consent from those who would be videoed. For example, this meant I had to limit the videoing to PE class time, which prevented me from documenting performances of gender taking place in 'unofficial' spaces, such as the boys' changing rooms and games of touch rugby played during breaks.

Although most studies to date have involved using pre-existing visual representations in the form of photo elicitation (e.g., Azzarito, 2009; Azzarito & Katzew, 2010; Curry, 1986; Gorely, Holroyd, & Kirk, 2003; Snyder & Kane, 1990), researchers using visual methods have recently started making visual representations in collaboration with the participants (i.e., Azzarito & Sterling, 2010). In this study, I used a participatory visual research approach (Pink, 2007; Prosser & Burke, 2008), in which PE classes were recorded on video by both me as the researcher and the participating boys. According to Prosser (2007), the use of participatory visual research methods in educational research is of importance because it shifts the focus from doing research on students to doing research with and by students. Participatory visual research methods "let the people speak for themselves" (Prosser & Burke, 2008, p. 408) and can provide a more intimate representation of the participants' contextually embedded everyday experiences. Whereas using existing visual material in the form of photo elicitation can provide valuable findings, more insights about the subjective dimensions of people's experiences may be generated by people's reflection upon their own visual representations of their experiences (Azzarito, 2010). By allowing the boys to create 'mini-documentaries' of their experiences in PE, the visual representations became a medium of communication between myself and the boys (Curry, 1986). The boys helped produce an ethnographic account that to some extent was 'co-created' (Robinson, 2009).

One of the reasons I decided to use video-based data is its permanence as a record and its accessibility/retrievability for me as the researcher. In particular, using digital video enabled the annotation of clips, making it easy to retrieve, select and edit for further discussion/analysis. However, Schuck and Kearney (2006) argue that video-based data is prone to the same issue of subjectivity as the selection and analysis of non-video-based data. Visual data is never neutral; it is always literally and socially constructed (Schuck & Kearney, 2006). For instance, Baker, Green and Skukauskaite (2008) contend:

> A video record of an event represents not the event in its complexity, but rather, it is an inscription of how the ethnographer chose to focus the camera. As a fieldnote, therefore, the video (re)presents an event selected by the ethnographer, making available for analysis a particular range of discourse and actions among members.
>
> (p. 82)

By handing over the video camera to the participating boys, I wanted to avoid the researcher being exclusively responsible for the production of the visual data. However, when editing and analysing the video data, I was aware that there was still the issue of what data would be used in the discussion/analysis. In particular, when the visual data is edited and produced, a level of distance between the participant, the researcher and the social context is still maintained (Schuck & Kearney, 2006). Kaplan and Howes (2004) claim that often "researchers interpret data collected from students and present researcher perspectives on the students' activity, but do not give the students the opportunity to have a voice in the interpretation" (p. 145).

To increase the level of intimacy between the researcher, the visual data and the social context, Banks (2001) suggests that the visual data produced by the participants can be used as a form of 'interview probing'. Schuck and Kearney (2006) state that using data in the form of video recordings can stimulate good conversation and produce rich data; a number of researchers have used this type of 'stimulated-recall interview' to generate data (e.g., Byra & Sherman, 1993). This is why the visual data recorded by both myself and the participating boys was used during the focus groups and individual interviews to help provide a more ethical and balanced presentation of results, giving the boys the chance to provide an interpretation of the visual data (Kaplan & Howes, 2004). Stimulated-recall interviews redress the imbalance of power when the researcher (exclusively) analyses the data's significance (Allen, 2008).

In my study, I particularly used visual data during the interviews to create a forum for the active construction of meanings. By engaging the boys in both the representation and interpretation of the visual material, I attempted to encourage meaning-making grounded in the boys' own specific context (Allen, 2008; Gauntlett & Holzwarth, 2006). Visual representations are not only produced by the maker but are continuously produced and reproduced by anyone who engages with them (Rose, 2007). That is, the same visual material can help produce an endless number of active constructions of multiple meanings. The boys' visual representations, together with their descriptions and interpretations of these in the focus groups and individual interviews, provided thick and rich accounts of boys' performances of gender in PE and generated an array of meanings. Their visual representations and interpretations particularly gave me an indication of what they wanted "others to see and think about; they draw attention and direct attention" (O'Donoghue, 2007, p. 66). By employing participatory visual research methods based on Foucault and Butler's work on power and gender, my research project provided an opportunity for these boys to critically examine their conditions of (im)possible gendered identities and pleasures in PE.

However, giving the boys a voice through participatory visual methods is not unproblematic. Finding the line between the participants' own stories and that of the researcher is a particularly important consideration (Luttrell, 2010). Yates (2010), for instance, argues that it is important not to focus on the participants' stories as the endpoint of research by providing a more theoretical engagement with such stories, which itself should be the object of further investigation in order to understand social distinctions, inequalities and power. Arnot and Reay (2007) in particular caution against conflating voice and message and instead accepting common sense understandings as themselves produced. In my study, it was also important to explore the tension between the boys' voices and the meanings they convey (Yates, 2010). This is also why it was important to use participatory visual methods in conjunction with other more 'traditional' ethnographic techniques, such as interviews/discussions and observations (Pink, 2007).

Having discussed my methodological assumptions, I will now address the practicalities of the research process relating to the research setting/participants, data generation methods and means of analysis.

The Research Setting and Participants

Kea College (Figure 3.1) is a single-sex, boys' secondary school in Auckland, New Zealand. The school is widely known for its strong focus on sports, especially rugby, and the school's 'First XV' team is the pride and joy of the school. In fact, the school seems to live and breathe for rugby, with rugby balls and rugby talk dominating physical and social spaces among both the boys and the teachers. This school was selected because it was the first one that agreed to participate in the study but also because of my previous knowledge of the school and it being located in close proximity to where I was living at the time of the study. The study did not set out to find a representative sample of all single-sex boys' schools in New Zealand. Both the principal and the PE teacher were sent copies of the participant information sheet, outlining the objectives of the study, along with the consent form.

Once I had been granted access to the two PE classes by the principal and the teacher, I visited the school and introduced the study to the boys and invited them to take part in my research. Although I stressed the fact

Figure 3.1 The Sports Fields, the New Sports Complex (right), the Multipurpose Astro-Court (Centre) and the Old Gym (Left) at Kea College.

that participation was voluntary, the notion of 'voluntary' consent in school environments is problematic and "this is due to the way authority operates in schools, so that any form of endorsement of the research can be interpreted by students as an expectation to participate" (Allen, 2005, pp. 40–41). Since the aim of my study was to carry out observations and interviews in two PE classes, there was an issue of all the students feeling compelled to take part in the study, particularly since both the principal and the teacher had already shown their support. This problem, however, is often difficult to remedy due to the nature of schools and the challenge of gaining access to schools.

After my introduction, I handed out participant information sheets to all the boys, describing what their involvement in the study would entail and pointing out that participation was strictly voluntary. The boys were also given the opportunity to ask questions before deciding to take part in the study. Before starting the focus groups and individual interviews, I once again emphasised that participating in these were entirely voluntary and they could leave the interview at any time or choose not to answer questions that they did not feel comfortable with. In addition, the boys were told that they had the right to turn off the digital audio recorder at any time during the interviews (Allen, 2005). The boys were also informed both verbally and in writing that they could withdraw from the research study at any time or withdraw information they had provided up until the conclusion of the study, without having to give a reason.

An important ethical consideration for my study was the fact that no harm should come to those who decided to participate in the study. The boys were assured that the identities of individuals and sources of information would not be made known to the reader. Indeed, Haywood and Mac an Ghaill (1996) assert that "one-taken-for-granted aspect of social research is the ethics of confidentiality" (p. 104). Any details of the students' individual responses were not made available to any of the school staff, and pseudonyms were used for the boys'/teacher's citations and the name of the school to minimise risk of identification (Miles & Huberman, 1994). However, in the participant information sheet, the boys were also made aware that the nature of the study made it difficult to guarantee confidentiality and/or anonymity (discussed further below).

Since all the participants were younger than 16, parental consent was also required. After both the boys and their parents/legal guardians had received a participant information sheet, all the boys and at least one parent/legal guardian for each boy signed consent forms.

Kea College's faith-based character and values underpin its programmes, systems and practices. For instance, classes at all levels from Year 7 to Year 13 receive formal instruction in the teaching of Religious Education (RE) each week, and tests are conducted each term. As part of the College's religious mission, there are also regular class and school masses, liturgies and reconciliation. In the principal's message in the school's prospectus,

Mr Andersson[1] states that the school's mission is to "produce educated, responsible, self-disciplined young men".

The school's religious profile also means that the boys come from diverse ethnic and cultural backgrounds. Although 63% of the students are grouped under the 'European/Pākehā'[2] category, this involves a wide range of nationalities and ethnicities. Many of the boys in my study were born in European countries before moving to New Zealand or had parents who had grown up across Europe. Yet, this group of boys also included those who came from families that have been in New Zealand for some generations. The second-biggest group was 'Asian' (16%), which also includes several nationalities, such as Chinese, Korean and Japanese. The 'Pacific Island' and 'Māori'[3] groups come third and fourth, with 7% and 5% respectively. The school also has a significant group of 'International Students' (5%), who mainly come from non-English speaking countries, such as China and Korea. The smallest group of students is labelled 'Other' (4%) and includes boys from countries not included in other categories, such as countries in North and South America and Africa. The boys participating in my study were, for instance, born in: New Zealand, Australia, England, China, Iraq, Hong Kong, Korea, the Philippines, Egypt, Saudi Arabia and South Africa.

Kea College is located in one the more affluent areas of Auckland and has a decile[4] rating of 9. This decile rating would indicate that most of the boys come from higher socio-economic backgrounds. However, since a decile rating is based on an average, it does not always capture the spread or diverse socio-economic circumstances of the students (Allen, 2008). This was substantiated when many of the boys in my study described their parents as being in low- to middle-income work (i.e., cleaner, nurse, secretary). Nevertheless, some boys came from wealthier backgrounds, with their parents being in higher-paid positions such as doctors, managing directors and architects.

The participants in this study were 60 boys aged 14–15 enrolled in two Year 10 PE classes. The two PE classes that took part in the study were selected by the PE teacher and head of department (HOD), Mr Whyte, who agreed to be involved in the study mainly for the reason that he was also responsible for teaching these two classes. Allen (2005) has raised concerns over the fact that when conducting research in schools, it is common that those participants made 'available' to the researcher by the school are those who "will make a good impression or who are more articulate" (p. 41). In my study, this means that the type of data generated might not be a good representation of all students at this particular school; however, the issues of representation and/or generalisation were not of concern to this study. Mr Whyte believed that examining these two PE classes would be of interest to my study because the two classes represented the highest and the lowest 'academic streams' respectively, out of a total of five classes within this year level. Kea College employs an 'academic streaming system', which is a very structured hierarchical system used across all subjects, in which students are put into different classes based on academic achievement (although their achievements in PE are not counted). This is reviewed every second term, when the students can move up or down depending on their academic results.

The participating boys were all aged between 14 and 15, which in New Zealand corresponds to Year 10. The reason why older students were not included is that in New Zealand, PE is not compulsory after Year 10, which means that only those who like the subject select to carry on. This also means that those who are not in favour of PE can drop the subject for the last three years of secondary school. Selecting Year 10 PE classes therefore ensured that the research participants consisted of boys with a wide range of attitudes towards the subject.

In the results chapters, chapters four to six, I also provide descriptors of the boys when they are referred to for the first time in the book. In addition to the age of the boys, these descriptors also include their ethnic/cultural background and sport involvement (if any) because these two factors seemed to be important in terms of shaping their experiences and understandings of PE. Any form of sport involvement appeared to be linked to more pleasurable experiences, but in particular, team sports such as rugby, soccer and basketball were linked with privileged and pleasurable masculinities. The ethnic/cultural background was important in terms of knowledge and experience in privileged (sporting) practices, with 'European/Pākehā' and 'Māori' boys particularly being the ones benefiting within this sociocultural PE context.

I will now discuss how I spent a total of 12 months with both PE classes generating data through observations, video recordings, focus groups and individual interviews.

Observations

In my study, I began with observations, or what is frequently described as 'participant observation' (Spindler & Hammond, 2000). In many respects, I pursued my work as would any social scientist writing a traditional ethnography. I fluctuated between the various classical roles of the participant observer: complete observer, observer as participant, participant as observer and complete participant (Gold, 1958; Junker, 1960). That is, at times I was quietly sitting/standing next to the lesson, taking notes or talking to the boys/teachers, whereas at other times I was taking part in the games/activities of the lesson, observing the boys' (inter)actions from within the game/activity or merely participating. This was a way to get started and allowed me as the researcher to engage with the research context. Initially, the purpose of these observations was to get to know the boys and gain some of their 'trust', which was seen as important prior to conducting the interviews (Denzin & Lincoln, 1998). Over the 12 months I spent at Kea College, I observed over 120 hours of PE classes.

The observations were of the 'naturalistic' kind, in the sense that they took place in the boys' natural setting during normal PE classes. The situation observed was thus not contrived for research purposes (Punch, 2005). Although both the boys and the teacher were well aware of my presence, the specific purpose of these observations was to some extent kept undisclosed, at least until the focus groups and individual interviews started. I adopted an approach similar to that employed by Pascoe (2007) by telling the boys and the teacher that I was writing a book about boys and PE. By doing so, I hoped that the boys would not change their behaviour significantly during their PE classes to somehow 'fit' within my research and that they would feel positive about my presence. In this way, I was also trying to deal with the (ethical) issue of communicating the worthiness of the study (Miles & Huberman, 1994) to the boys and the teacher. In my introduction and throughout this period of initial observations, I conveyed the argument that many previous studies had already investigated girls' (lack of) participation and enjoyment in PE and that it was time to also focus on boys' experiences of PE, with the goal of ensuring that (more) boys also receive a meaningful and enjoyable PE experience. However, the mere presence of me as a researcher and the fact that I am also a male PE teacher may still have influenced the boys' behaviour. For instance, I believe that it initially made it difficult to gain the trust of those boys who were perceived—or identified— as 'non-sporty'. It also resulted in intensified displays of dominant gender performances from those boys who were possibly looking to gain my respect due to the stereotypical assumptions aligned with being a male PE teacher (Piotrowski, 2000).

As the study progressed, the observations specifically focused on the boys' performances of gender during PE and whether there were any patterns that suggested the presence of dominant discourses of gender. The observations looked for certain key signifiers of gender and how these might relate to a certain discourse of gender. This included, for instance, how the boys were dressed (i.e., sporty, non-sporty), body language (i.e., aggression, submission), language use (i.e., humour, bullying, swearing), student interaction (i.e., inclusive, exclusive) and participation (i.e., competitive, bystander).

I was particularly interested in how the boys' performances of gender could be seen to either articulate with or disrupt discourses related to masculinity, sport, fitness and health. That is, did the boys' behaviour and actions during PE align with masculine ideals of competition, aggression and physicality, or did they seem to focus more on participation and inclusion? How did different groups of—or individual—boys' behaviour and actions vary between different games/activities, such as dodgeball and rugby, that could indicate certain discursive links between masculinity and the types of games/activities engaged in during PE? I also observed what kind of boys seemed to occupy either privileged/dominant or subordinate positions. What were some of their characteristics, and what kind of behaviour/ actions seemed to reaffirm those positions?

Based on my research questions, I also placed particular emphasis on the production of pleasure, the spaces of PE and the boys' bodies. In terms of pleasure, I focused on when and how the boys seemed to be particularly enjoying their PE. For instance, at what point during the lessons and while doing what kinds of games/activities did they show enjoyment? In addition, I tried focusing on both the physical and social spaces of PE. What spaces were used and in what way? How did the boys' and the teacher's use of those spaces (re)produce PE as a meaningful and enjoyable space? When it comes to their bodies, I observed both how the boys presented their bodies/bodily appearances (i.e., tall, short, muscular, lean) and how their bodies were used (i.e., running, performing various sporting skills). Did the boys' participation in and through PE seem to reaffirm the importance of fit, healthy and sporty masculine bodies in PE?

The (gendered) patterns/themes identified during these initial observations were then explored during the focus groups and individual interviews. Follow-up observations were also conducted after the interviews had been completed, as a way of further exploring issues/themes raised in the focus groups and individual interviews. These observations gave me an opportunity to confirm the boys' responses and to observe through the lens of the boys' own perceptions what goes on during PE classes. Indeed, this second series of observations allowed me to look for new/alternative performances of gender in light of insights gained during the initial data collection and analysis. More importantly, this also led to new issues being identified, which can be explored in future research projects. All the observations were documented with written notes and video recordings.

Video Recordings

Video recordings were used instead of other visual imagery, such as still photography, in order to more fully capture the movements and (inter)actions of the boys during PE. This was seen as important in terms of generating data that would allow me to interrogate the multiple and fluid nature of the boys' (gendered) performances. The inclusion of both video and audio provided me with a format in which I could (re)watch shorter and longer recordings of the boys' PE and in particular focus on moments when the boys' excitement (or discontent) about learning in, through and about movement was evident. In relation to answering my main research questions, the video recordings also importantly captured how the spaces of PE and the boys' bodies intermeshed/interweaved with the boys' (gendered) performances and the pleasures those produced/induced.

The fact that the observations were recorded using video had its advantages and disadvantages. The video camera provided an instrument for accurate and detailed observations that is in some ways unparalleled. This freed me to act as a complete participant in numerous situations, knowing that the video camera was capturing the events in which I was participating.

Moreover, the video camera recorded information in quantities and at speeds that were exponentially larger and faster than I could ever achieve through conventional note-taking. However, as noted by Togman (2011), cameras, microphones and other filmmaking equipment are more obtrusive than the ethnographer's traditional pad and pen. The presence of a video camera during the observations inevitably intruded on the 'natural' environment of these PE classes (Schuck & Kearney, 2006). Although all ethnographers disrupt to some extent that which they observe, the presence of a video camera can change the subject's behaviour in more noticeable ways (Bogdan & Biklen, 1998). I noticed that bringing a video camera into the classroom initially gained some extra attention from some of the boys who started 'acting up' in front of the camera by, for example, throwing balls at each other or harassing each other in different ways. However, the novelty of having a video camera in the classroom quickly disappeared, and most boys seemed to go back to 'normal' behaviour after a short time. The video camera was permanently fixed in a location where most of the interaction that took place during the PE classes could be recorded. I also decided not to stand behind the camera or, for instance, change the focus of the camera to follow particular groups of boys (Schuck & Kearney, 2006).

After an initial period of recording observations lasting a couple of weeks, I then allowed the students control of the video camera. Although Pink (2007) suggests that giving the camera to the participants right away might be useful to quickly gain the trust and collaboration of the participants, I found it important to begin with an observational period to familiarise myself with both the context and the two PE classes. This also meant that the boys got used to the presence of a video camera in the classroom. The only instruction I gave them before handing over the video camera was that they were supposed to produce a 'mini-documentary' of their PE. The 'gaze' of the boys' camera was thus random, not systematic, but following Prosser and Schwartz (1998), these boys sought to use the camera as a way to "discover and demonstrate relationships that may be subtle and easily overlooked" (p. 116). They were particularly encouraged to consider aspects and situations of PE that they were interested in and wanted to highlight with visual representation. Each student got to use the video camera for about 20–30 minutes, resulting in a mixture of longer and shorter video clips. Their clips, along with the ones I had recorded, in total over 50 hours, were then transferred to my computer and, without any editing taking place, used during the focus groups and individual interviews. The video recordings were also transcribed, comprising narratives and still images.

The fact that video recordings were used made it more difficult to ensure anonymity (Flewitt, 2005). When using video recordings, there is also an issue of capturing people who have not agreed to participate in the study (Broyles, Tate, & Happ, 2008), which meant that the videoing was strictly limited to the two participating PE classes from which all the boys had given their consent and did not at any point include other students from the school. In the participant information sheet and consent form, I also assured the boys that any images of them would not be shown in any publications of the research unless permission had been given by each and every individual in the images. In order to conceal the identity of both the boys/teachers and the school, I also had the visual images blurred (Schuck & Kearney, 2006).

I will now outline the details of the focus groups and individual interviews before discussing my rationale behind conducting the interviews.

Focus Groups

The focus groups consisted of 4–6 boys who had been doing an activity together at some point in one of the lessons, such as playing on the same volleyball team. The group stayed the same for the second interview. Each group had a photo taken and chose a name for the group, as a way of involving the boys in the research process and enabling them to take further ownership of the research. My reason for selecting the focus groups in this way was both to have something for them to relate to as a group and also to address some ethical concerns.

The boys were, for instance, told that confidentiality could not be guaranteed when they would meet together with other boys in the focus group interviews. In particular, there was an element of risk associated with boys disclosing sensitive information in the focus groups that could lead to individuals being harassed (Frosh, Phoenix, & Pattman, 2002). Having already spent some time with the boys during the initial observations, I knew a bit about the dynamics of the two classes and was able to put some extra thought into the composition of the groups. Care was taken to ensure that the focus groups did not include participants who were considered to be from different status groups in this PE setting. For instance, 'sporty' boys were not to be grouped together with 'non-sporty' ones and so on because this might have resulted in 'low status' individuals being harassed or bullied by 'high status' individuals.

Focus groups involve participants discussing a chosen topic collaboratively rather than engaging in a two-way conversation with the researcher. The focus group format was chosen because the hallmark of a focus group is "the explicit use of the group's interaction to produce data and insights that would be less accessible without the interaction found in the group" (Morgan, 1998, p. 12). Watts and Ebbutt (1987) further claim that focus groups are more likely to produce critical comments than when individuals are interviewed. Indeed, I found that the focus groups encouraged the exploration of complex motivations and behaviours because the nature of the groups made the boys concentrate on one another, not me. The focus group, therefore, enabled the boys themselves to engage in discussions and negotiations about the complex and contradictory nature of performances of gender in PE. Arguably, it is the collective interaction that characterises the focus group method that generates rich data in terms of the production of discourse because focus groups reveal information about "how accounts are articulated, censured, opposed and changed through social interaction and how this relates to peer communication and group norms" (Kitzinger & Barbour, 1999, p. 5). When the boys questioned each other, asked for clarification and laughed at or contested certain responses, it was possible for me to see how gendered knowledge and 'truths' were constructed in these focus groups. For instance, on many occasions we would get into discussions about what the content of PE should be, and the way the boys argued for or against the inclusion of certain games/activities provided important data in terms of what 'normal' boys should (and should not) find desirable in PE (i.e., rugby and soccer, not netball and dance).

The boys also appeared to carefully police the information they revealed about themselves, giving acknowledgement that what they said and how they said it differed according to context. I also quickly recognised that what was not said was as crucial as what was actually spoken. Foucault (1978) points out that silence itself conveys a great deal of meaning:

> Silence itself—the things one declines to say, or is forbidden to name, the discretion that is required between different speakers—is less the absolute limit of discourse, the other side of which is separated by a strict boundary, than an element that functions alongside the things said, with them and in relation to them in the overall strategies.
>
> (p. 27)

By employing silences and leaving certain details unspoken, the boys demonstrated careful self-surveillance of their gendered (masculine) selves. The focus groups were not just about giving representations and interpretations of their gendered experiences in PE but also provided an important site for the constitution and management of their own gendered (masculine) identities (Allen, 2005). From this perspective, the focus groups offered another site for observation of the performances of gendered identities and added another layer of data and analysis that moved beyond what the boys reported directly about their gendered experiences in PE. In this sense, the focus groups provided a context in which the boys presented or performed gendered selves. That is, the interviews themselves became sites for performances of gender, in which the boys' (body) language, behaviour and (inter) actions shed more light on the different facets of their gendered identities (Frosh et al., 2002). For instance, the type of language used by the boys to talk about gender and their own bodies was an important source of data. This included the use of humour since it has previously been suggested that humour is used as a "regulatory technique, structuring the performance of masculine identities" (Kehily & Nayak, 1997, p. 84). However, in accordance with Frosh et al. (2002), the types of performances of gender demonstrated in, for instance, the individual interviews were not seen as more 'authentic' than those observed in the group interviews. Instead, these were regarded as different ways of performing gender because boys may perform different kinds of gendered identities in different contexts (Daniels, 2009).

The first focus groups began with me showing a video clip of a particular situation recorded during the observations containing a (gendered) pattern or theme that I had identified as of relevance to the study. I was aware of Azzarito's (2010) concern that the visual material selected by me as the researcher might lead to a "displacement from the personal to the social" (p. 156), in which the boys might disavow strong feelings or issues of personal relevance on the topic researched. Consequently, I also let the boys themselves decide what visual material to discuss during the interviews. The clips were then played on my computer, and I asked the boys to talk about what was happening in the particular clip. The focus groups thus explored how the boys experienced these particular situations. Similar to Mousley's (1998) study, I found that some of the boys got distracted by their own appearance, clothing, expressions, vocal tenor, etc., which is why I decided to also use still images captured from the video recordings as stimulation during the focus groups. Hence, a combination of video clips and still images was used in this study.

Individual Interviews

All the boys also took part in one individual interview. Everyone was invited to take part in the individual interviews in order to eliminate the risk of individual students being questioned by their peers as to why they were chosen, which could potentially lead to these students being harassed or ridiculed. In these individual interviews, both the boys and I selected more video clips to look at and explored patterns/themes identified during the focus groups. Data analysed from the focus groups was thus used in the individual interviews to inform a more in-depth discussion around issues that could not fully be addressed in the group setting. These themes were then used in the individual interviews in order to continue discussion and ask for clarifications and elaborations. This often involved going back to particular video clips individuals had selected and asking them to look at them again, either reaffirming or amending their interpretations.

Issues of a more sensitive nature that could not be addressed during the focus groups due to the risk of the involved boys being ridiculed or harassed were particularly discussed in the individual interviews. The individual interviews allowed me to ask more sensitive and intimate questions about, for instance, the boys' understandings/experiences of their own bodies and how this might impact their performances of gender. These questions also included important issues such as vulnerability, body image, high/low self-esteem and peer pressure, which formed an integral part of a more in-depth analysis/discussion concerning the complexities of performing gender in PE. The individual interviews also revisited statements made by the boys during the focus groups that I had found interesting and/or that seemed contradictory or hesitant. Issues around simultaneous and contradictory/competing performances of gender were of particular interest.

Throughout the study, I gave careful consideration to when and how I should intervene if some boys ended up being ridiculed or harassed as a result of my research. My intention was to report any cases of bullying to the school authorities (Pascoe, 2007), but fortunately this was not needed. However, due to the sensitive nature of some of the topics discussed (especially in the individual interviews) and the inclusion of visual material, there were moments when I was put in ethically difficult situations. For instance, when talking about their bodies, some boys disclosed serious issues such as misuse of alcohol and drugs. On the one hand, I was obliged to maintain confidentiality and the trust established with the boys and not pass this information on to the school, but on the other hand, I was left with the ethical dilemma of 'doing the right thing'.

Conducting the Interviews

The interviews typically took place in one of the PE teachers' offices, behind closed doors. The boys participated in two focus groups and one individual interview, taking place between July and December 2010. In total, I conducted 24 focus groups and 60 individual interviews. The time length of each interview varied between 30 and 45 minutes. No scribe was used during the interviews, as this could inhibit the discussion. However, the interviews were recorded via digital audio and transcribed verbatim by myself. In subsequent interviews, I asked the boys to help clarify points raised and to ask further questions. In addition, while I was analysing and writing up the findings of the study, I continued to visit the school and seek further information from the boys about their (gendered) experiences and understandings of PE.

During the interviews, I attempted to adopt a 'friendly' and 'relaxed' style (Frosh et al., 2002). This interview style was achieved by sitting together in a circle in the focus groups and, in the case of the individual interviews, directly opposite the boy, with no tables or desks in between. The fact that video recordings were used during the interviews can also be seen as a way of stimulating conversation with the boys as a 'fun' and less formal way of conducting interviews. In addition, this meant that for most of the interview, focus was on the computer monitor rather than on the boys themselves, so the boys were not put too much in the 'spotlight'. At times, it felt like sitting down with a group of friends, having a discussion about what was happening on TV. At the start of the interviews, the boys were thanked for taking part, and I emphasised that I was there trying to learn from them what it is like being a boy in PE and that there were no right or wrong answers. I saw it as important, as noted by Frosh et al. (2002), that the boys did not see me as a kind of 'scientist' who turned them and their behaviours into "objects of a 'scientific' discourse" (p. 30), but that I was there to learn from them; they were the 'experts'. For instance, at the end of the interviews, I often told them how deeply interested and passionate I was about knowing more about their experiences of PE. I said they could come and talk to me at any time about any thoughts/ideas/feedback they wanted to share. I also gave them the opportunity to ask me about my research and what I was hoping to achieve.

My interview approach was underpinned by the belief that knowledge production is a subjective process and that the interview is an inter-play between people "conversing about a theme of mutual interest" (Kvale, 1996, p. 2). During the focus groups and the individual interviews, a schedule or interview guide containing open-ended questions/prompts was used in order to make sure that the data collected addressed issues related to the research questions. The interview guide was developed in relation to my review of literature and themes/issues that I had identified during the observations and video recordings. In conducting the interviews, I used a semi-structured approach, which typically has a sequence of conversation themes to be explored, as well as suggested questions, but "there is an openness to changes in sequence and forms of questions in order to follow up the answers given and the stories told by subjects" (Kvale, 1996, p. 124). When it comes to focus groups and individual interviews, there is sometimes an issue with the researcher taking control of the interview and dictating the topics discussed in order to obtain responses that are of particular interest for the study (Frosh et al., 2002). Consequently, the open-ended questions/prompts were only provided to introduce topics for discussion when needed in order to allow the boys to talk and exchange ideas with each other, so as not to overly influence responses.

The open-ended questions/prompts included topics such as the boys' feelings and embodied experiences of particular situations in PE, whether any problems or conflicts ever arose as a result of particular situations in PE and how the other boys and the teacher typically respond to particular situations. They also included other key areas, such as the family background of the boys (i.e., ethnicity, parents' education and occupation, religious views), the boys' views on gender, masculinity, femininity and body image and their involvement in sport and other pastimes. Given the overlap between these topic areas, the interviews did not progress in linear fashion, and each interview developed its own distinctive shape. However, the interviews were typically initiated by me asking the boys to talk about something that had come up during class or that was recorded in the video clips. Once a topic had been introduced, I attempted to discuss/negotiate the boys' views, perceptions and experiences of these particular situations. It is important to note that it was the boys' interpretation and discussion/negotiation of these particular situations that formed the data of crucial importance in answering my study's research question.

Overall, I attempted to facilitate a discussion around this series of open-ended questions about the boys' gendered experiences of PE. The purpose here was to explore how boys conceptualise gendered experiences in terms of their positive and negative consequences/outcomes and their construction and articulation of these during the interviews. When using video clips, I particularly wanted to encourage the boys' critical engagement with the gendered messages communicated/portrayed. For instance, one of the video clips offering a dominant construction of male gender represented a boy quickly getting back onto his feet and getting back to into a game of rugby after being tackled to the ground and visibly being seriously hurt. After looking at this video clip, the boys were asked to describe what they thought it conveyed about being a boy and whether they believed this to reflect the experiences of other boys.

More generally, I viewed the interviews as a two-way, rather than a one-way, exchange of information. Denzin (1989) warns that if an interviewer only listens without sharing, this could create distrust and stunt the depth of the conversation. As pointed out by Mac an Ghaill (1994), "male ethnographers of young men's schooling have systematically failed to acknowledge the implicit male knowledges, understandings and desires that we share with male research participants' schooling experiences" (p. 174). This means that I needed to scrutinise my own schooling and PE experiences (see preface) and become aware of how this may influence the interaction with different boys. For instance, as a male PE teacher, I needed to be careful not to 'bond' only with those boys who shared similar perspectives and views on boys, gender and PE. Accordingly, I did not remain neutral or passive throughout the study but attempted to share my own personal experiences of PE, both as a student and a teacher. In this way, I attempted to share my own experiences of what it means to be a boy in PE. I also deliberately told them stories about some of my own anxieties and failures in PE as a way of trying to lower my own 'male status'. I also believe that the fact that I was not that much older than the students helped me to relate to their 'life-world' in PE.

Data Analysis

Data consisted of field notes, video recordings and transcripts from focus groups and individual interviews. All field notes and interview transcripts were written up and prepared for detailed analysis. The video recordings were edited and organised, with those video clips identified as most relevant for the research questions also transcribed with both narratives and still images. Unfortunately, because of the limitation of the conventional format of a book, this video material is not incorporated into the book since it is not possible to explore the very rich nature of this data, nor conduct an in-depth analysis of it, because the boys' movements it demonstrates/represents cannot be easily conveyed by written text. In the presentation of findings, I therefore use only narratives and still images to represent the video material being discussed/analysed during the interviews.

In order to analyse this data, I used a qualitative method known as 'thematic analysis' (Braun & Clarke, 2006), a method that is compatible with a Foucauldian poststructural approach. Thematic analysis involves the identification, analysis and presentation of themes within data to go beyond common sense accounts. I also used thematic analysis as a form of Foucauldian analysis of discourse (Burman & Parker, 1993). Gee, Michaels and O'Connor (1992) articulate discourse analysis as any study that "may be concerned with any part of the human experience touched on or constituted by discourse" (p. 228).

I decided to use both thematic analysis and discourse analysis because it provided a broad framework that enabled me to focus on the practical implications of discourse, particularly with regards to power relations.

Thematic Analysis

Thematic analysis involves exploring all data guided by the theoretical underpinnings of the study and by key themes that arise from close reading of the research data. A theme is defined as something that "captures something important about the data in relation to the research question, and represents some level of patterned response or meaning within the data set" (Braun & Clarke, 2006, p. 82). The flexibility of thematic analysis means that there are a number of ways of determining themes and their prevalence. There is no fixed frequency or proportion of the data that needs to display evidence of a particular theme for it to be considered a theme. However, it is important to be consistent in the way this is decided. Braun and Clarke (2006) describe two broad data approaches: 'inductive' or 'deductive' analysis. An inductive analysis is ostensibly not driven by the researcher's theoretical interest, whereas a deductive approach is driven more clearly by the researcher's theoretical interest. In making these distinctions, it is emphasised that "in reality" it is not possible to analyse data in an "epistemological vacuum" (Braun & Clarke, 2006, p. 84). I agree with these authors' assertion that it is impossible for researchers to be outside of some sort of theoretical position. Similarly, Ramazanoglu and Holland (2002) assert that any interpretive approach inevitably has constraints shaped by the researcher's politics.

All the data generated was coded according to emerging themes in relation to the boys' performances of gender. The themes, or 'analytical categories' (Miles & Huberman, 1994), were carefully selected in relation to my prime research questions. The analysis of the themes involved going from an analysis at a 'semantic level' to a 'latent level' (Braun & Clarke, 2006), in which I attempted to understand how these themes, in relation to the performances of gender, ended up with their particular form and meaning. That is, once these broad themes had been identified, I conducted a *Foucauldian discourse analysis*.

Foucauldian Discourse Analysis

My discourse analysis was guided by Foucault's (1978) 'cautionary prescriptions' for identifying and understanding the workings of discourse.

Foucault warned that it was not a simple task to identify a specific discourse and explained that discourses are difficult to decipher, in part because "multipl[e] discursive elements . . . can come into play in various strategies" (Foucault, 1978, cited in Markula & Pringle, 2006, p. 215). Indeed, identifying with any certainty the prevailing or dominant discourses of boys' PE is a difficult (if not impossible) task.

In my discourse analysis, and drawing on for instance the work of Wright (1996, 2004), I was particularly interested in how various (gendered) discourses constitute PE and how particular discourses work ideologically to position boys. My analysis of the data therefore explored how the boys differentiate between diverse gendered meanings and how they may position these in a hierarchical order. Thus, the analysis examined how different discourses of gender may be in competition with each other. In particular, I attempted to highlight the relationship between power and knowledge and how certain forms of knowledge emerge and produce 'gendered truths', such as 'boys will be boys'. An important part of this involved examining how these discourses construct boys and how these constructions impact on the boys' performances of gender in PE. That is, how do boys embody and appropriate these discourses through their participation in PE (Clarke, 1992)? For example, the strong prevalence of rugby at this school impacted many of the boys' performances of gender, through outwardly hyper-masculine performances of gender, often involving reaffirming a particular privileged hyper-heteronormativity.

In my analysis of (gendered) discourses in PE, I also focused on the linguistic patterns (Wright & King, 1990) used by both the teachers and the students. Indeed, the different speech patterns used by the teachers and the students seemed to contribute to the construction of particular gendered ways of thinking and behaving within the PE classroom. For instance, the constant reproduction of boys and girls as natural opposites and inherently different, and the repudiation of stereotypical feminine acts and gestures, was a recurring pattern in much of the boys' language. This also intersected with issues of sexuality, in which the boys, through the use of language, reaffirmed their heterosexual status by positioning homosexuality as opposite and 'other' (Hunter, 2004).

In particular, I was aware that the language available to the boys to describe their experiences of PE is shaped by contextually specific discourses. That is, the language used by the boys to describe their experiences simultaneously defines them (Foucault, 1972). One of my key analytical tasks was therefore to identify and analyse the discursive resources that the boys used in their representations and interpretations of PE. My process of analysing the discourses was thus guided by Foucault's (1972) definition of discourse and discursive resources, which helped identify various social practices (e.g., 'doing what boys do' or 'scoring chicks'), subjects (e.g., 'sporty boys' or 'non-sporty boys') or objects (e.g., 'changing room' or 'dodgeball'). Furthermore, the particular way that boys might describe (pleasurable) experiences, such as "I love sweating" and "working hard", might reify dominant discourses related to discipline, fitness and health. The important thing here is that the boys are never outside of discourse; they make sense of their experiences through the discourses available to them.

In analysing the data, and based on my prime research question's focus on the articulation between performances of gender and pleasure, I was particularly guided by Foucault's (1978) work in the history of sexuality in which he aimed:

> to locate the forms of power, the channels it takes, and the discourses it permeates in order to reach the most tenuous and individual modes of behavior, the paths that give it access to the rare or scarcely perceivable forms of desire, how it penetrates and controls everyday pleasure.
>
> (p. 11)

I was interested in examining the workings of discourse and power to understand the constitution of boys' performances of gender and their articulations with (dis)pleasures. In particular, I wanted to identify the discourses that encouraged or demanded boys' participation in and enjoyment of PE. I was also interested in exploring whether some boys problematised their experiences of gender and pleasures in PE. Overall, I examined how the workings of discourse and power constituted the boys as gendered subjects who derive pleasures from participating in PE but also how the boys (re)negotiated those pleasurable experiences. That is, my research intention was not to simply explore boys' performances of gender and their articulations with (dis)pleasures but also to problematise them by revealing the discourses that they are constituted within.

The remainder of this book explores how the lives of Kea College boys constitute and are constituted by these discourses via the following thematic chapters.

Notes

1   All names of staff, teachers and students are pseudonyms.
2   Pākehā is the Māori name for European or non-Māori. It is commonly used in New Zealand alongside European.
3   Māori are the indigenous people of New Zealand
4   Differentiated funding of New Zealand schools is based on a 1–10 'decile' rating, which uses census data to measure socio-economic differences between school communities. Schools in wealthier communities, defined as 'high decile' schools, receive incrementally less funding.

References

Allen, L. (2005). Managing masculinity: Young men's identity work in focus groups. *Qualitative Research, 5*(1), 35–57.

Allen, L. (2008). Young people's 'agency' in sexuality research using visual methods. *Journal of Youth Studies, 11*(6), 565–577.

Allen, L. (2009). 'Snapped': Researching the sexual culture of schools using visual methods. *International Journal of Qualitative Studies in Education, 22*(5), 549–561.

Arnot, M., & Reay, D. (2007). A sociology of pedagogic voice: Power, inequality and pupil consultation. *Discourse, 28*(3), 311–326.

Azzarito, L. (2009). The panopticon of physical education: Pretty, active and ideally white. *Physical Education and Sport Pedagogy, 14*, 19–40.

Azzarito, L. (2010). Ways of seeing the body in kinesiology: A case for visual methodologies. *Quest, 62*, 155–170.

Azzarito, L., & Katzew, A. (2010). Performing identities in physical education: (En)gendering fluid selves. *Research Quarterly for Exercise and Sport, 81*, 25–37.

Azzarito, L., Solmon, M. A., & Harrison, L. (2006). '. . . If I had a choice, I would. . . .': A feminist poststructuralist perspective on girls in physical education. *Research Quarterly for Exercise and Sport, 77*(2), 222–239.

Azzarito, L., & Sterling, J. (2010). 'What it was in my eyes': Picturing youths' embodiment in 'real' spaces. *Qualitative Research in Sport and Exercise, 2*(2), 209–228.

Baker, D. W., Green, J. L., & Skukauskaite, A. (2008). Video-enabled ethnographic research: A microethnographic perspective. In G. Walford (Ed.), *How to do educational ethnography* (pp. 76–114). London, UK: Tufnell Press.

Banks, M. (2001). *Visual methods in social research*. London, UK: Sage.

Bogdan, R. C., & Biklen, S. K. (1998). *Qualitative research for education: An introduction to theory and methods*. Boston, MA: Allyn and Bacon.

Braun, V., & Clarke, V. (2006). Using thematic analysis in psychology. *Qualitative Research in Psychology, 3*, 77–101.

Broyles, L. M., Tate, J. A., & Happ, M. B. (2008). Video recording in clinical research. *Nursing Research, 57*(1), 59–63.

Burman, E., & Parker, I. (1993). *Discourse analytical research*. London, UK: Routledge.

Byra, M., & Sherman, M. (1993). Preactive and interactive decision-making tendencies of less and more experienced preservice teachers. *Research Quarterly for Exercise and Sport, 64*, 46–55.

Clarke, G. (1992). Learning the language: Discourse analysis in physical education. In A. C. Sparkes (Ed.), *Research in physical education and sport: Exploring alternative visions* (pp. 146–166). London, UK: Falmer Press.

Curry, T. J. (1986). A visual method of studying sports: The photo-elicitation interview. *Sociology of Sport Journal, 3*, 204–216.

Daniels, D. B. (2009). *Polygendered and ponytailed: The dilemma of femininity and the female athlete*. Toronto, Canada: Women's Press.

Delamont, S. (2003). Ethnography and participation observation. In C. Seale (Ed), *Qualitative research practice* (pp. 217–229). London, UK: Sage.

Denzin, N. K. (1989). *Interpretive biography*. Newbury Park, CA: Sage.

Denzin, N. K., & Lincoln, S. (1998). *Collecting and interpreting qualitative materials*. Thousand Oaks, CA: Sage.

Denzin, N. K., & Lincoln, Y. S. (2005). *The SAGE handbook of qualitative research* (3rd ed.). Thousand Oaks, CA: Sage.

Eisner, E. (2005). *Reimagining schools: The selected works of Elliot W. Eisner*. London, UK: Routledge.

Erickson, F., & Shultz, J. (1992). Students' experience of the curriculum. In P. Jackson (Ed.), *Handbook of research on curriculum* (pp. 465–485). New York: Macmillan.

Flewitt, R. (2005). Conducting research with young children: Some ethical considerations. *Early Child Development and Care, 175*(6), 553–565.

Foucault, M. (1972). *The archaeology of knowledge and discourse on language* (1st
American ed.). New York: Pantheon Books.

Foucault, M. (1978). *The history of sexuality, volume one.* Harmondsworth, UK:
Penguin.

Frosh, S., Phoenix, A., & Pattman, R. (2002). *Young masculinities: Understanding
boys in contemporary society.* Hampshire and New York: Palgrave.

Gauntlett, D., & Holzwarth, P. (2006). Creative and visual methods for exploring
identities. *Visual Studies, 21,* 82–91.

Gee, J. P., Michael, S., & O'Connor, M. C. (1992). Discourse analysis. In M. D.
LeCompte, W. L. Millory & J. Preissle (Eds.), *The handbook of qualitative
research in education* (pp. 227–291). San Diego, CA: Academic Press.

Gold, R. L. (1958). Roles in sociological field observations. *Social Forces, March,*
217–223.

Gorely, T., Holroyd, R., & Kirk, D. (2003). Muscularity, the habitus and the social
construction of gender: Towards a gender-relevant physical education. *British
Journal of Sociology of Education, 24*(4), 429–448.

Grossberg, L., Nelson, C., & Treichler, P. A. (1992). *Cultural studies.* New York:
Routledge.

Haywood, C., & Mac an Ghaill, M. (1996). Schooling masculinities. In M. Mac an
Ghaill (Ed.), *Understanding masculinities* (pp. 50–60). Buckingham, UK: Open
University Press.

Hills, L. (2007). Friendship, physicality, and physical education: An exploration of
the social and embodied dynamics of girls' physical education experiences. *Sport,
Education and Society, 12*(3), 317–336.

Hunter, L. (2004). Bourdieu and the social space of the PE class: Reproduction of
doxa through practice. *Sport, Education and Society, 9*(2), 175–192.

Junker, B. (1960). *Field work.* Chicago, IL: University of Chicago Press.

Kaplan, I., & Howes, A. (2004). Seeing through different eyes: Exploring the value
of participative research using images in schools. *Cambridge Journal of Education, 34*(2), 143–155.

Kehily, M. J. (2002). *Sexuality, gender and schooling: Shifting agendas in social
learning.* London, UK: Routledge Falmer.

Kehily, M. J., & Nayak, A. (1997). 'Lads and laughter': Humour and the production
of heterosexual hierarchies. *Gender and Education, 9*(1), 69–87.

Kitzinger, J., & Barbour, R. (1999). Introduction: The challenge and promise of focus
groups. In R. Barbour & J. Kitzinger (Eds.), *Developing focus group research:
Politics, theory and practice* (pp. 1–20). London, UK: Sage.

Kvale, S. (1996). *InterViews: An introduction to qualitative research interviewing.*
Thousand Oaks, CA: Sage.

LeCompte, M. D., & Preissle, J. (1993). *Ethnography and qualitative design in educational research* (2nd ed.). New York: Academic Press.

Luttrell, W. (2010). 'A camera is a big responsibility': A lens for analysing children's
visual voices. *Visual Studies, 25*(3), 224–237.

Mac an Ghaill, M. (1994). *The making of men: Masculinities, sexualities and schooling.* Buckingham, UK: Open University Press.

Markula, P., & Pringle, R. (2006). *Foucault, sport and exercise: Power, knowledge
and transforming the self.* New York: Routledge.

Miles, M. B., & Huberman, A. M. (1994). *Qualitative data analysis.* Thousand
Oaks, CA: Sage.

Mitchell, C., & Weber, S. (1998). Picture this! Class line ups, vernacular por-
traits and lasting impressions of school. In J. Prosser (Ed.), *Image-based*

research: A sourcebook for qualitative researchers (pp. 197–213). London, UK: Falmer Press.

Morgan, D. L. (1998). *The focus group guidebook.* Thousand Oaks, CA: Sage.

Mousley, J. (1998). Ethnographic research in mathematics education: Using different types of visual data refined from videotapes. In C. Kanes, M. Goos, & E. Warren (Eds.), *Teaching mathematics in new times* (pp. 397–403). Brisbane, Australia: Mathematics Education Research Group of Australasia Inc.

O'Donoghue, D. (2007). 'James always hangs out here': Making space for place in studying masculinities at school. *Visual Studies, 22*(1), 62–73.

Pascoe, C. J. (2007). *Dude, you're a fag: Masculinity and sexuality in high school.* Los Angeles, CA: University of California Press.

Pink, S. (2001). *Doing visual ethnography: Images, media and representation in research.* London, UK: Sage.

Pink, S. (2007). *Doing visual ethnography.* London, UK: Sage.

Piotrowski, S. (2000). The concept of equal opportunities in physical education with reference to gender equality. In S. Capel & S. Piotrowski (Eds.), *Issues in physical education* (pp. 25–46). London, UK: Routledge Falmer.

Prosser, J. (1998). The status of image-based research. In J. Prosser (Ed.), *In image-based research: A sourcebook for qualitative researchers* (pp. 97–112). London, UK: Falmer Press.

Prosser, J. (2007). Visual methods and the visual culture of schools. *Visual Studies, 22*(1), 13–30.

Prosser, J., & Burke, C. (2008). Image-based educational research: Childlike perspectives. In J. G. Knowles & A. L. Cole (Eds.), *Handbook of the arts in qualitative research* (pp. 407–419). London, UK: Sage.

Prosser, J., & Schwartz, D. (1998). Photographs within the sociological research process. In J. Prosser (Ed.), *Image based research: A sourcebook for qualitative researchers.* London, UK: Falmer Press.

Punch, K. (2005). *Introduction to social research: Quantitative and qualitative approaches.* London, UK: Sage.

Ramazanoglu, C., & Holland, J. (2002). *Feminist methodology: Challenges and choices.* London, UK: Sage.

Robinson, J. (2009). There's no place like home. *Studies in Symbolic Interaction, 33,* 47–57.

Rose, G. (2007). *Visual methodologies: An introduction to the interpretation of visual materials.* London, UK: Sage.

Schuck, S., & Kearney, M. (2006). Using digital video as a research tool: Ethical issues for researchers. *Journal of Educational Multimedia and Hypermedia, 15*(4), 447–463.

Snyder, E. E., & Kane, M. J. (1990). Photo elicitation: A methodological technique for studying sport. *Journal of Sport Management, 4,* 21–30.

Sparkes, A. (1992). *Research in physical education and sport: Exploring alternative visions.* London and Washington, DC: Falmer Press.

Spindler, G., & Hammond, L. (2000). The use of anthropological methods in educational research: Two perspectives. In B. Brizuela, J. Stewart, R. Carrillo, & J. Berger (Eds.), *Acts of inquiry in qualitative research* (pp. 39–48). Cambridge, MA: Harvard Educational Review.

Togman, J. M. (2011). A home in brick city. *Studies in Symbolic Interaction, 36,* 183–199.

Wang, B. (1977). *An ethnography of a physical education class: An experiment in integrated living* (Unpublished doctoral dissertation). University of North Carolina, Greensboro.

Watts, M., & Ebbutt, D. (1987). More than the sum of the parts: Research methods in group interviewing. *British Educational Research Journal, 13,* 25–34.

Weber, S., & Mitchell, C. (1995). *'That's funny, you don't look like a teacher': Interrogating images and identity in popular culture.* London, UK: Falmer Press.

Whyte, W. (1997). *Creative problem solving in the field: Reflections on a career.* Walnut Creek, CA: Alta Mira Press.

Wright, J. (1996). The construction of complementarity in physical education. *Gender and Education, 8*(1), 61–79.

Wright, J. (2004). Post-structural methodologies: The body, schooling and health. In J. Evans, B. Davies, & J. Wright (Eds.), *Body knowledge and control: Studies in the sociology of physical education and health* (pp. 19–31). London, UK: Routledge.

Wright, J., & King, R. C. (1990). 'I say what I mean,' said Alice: Analysis of gendered discourse in physical education. *Journal of Teaching in Physical Education, 10*(2), 210–225.

Yates, L. (2010). The story they want to tell, and the visual story as evidence: Young people, research authority and research purposes in the education and health domains. *Visual Studies, 25*(3), 280–291.

Part II

A Visual Ethnography of Kea College

4   Sporting and Masculinising Spaces
The Performative and Pleasurable Spaces of Boys' PE

This chapter explores the spatiality of boys' performances of gender in PE and argues that the spaces of PE (re)produce not only gendered meanings and identities but also (dis)pleasures. In particular, the findings presented in this chapter show how the boys' performances of and within PE spaces both conform with and disrupt discourses of sport and masculinity, pointing towards the unstable and fluid nature of both spaces and gender. I argue that the boys derive pleasures as the productive effect of the power articulated in and through the spaces of PE. In particular, I demonstrate how, through their performances of gender, as shaped by discourses and relations of power associated with sport and masculinity, the boys capitalise on the material features of PE to highlight them as productive and pleasurable spaces.

The 'Old' Gym and the Boys' Changing Rooms—The Performative Spaces of PE

The following visual representations (Figure 4.1) introduce the spaces of PE at the research setting and provide a 'glimpse' of what it is like coming to PE for the participating boys at this particular school. The spaces used for PE at Kea College include: the 'old' gym, the 'new' gym, the rugby field, the soccer field and the multipurpose sports field. Although these spaces undeniably exist, this section starts exploring how the spaces come to matter or become meaningful through the boys' performances of gender as the 'performative spaces' (Gregson & Rose, 2000) of boys' PE. Although the visual representations below serve as examples of what a 'typical' PE class at this school involves, every PE class I observed and participated in developed in its own unique way.

In spatial terms, this PE context can be viewed as at once 'material', 'discursive' and 'performative'. Firstly, PE takes place in material spaces. In a material sense, PE exists: it is a 'real' space with actual buildings and a specific location. However, the narrative and visual imagery above also illustrate how the spaces to which the boys come for PE are not merely pre-existing and material spaces they simply go to. Although in a material sense, spaces like the gym exist as buildings, space only begins to matter in

Figure 4.1 A Visual Representation of a PE lesson at Kea College: The 'Old' Gym Before the Lesson (Top Left), Mr Whyte Briefing the Class (Top Right), Warm-Up/Fitness Drills (Middle Left), Picking Teams (Middle Right) and Playing Dodgeball (Bottom).

discursive terms (Rose, 1993). That is, despite having certain material characteristics such as walls, a roof, lines and basketball hoops that temporally have been fixed in that locality, this does not mean that as a space it matters or is meaningful (Pink, 2011). For instance, the spaces of PE exist in and of themselves but also relative to their purposes and usages over time. Although this gym is mainly used for PE, it might also be used for other events such as extra-curricular sports, school assemblies and voting venues during elections. That is, material spaces do not acknowledge the socio-cultural production of space or the lived experiences of those spaces (Foucault, 1980). A discursive space is therefore one where particular meanings are made according to the discourses shaping that space.

When talking to Ben and Adam (both 14 years old, European/Pākehā, active in multiple team sports) about doing PE in the 'old' gym depicted above, they say:

Ben: Yeah, as soon as you walk into this gym, you feel like running around, you know, getting fit and stuff and competing against the other boys.

Göran: What makes you say that?

Ben: Well, it's like, you know, being inside that big open space with lines and stuff instead of desks and chairs makes you want be active and to play sports and stuff. I love it!

Adam: I love having PE in the old gym. I mean, it is pretty grotty and stuff but cool to have PE in the same gym as my dad.

Göran: Ah, so your dad went to this school as well?

Adam: Yeah, so pretty cool.

Ben: It is also awesome how we just get changed right there in the gym. You know, just having boys and stuff, so we don't have to worry about girls being there.

Firstly, the boys' comments draw attention to this 'old' gym as an enjoyable PE space. Ben's statement, in particular, points towards the material nature of the gym ("big open space") affording them with certain bodily pleasures because the space allows the boys greater freedom of movement than is possible, for instance, in classrooms filled with "desks and chairs". In contrast to Bale (1996), it is not movement in an aesthetically pleasing environment (as evidenced by the description of the gym above) but the open spaces of this gym that produces this gym as a meaningful and enjoyable space. Throughout my year with these boys, I frequently observed how the space of PE for the majority of boys seemed to be defined by "a common delight in bodily movement—a biological exuberance" (Tuan, 1986, p. 13). The discourses of (bodily) (dis)pleasures in PE are explored further in chapters five and six.

The boys' comments also highlight the discursive nature of this space. The discursive space of this PE class comprises discourses around fitness ("running around and getting fit and stuff"), performance ("competing against the other boys"), sport ("play sports") and heteronormativity ("getting changed right there in the gym" and "not worry about girls being there"). Drawing on the dynamic, contested and multiple meanings associated with particular spaces, Harvey (2006) argues that it is the actions or performances that take place in material spaces that determine how spaces make sense or come to matter for individuals within them. The way PE spaces come to matter is located within—and performed by—the relationships among the boys and between the teacher and the boys. The social relations and practices of the boys and the teacher in PE simultaneously perform (gendered) identities and spaces. In this way, the spatial and the social are reciprocally constructed through materially embedded practices and performances that create and maintain everyday social relations, including the boys' performances of gender (Rose, 1993). The space of PE is literally made or performed through the actions and interactions of the boys and the teacher within the material and discursive space of PE.

The visual representations above also illustrate how the spaces of PE are endlessly made and remade (and sometime undone) (Crang, 2005). The types of activities, for instance fitness drills and dodgeball, which the boys engage in continuously help construct and reconstruct the meanings and values associated with this space. In this sense, the spaces of PE are not fixed or rigid but rather open and shifting, "the simultaneity of stories so far" (Massey, 2005, p. 9). The spaces of PE constitute and are constituted by many and conflicting meanings and values, as interpreted, lived, challenged and performed by the boys in different ways. The way the boys participate in these activities also alters both the nature of the activity and the space where is it practiced (Raitz, 1995). PE is both determined by space and also the producer of space (Eichberg, 1990). Drawing on Massey's (2005) notion of 'place-event', it could be argued that each PE class reproduces the spaces of PE. It is not just that the PE classes are different each time they are performed, and it is not simply the way the boys' experiences of participating in that PE class are different; rather, the PE class as a 'place-event' is each time (re)performed. Although it is similar to previous PE classes and thus recognisable as the same event, it actually constitutes a new PE space.

One particular space that was identified as important and inquisitive in my study was the boys' changing room, located in the 'new' gym at Kea College. As discussed in chapter three, ethical restrictions prevented me from documenting certain 'off-limit' or 'unauthorised' spaces (Epstein & Johnson, 1998; Kehily, 2002), such as the boys' changing rooms. However, after analysing both the verbal and visual data, I soon recognised that the changing rooms play an important role in the boys' management of gendered identities. Indeed, in one of the focus groups, prompted by me showing a still image of the door leading into the boys' changing rooms (Figure 4.2), Matthew (15 years old, European/Pākehā, active in multiple team sports), one of the seemingly popular rugby boys, says the following about what goes on inside this space:

Matthew:	Well, it is the time [the changing rooms] when there is a lot of bonding going on [laughter].
Göran:	What do you mean by bonding?
Matthew:	You know, boys doing boys' stuff. You know, talking about scoring girls, playfighting, playing practical jokes on each other

Figure 4.2 Door Leading into the Boys' Changing Rooms in the 'New' Gym.

and showing who is stronger or weaker, you know. It's a bit like the survival of the fittest [laughter].

Göran: And who are the winners?
Matthew: Well, most of the time, all of us rugby boys [laughter].

While no actual visual data existed of the inside of the changing rooms, Matthew explains the significance of this physical space in the discursive constitution of meanings about gender. In particular, Matthew's statement draws further attention towards the type of gender, disciplinary and heteronormative work that takes place in changing room spaces (Atkinson & Kehler, 2010; Burstyn, 1999; Caudwell, 2006). In contrast to previous PE studies (e.g., Atkinson & Kehler, 2010), my data analysis also reveals some contradictory statements about the role that the changing rooms play in the boys' performances of gender. For example, one of the other 'sporty' boys, Thomas (14 years old, European/Pākehā, active in a number of team and individual sports) explains how the changing rooms act as a space away from the surveilling gaze of the teacher, a form of haven where the boys can escape some of the pressures involved when out in the gym and in the official school grounds:

Thomas: Well, you know, I like just being with the other boys and talking to each other before and after PE since it is the only time really that we get to be somewhere at this school without the teachers watching you. You know, we can be ourselves and talk about whatever we want. I mean, some of the boys get a bit mean to each other, you know, say stuff about the other boys' bodies and stuff. But most of the time, you know, we have a good time in there.

Göran: So what do you do and talk about in there?

Thomas: Well, all kind of stuff. You know, sometimes just good old boys' stuff, but yeah, I guess sometimes we also behave a bit like girls.

Göran: What do you mean?

Thomas: Well, you know, talk about who is seeing who. I mean girls. Sometimes we talk about problems that some might have with their girlfriends and stuff. I mean, we are not always trying to be all macho and stuff like some people might think. We actually look out for each other. And I think the changing rooms, to be honest, is one of those places where we are able to do so without worrying about keeping up some kind of image.

Thomas's account of what goes on in the changing rooms offers a somewhat different glimpse of boys negotiating and regulating dominant discourses of gender, similar to that observed by Curry (1991). It seems as if unofficial spaces such as the changing rooms also function as spaces where some boys are able to contradict common stereotypes of boys' behaviour (Curry, 1991). In this sense, the space of the changing rooms acts not only as a gender disciplinary space but also as an alternative or 'safe space' (Renold, 2004), where some boys inhabit or perform the changing rooms as a way of disrupting the disciplinary gaze of the school in which gendered norms and behaviours are policed more closely. The (re)performing of the boys' changing rooms from a 'hyper-masculine' space (Atkinson & Kehler, 2010) into a form of 'caring', 'sensitive' space, gives further evidence of boys as active subjects in negotiating power relations (Azzarito & Solmon, 2006; Markula, 2003). In this case, this means that the boys are able to display empathy for other boys and sensitivity to their emotions and feelings, not commonly 'expected' from a group of teenage boys (Frosh, Phoenix, & Pattman, 2002).

This finding is further substantiated when the same boy (Thomas) says the following when a photo of my family comes up on the computer screen in between video clips in one of the focus groups:

Thomas: Ah, how cute!
Göran: Oh thank you, yeah, that is my family.
Thomas: Cute family!

Some boys are performing gender differently to what might be expected and thus pointing towards the unstable nature of both spaces and gender. The spaces of PE, such as the boys' changing rooms, need to be understood as not only pre-existing spaces but as spaces that the boys' own performances of gender constitute and (re)produce as meaningful (Bell, Binnie, Cream, & Valentine, 1994; Massey, 1994). In contrast to previous studies (e.g., Atkinson & Kehler, 2010), it is argued that it is not the space of the changing rooms *per se* that determines boys' performances of gender, but the boys' own performances of gender also constitute this space. The boys' performances of gender and the space of the boys' changing rooms in PE are mutually constitutive (Grosz, 1992). However, it is important to note that the material aspect of this space also matters. The fact that the boys' changing room is removed from the gaze of the teacher affords the boys more 'freedom' to negotiate these issues because teacher surveillance is rendered more problematic in this context (Allen, 2008). The boys' performances of gender and the materiality of the changing rooms are mutually constitutive of gendered identities and meanings.

However, while the boys can be seen as active agents in making use of the discursive resources at their disposal to perform gender and space, they must locate their discursive activities within a meaningful context (Hardy, Palmer, & Phillips, 2000). The spaces of PE, such as the old gym and the boys' changing rooms, offer both opportunities and constraints in the expression of self and in the making of different kinds of lives and subjectivities (Massey, 1994), as shaped by the workings of discourse and relations of power (Gregson & Rose, 2000). Drawing on the notion of socially produced (Massey, 1994) and performative spaces (Gregson & Rose, 2000), it could be argued that the meanings and values constructed in the PE spaces described and represented above impact on the boys in particular ways, both inhibiting and allowing particular ways of being within space. The spaces of PE, with their particular attributes, meanings and values, 'teach' the boys about how the world works and their place within it (Gruenewald, 2003a, 2003b). At Kea College, as indicated in chapter one, the spaces of PE are particularly influenced by the prominent role that sport plays in the education of boys. In the next section, I illustrate both how the boys' performances of space and gender in my study can be seen as articulations of discourses and relations of power associated with sport and their discursive links with masculinity.

'Sport for Its Own Sake'—Sporting and Masculinising Spaces

Logbook entry from my first day of fieldwork at Kea College:

> On my first day at Kea College, I park my car and walk across the sport fields, making my way over to the 'PE blocks', where Mr Whyte, the main teacher participating in this study and also the head of department (HOD) for PE, is waiting for me to arrive. The first thing that I am struck by is the brand new sports complex at the end of the rugby and soccer fields, named after the long withstanding school principal, Mr Andersson. Next to this new sports complex, there is a multipurpose 'astro-court' (artificial grass) with lines for tennis and hockey, including a smaller fenced-off area for basketball. Behind the new sports complex and the multipurpose astro-court, there is an older gym, which is a two-story building with changing rooms, gym and PE staff room downstairs and an indoor multipurpose gym with lines for indoor soccer and hockey, basketball, etc. upstairs. Up over the hill, there is another sports field with stands that is used for the school's top rugby, cricket and soccer teams. Adjacent to this sports field are the other main school buildings, including 'blocks' for art, science, technology, language, etc. Straight away, you get a sense of this school 'living and breathing for sports'.
>
> Logbook entry 03/04/2010

The sports-oriented nature of this school and the discursive links with masculinity are also evident in other spaces. On the school's official webpage, there is a slideshow consisting of a number of images related to sport. The first one shows the principal, Mr Andersson, sitting at a table in his office together with a group of smiling boys and some sporting trophies showing in the background. In the second image, the school's 'First XV' rugby team is showcasing one of its winning trophies. The third is of a big group of boys running races on the beach. The fourth image shows some of the school's soccer players in action and the fifth an athletic looking boy in mid-air while completing a long-jump. Out of the seven images in the slideshow, only two are not directly sport-related. In one of those images, an older student is seen 'mentoring' some younger students, and the other one is a photo from a Christmas play, which also contains girls from Kea College's sister school. The sport-oriented nature of this school is further seen by the content of the 'upcoming events' section on the front page of the school's website, all relating to various sporting events such as basketball, swimming and rugby.

By examining the spaces of Kea College, and by coupling this analysis with Butler's attention to the performative effects of discourse, a process of materialisation in which both spaces and gender are shaped by discourses of sport and masculinity is revealed. Indeed, in some of my earliest conversations with Mr Whyte, he expresses the belief that most students, once they leave Kea College, should have 'found' at least one sport that they will continue doing later in life. As I will discuss in chapter five, this focus on sport is also something that has a major impact on the content and practices of PE at this school. Throughout my year at Kea College, it soon became clear that through everyday practices, such as encouraging physical fitness/health and participation/excellence in and through sports, the school instils the boys with certain forms of masculinity. According to Mac an Ghaill (1994), schools are important social spaces and, outside the family, are key sites for identity construction. In particular, he argues that within schools "the administration, regulation and reification of gender roles is institutionalised through social and discursive practices of staff rooms, classroom and playground microcultures" (Mac an Ghaill, 1994, p. 9). Philips (1997) further suggests that "masculinities are spatially constituted; they reflect the characteristics of the spaces in which they are constituted" (p. 18). That is, the materialisation of discourses of sport and masculinity into 'sporting' and 'masculinising' spaces shapes both how the boys understand/experience PE at this school and their performances of gender.

There are two discourses related to sports at Kea College, one that relates to excellence or 'performance' and the other one to 'participation' (Tinning, 2010). In the school's prospectus for future students, "sporting excellence" is one of the main headings, under which it states that "Sport has always had a high profile at [Kea] College and many of our Old Boys, as well as some current pupils, are in National Representative teams". However, in the school prospectus, it is further stated that at Kea College:

> We stress the importance of sport in the all-round development of healthy young men, believing it to be as important for their social development as classroom activities are for their academic progress. All boys are encouraged to participate and develop skills in some form of sporting activity as well as taking part in Physical Education lessons at all year levels. . . . Although the importance of competition is acknowledged, we are more concerned in encouraging enjoyment of *sport for its own sake*. While success is always gratifying, [Kea] College is proudest of its tradition of sportsmanship and fair play. [emphasis added]

In addition to sporting performance and achieving excellence through sports, participation in sport is valued as important "for its own sake". For instance, in contrast to many other schools across New Zealand, PE at Kea College is compulsory throughout the entire schooling (Year 7–13) whereas in most other schools (and indeed the curriculum stipulates this), it is only compulsory until Year 10. Many of the boys and teachers at this school seem to conflate school sports, such as rugby, with PE. This is a conflation that neither I nor the official Health and PE curriculum in New Zealand (Ministry of Education, 2007) would promote but that seems to be a recurring feature of the boys'/teacher's commentary in this study. The above statements from the school prospectus also highlight Butler's (1997) proposal regarding the potentially productive power of discourse and representation in the process of materialisation. Drawing on Butler, it could be argued that a statement such as the "enjoyment of *sport for its own sake*" is all that is needed to (re) produce sport as a desirable or even expected masculine endeavour. That is, *any* form of involvement in sport is juxtaposed with *no* involvement because it helps boys reaffirm/conform to 'normal' masculine identities.

When I talk to the boys about the best things about going to this school, this focus on involvement in sport, as an expected and normal masculine venture, is a recurring theme. However, it is also an important source of enjoyment, as the following quotes reveal:

Mitchell: It's good, it is really sport orientated.
Logan: The rugby, the sports.
Dominic: Really sporty school . . . play rugby for the school . . . cool playing the national sport for the school.
Matthew: Games, sports.
James: Lots of sports.
Logan: Good sports team.

The opportunities to engage in various sporting activities and represent the school, particularly, as Dominic (14 years old, Pacific Island, active in multiple team sports) points out, in the "national sport" of rugby, are an important feature of schooling at Kea College for the boys participating in my study. When the same boys as above talk about why they enjoy sport, they mainly refer to the nature of sport being associated with certain desirable (masculine) characteristics:

Mitchell: Sports build character, you know, respect others and stuff.
Logan: You learn how to work hard . . . discipline.
Dominic: Cooperating with others.
Matthew: Competing and measuring yourself against others.
James: Learning certain skills . . . you know, like running and stuff.
Logan: Teamwork and that sort of stuff.

The boys' comments draw attention to how their enjoyment of sport coheres around the development of psychological traits ("working hard", "discipline" and "competing") but also social values ("respecting others", "cooperating" and "teamwork"). Participating in and achieving excellence through sports is regarded by boys such as Mitchell and Logan (both 14 years old, European/Pākehā, active in multiple team sports) and Dominic, Matthew and James (15 years old, Other, active in multiple team sports) as playing a vital role in their construction of masculine identities. However, rather than merely viewing sport as important masculinising spaces (Hickey, Fitzclarence, & Matthews, 1998; Messner, 1992) that attempt to turn boys into the right way of being masculine (Connell, 2008; Markula & Pringle, 2006), sport is also seen by the boys themselves as a desirable aspect of boys' schooling. The discourses of sport and masculinity as materialised through the spaces of schooling and PE also intersect with discourses of pleasure.

What is important to remember, though, is that in poststructural perspectives on pleasure, there are no pre-existing, inherent pleasurable feelings; rather, pleasure is interpreted by people in relation to the discourses circulating in a given socio-cultural context (Foucault, 1978; Pronger, 2000). In this sense, pleasure is also discursively constructed and thus "cannot be separated from the words and concepts that are already in circulation to define and describe them" (Coveney & Bunton, 2003, p. 164). The pleasures these boys derive from being involved in sport can be seen as discursively constructed, in which being and performing 'sporty boy' is closely related to the development of certain sporting (masculine) identities. The discourses of PE (dis)pleasures and their articulations with boys' performances of gender are explored further in the next chapter.

However, many of the boys in my study also reveal how their schooling activities do not (only) involve sport, thus blurring the discursive links between sport and masculinity. For instance, the boys talk about playing various "instruments", being involved in "graphics/arts" and "computer games". One of the boys, Jack (15 years old, European/Pākehā, active in multiple individual sports), says that the main reason he goes to Kea College is because of its "awesome music department and teachers" so he can pursue his passion for playing the piano. Indeed, Mr Whyte runs computer games programming courses both during the school terms and in the school holidays. While in the final stages of writing up the findings of this research project, he had just taken over the IT department, which can be seen as a sign of disrupting the link between sport, PE teachers and masculinity. Reporting on the lived experiences of PE teachers such as Mr Whyte can be important in order to provide further disruptions to the enduring discourses of masculine hegemony that pervade all-boys schooling and PE (Mooney & Hickey, 2012).

Nevertheless, the prevailing sporting discourse at Kea College not only shapes the way the boys talk about and understand boys' schooling but also influences social relations and practices. In particular, the boys account for the (dis)pleasures of how sport largely defines social groups and who the boys spend time with during breaks:

Latham:	You hang out with the people who play same sports as you.
Alex:	In the breaks, people get into groups, sporty and not sporty.
James:	Rugby people hang out with rugby people . . . hang out in different spaces depending on the group.
Ben:	Rugby players group. . . . Not sporty people who hang out at the library.

James and Ben indicate that the sports you belong to, such as rugby, determine not only what people you mostly spend time with but also what spaces you occupy. In this sense, the gendered identities of the boys are also filled with spatial metaphors (Gilroy, 1993). Foucault (1995) alerts us to the ways in which even physical spaces are power processes that produce effects in people. In relation to education, Allen (2013) more specifically argues that this is how "temporal and spatial configurations of power that are often inconspicuous, unacknowledged and/or mundane affect students' experiences of education" (pp. 59–60). Oliver (15 years old, European/Pākehā, active in multiple individual sports) cites this socio-spatial grouping dependent on sports as being one of the negatives or "downsides" of attending Kea College:

Oliver:	Well, you know, the downside is that there are a few people I don't like. . . . Some people show off too much. . . . Groups of really sporty people always hang out together. . . . They think they are good at everything . . . telling everyone what to do and stuff.

One of the other boys, Timothy (14 years old, Pacific Island, not involved in any sport), tells me how this grouping of people is also related to issues of bullying:

Timothy:	Yeah, bullying is definitely one of the negatives of Kea College. . . . People who are not very social and not into sport [are bullied].

Oliver and Timothy illustrate how sport acts not only as an important space for the development of masculine identities but also in the production and maintaining of unequal power relations between and among boys.

These findings add to Connell's (e.g., Connell, 2005), Kehler's (e.g., Kehler & Atkinson, 2010) and others' (e.g., Martino, 1999, 2000; Martino & Pallotta-Chiarolli, 2003; O'Donoghue, 2007; Rawlings & Russell, 2012; Renold, 1997, 2004; Ringrose & Renold, 2010) studies on masculinity and bullying. The way bullying is often framed as consisting of a 'bully' and a 'victim'—each with specific attributes and performances—simplifies and reduces the complexity of such practices rather than attempting to deconstruct the gender/sexuality regulation framework involved (Rawlings & Russell, 2012). Indeed, bullying research and policy has been largely 'gender blind' (Ringrose & Renold, 2010), failing to note the socio-cultural context of bullying and ways in which exclusion and violence are often rooted in reinforcing 'rules' for heteronormative gender (Payne & Smith, 2013). At Kea College, discourses of masculinity, sport, fitness and health played an important role in and shaped the boys' performances of gender and, more specifically, what types of performances of gender were (im)possible (Youdell, 2006). It was in particular the boys who were not outwardly 'sporty' who became the targets of various forms of abuse and harassment.

For instance, on a couple of occasions, I observed how groups of 'sporty' boys before/during/after PE bullied/intimidated other less 'sporty' or 'non-sporty' boys by tackling them against the wall/fence/to the ground or passing the ball to someone who clearly was not ready to receive it. Just as the boy James in O'Donoghue's (2007) study used a particular schoolyard place to bully other students, the materially and discursively constructed sporting space is used by some boys to intimidate other boys.

Whereas the 'sporty' boys were able to claim dominant spaces by occupying both social and physical space (Connell, 2005), some of the other boys were subjugated to spaces away from the interaction of these boys. Size, muscularity, athletic physicality and skill in popular male sports such as football/rugby were fundamental masculine features, providing a high status and popular form of masculinity among the boys in the school culture (Renold, 1997, 2004). Dominant masculine ideals as related to sport, fitness and health can be seen to constitute a form of 'bullying' discourse (Ringrose & Renold, 2010), which acts as the further policing of 'intelligible' heteronormative masculinities by positioning some boys as deviant or 'other' when not adequately performing normative ideals of masculinity.

However, it is important to note that it is not the sporting spaces *per se* that determine these actions; it is the boys' repeated use of these spaces, as shaped by discourses of sport and masculinity and relations of power, that performs these spaces as 'bullying' spaces. Being and performing 'sporty' boy, importantly, has the double function of giving access to particular spaces associated with privileged social peer group status and (re)produces the position of the 'non-sporty' boys as the 'other' (Hunter, 2004). In this sense, the spaces of schooling and PE as constitutive of discourses of sport and masculinity simultaneously produce certain (dis)pleasures.

The language available to these boys to describe their understandings and experiences of schooling and PE is shaped by the socio-spatial context of sport. One of Foucault's (1972) primary assertions about discourse is that language not only describes a thing but simultaneously produces it: "Discourses are not about objects; they constitute them and in the practice of doing so conceal their own intervention" (p. 49). The particular way these boys describe how sports define social groups and who they spend time with during school, such as 'sporty' and 'non-sporty' boys, might reify discursive links between discourses of sport and masculinity. However, their description, as in Oliver's case, might also provide evidence of some sort of resistance to dominant ideas associated with these particular kinds of experiences. The important thing here is that these boys are never outside of discourse; they make sense of their experiences through the discourses available to them.

In summary, the spaces of Kea College can be seen as the concretisation of power (Markus, 1993) associated with discourses of sport and masculinity, along with other discourses such as education and sexuality. In particular, as spaces for the accumulation of 'masculine capital' (De Visser & McDonnell, 2013), boys perform gender in and through sporting spaces to reaffirm (privileged) normal masculine identities. Having identified the spaces of both schooling and PE as sporting and masculinising spaces, I now turn my attention to how the boys' performances of gender within those spaces might articulate with (dis)pleasures. That is, how do the performative spaces of PE, as sporting and masculinising spaces, contribute to (dis)pleasures? In the next five sections, I will use Foucault's (1995) "art of distributions" (p. 141) to explore not only how the spaces of PE create disciplined and docile (sporting and masculine) bodies but also how the performative spaces of PE produce (dis)pleasures.

Enclosed Spaces—Focusing on 'Doing What Boys Do'

When observing the boys' PE classes, I would typically arrive 5–10 minutes early because I was interested in what goes on before lessons start. One thing I quickly noted is that the teacher, on almost every occasion, would be waiting at the door or gate where the students arrive. The still image in Figure 4.3 demonstrates how Mr Whyte is standing by the gate of the fenced-off area for the PE lesson, almost like a shepherd rounding up all the students and making sure that they are all inside before the lesson begins. As soon as everyone has arrived, he or one of the boys then closes the gate or door. This 'closing the gate/door' routine seems important not only to the

Figure 4.3 Mr Whyte 'Rounding up the Students'.

teacher but also to the students, who are quick to point out if the gate/door is not closed properly.

When asked about the significance of this routine, Mr Whyte says:

Mr Whyte: Well, you have to make sure that all the students are in and not somewhere else in the school grounds, and also it stops other students from coming in or interfering with the lesson. It also means that the students cannot try and escape the lesson [laughter].

Drawing on Foucault's (1995) theorising of the disciplinary use of space, it could be argued that this routine (although also applicable to other school subjects) is related to controlling and coordinating the boys' actions by ensuring that they remain in the space allocated for this particular lesson and for the length of time required. More specifically, this routine can be explained by the disciplinary technique of "enclosure" (Foucault, 1995, p. 141). By locating the boys in a space protected from the rest of the school and its students, the teacher can make sure that the boys are placed together and doing the same or similar activities (Foucault, 1995). This point is further exemplified by the boys' visual imagery represented by the still images in Figure 4.4 but also draws attention to ways in which boys' performance of gender and (dis)pleasures in PE emerge as a result of particular enclosed spaces, such as the gym. When the video clip containing the still images in Figure 4.4 is discussed in one of the focus groups, a group of boys who can be said to belong to the 'sporty' group explain why they enjoy having PE inside this gym:

Matthew: I love having PE in the gym!
Dominic: Yeah, me too!
Göran: Why is that?
Matthew: Well, I mean it is great being inside the gym compared to being outside on the fields, especially in winter when it gets too wet all the time. In here, we can just focus on playing games and

Figure 4.4 The Enclosed Spaces of the Gym.

	competing without having to worry about the wind, cold or the rain and getting injured from slipping in the mud and stuff.
Dominic:	Yeah, we can focus more on what we are supposed to do in PE.
Göran:	And what is that?
Dominic:	You know, getting fit by competing and play lots of different sports. You know, doing what boys do.

Although Foucault (1995) argues that the aim of enclosed spaces (such as this PE gym) is to derive maximum advantages and to neutralise inconveniences (i.e., interruptions and disturbances from other students or teachers), making the workings of disciplinary practices more efficient and concentrated, Matthew and Dominic experience the gym as a 'sheltered' space removed from the potentially interruptive outdoor environment. Matthew and Dominic draw attention to the enclosed space of the gym as a space where they can focus more on the productive and pleasurable aspect of PE such as "getting fit", playing sports and "doing what boys do". The boys' comments demonstrate how this particular enclosed space affords pleasures that are associated with and produced by discourses of masculinity related to the fit, competitive and sporty boy (Swain, 2006). The material aspects of the gym, combined with the discursive space of this PE context, enable boys' performances of and within this space to be pleasurable.

What also makes these comments interesting is that they seem to go against Shropshire, Carroll and Yim's (1997) claim that boys are somehow less affected by 'environmental' factors in PE. Caleb (14 years old, European/Pākehā, active in multiple individual sports) also comments on this: "[I] don't like going outside in winter when [it's] muddy on rugby fields and [I] get prickles and stuff". The fact that boys are also aware of and affected by the environment and surroundings they find themselves in during PE is substantiated by Sam (14 years old, Asian, not involved in any sport) when I ask him about the significance of the particular space represented by the still images in Figure 4.5. He says:

Figure 4.5 The Enclosed Spaces of the Multipurpose Field.

Sam:	I really don't like being inside this space!
Göran:	What do you mean?
Sam:	You know, being fenced in like that. It feels like we are in prison or like caged animals or something.
Göran:	How does that make you feel?
Sam:	It kind of makes you feel uncomfortable, you know, being closed in like that.

One of the other boys, Joseph (14 years old, European/Pākehā, active in multiple individual sports), who tells me he does not like traditional masculine sports such as rugby and soccer but instead prefers alternative activities such as "BMXing" and "mountain biking", recounts similar experiences to Sam. Joseph also goes on to explain in more detail the (dis)pleasures of enclosed spaces of PE:

Göran:	So, Joseph, tell me something about your video clips?
Joseph:	Well, you know, I hate being stuck inside these four walls of the gym.
Göran:	What do you mean?
Joseph:	Well, I just don't feel comfortable being trapped like this; I'd rather be out in the open, like when I go BMXing or mountain biking with my friends on the weekend. Then we just go anywhere we want, there are no stupid walls to keep us in!
Göran:	So how does this affect your participation in PE?
Joseph:	Well, I guess I don't really get amongst it like some of the sporty boys who like being all aggressive and competitive and stuff, you know, tackling each other. I mean, I don't really have the right body for that anyway, so why should I even try? I guess it also means I am considered one of the non-sporty ones that don't really like PE . . . ummm, not like most of the other boys.
Göran:	Being sporty and liking PE is important if you are a boy?
Joseph:	Yeah.

In contrast to Matthew's and Dominic's experiences of enclosed spaces, Sam's and Joseph's comments about being "fenced in" or "trapped" during PE also have other consequences for the boys' performances of gender and space. Through physical and geographical mechanisms, these enclosed spaces become "uncomfortable" spaces in Sam's and Joseph's experiences, which simultaneously enable and constrain both performances of gender and pleasures. What Bale (1996) recalls as being a "landscape of fear" (p. 169), this rectangular gym with hard floors and walls is more specifically experienced by Joseph as providing the 'sporty' boys with an opportunity to exercise power through performing masculine ideals such as aggression, competition and physical dominance. Conversely, he positions himself as one of the 'non-sporty' boys and someone who does not have the "right body" and dislikes aggression/competition in PE, which are seen as ideals not compatible with "most other boys". As pointed out by Bale (1996), boys such as Joseph in this way learn and construct meanings about the spaces of PE through the body. The body becomes the vehicle in and through which the spatiality of power is performed. In chapter six, I will explore further how power articulated in and through the body produces (dis)pleasures at the intersection with boys' performances of gender.

Public (Panoptic) Spaces—Stopping Boys from 'Playing Up' or 'Mucking Around'

In contrast to enclosed spaces, some of the boys' responses draw attention to the (dis)pleasures of PE spaces as public (or even panoptic) spaces. Being able to display or perform (sporting) skills in front of the teacher(s) or other boys is regarded by some of the boys as one of the highlights of PE. PE spaces are often constructed and produced so that the students are clearly visible to the teacher and the other students. For instance, during PE, the teachers often tell their students to sit on the floor in front of them while they are standing up giving instructions, so everyone is clearly visible to the teacher (Figure 4.6). The same can also be said to apply when the teachers are setting up and organising activities in such a way that at least the majority of the students are visible throughout the activities. That is, the obvious direction of how surveillance works in PE is 'top-down': from teachers to students (Webb, McCaughtry, & MacDonald, 2004).

Although it can be argued that this disciplinary arrangement is not different from any other school subjects, such as English or Maths, the teaching of PE often also takes place in open spaces like fields and multipurpose sports

Figure 4.6 Spaces of (Self-)Surveillance.

fields. PE spaces are therefore public, which is partly due to the organisation of material or 'absolute' spaces (Harvey, 2006). For instance, Figure 4.7 (below) shows how many of the PE lessons I observed take place on one of the multipurpose sports fields, where the boys are clearly visible to the rest of the school (many of the classrooms look out over this particular sports field).

In contrast to other classroom-based lessons, the visibility of practical PE classes puts pressure on the boys in different ways. For instance, drawing on Foucault's (1995) notion of the "panopticon" (p. 208), it could be argued that despite not being able to single out who is actually watching whom, everyone is being watched by everyone, which becomes one of the major disciplinary means of power by which the boys' performances of gender are monitored and regulated. That is, the biggest pressure exerted on these boys does not come from the teachers but from themselves and other boys. Being on display, to a greater extent than for instance in the Maths classroom, means that all the boys become part of this disciplinary (panoptic) arrangement.

However, in contrast to previous research, the majority of the boys in my study do not experience this panoptic (self-)surveillance by the teacher, themselves and other boys or being on display in front of the rest of the school as something negative. The following conversation takes place in one of the focus groups while watching the video clips containing the still images in Figures 4.6 and 4.7:

Göran: So what is it like having your teacher Mr Whyte?
Adam: Well, Mr Whyte is awesome because he is always on top of us, you know, watching us and making sure we are doing what are supposed to.

Figure 4.7 Public (and Panoptic) Spaces.

Ben: Yeah, making sure that people are not playing up or just mucking around, you know, not taking it seriously.

Göran: What do you think it would be like having PE without a teacher?

Adam: No fun.

Ben: Yeah, people would probably just muck around; that would suck.

Göran: And what about doing PE in front of the rest of the school?

Ben: I quite like it because when you know that people might be watching, you try harder and stuff. Yeah, definitely more fun that way.

The boys' comments illustrate how the disciplinary use of space related to panoptic (self-)surveillance is not only disciplinary but also productive. In particular, they draw attention to how this is related to making sure people are not "playing up" or "mucking around" and interfering with the PE lesson. This demonstrates how disciplinary spaces are turned into "fun" or pleasurable spaces in PE for boys such as Ben and Adam. However, in two different individual interviews, we get into a conversation about the pressures and (dis)pleasures involved in being on display and constantly having to live up to masculine (heterosexual) ideals in PE:

Logan: In PE, you always have to watch out for being called gay and a poofter and stuff because otherwise it kind of sticks with you forever.

Göran: So what do you do to avoid that?

Logan: Well, you know, you got to make sure you go all out and be competitive and stuff with the other boys. To be one of the boys, you have to like playing sports, well, certain sports anyway. You also have to make sure you are not afraid of getting tackled and stuff. You need to look strong and not weak, otherwise, well, you know, you get called a poofter.

Göran: So being one of the boys means showing them you are not gay?

Logan: Yeah, definitely.

Randy: Well, I just don't like having PE in front of so many other people, you know, like the whole school sometimes. I just feel uncomfortable with so many people watching you. What if you mess up or do something that makes people think you are gay?

Both Logan and Randy (15 years old, Asian, not involved in any sport) draw attention to the public (panoptic) spaces of PE as spaces where they feel that they are constantly being watched. It is particularly the internalisation of this panoptic gaze, as evidenced by both Logan's and Randy's statements above, and regulation of their own behaviours, irrespective of the actuality of the gaze, that gives surveillance such deep-rooted and enduring potency as a technique of power (Webb et al., 2004). That is, the disciplinary technique of enclosure, combined with the public (panoptic) arrangement of PE spaces that allows for maximum (self-)surveillance of the boys by both the teacher and the other boys, simultaneously produces (dis)pleasures.

Partitioned (Cellular) Spaces—Picking 'The Sport You Like' and Making 'Even' Teams

Another way the spaces of PE produce (dis)pleasures in this setting is related to the allocation and distribution of the students into different locations depending on (sporting) activity and ability. The allocation and distribution of the boys in this way also serves to reaffirm (less) privileged and desirable masculine identities associated with different (sporting) activities and abilities. For instance, during many of the lessons I observed, the boys could pick between different sports such as basketball, rugby or soccer. Different groups of boys then played these sports separate from the rest of the class. In one of the group interviews, we talk about this lesson structure:

Göran: So tell me more about how you sometimes get to pick what sport you want to play in PE?

Matthew: Well, I think it is great because then you get to play the sport you like.

Ben: Yeah, it is more fun that way.

Göran: Why is that?

Ben: Well, then people pick the sport they are good at.

Matthew: Yeah, but some people are not good at any of them [laughter].

Göran: So what do they do?

Matthew: Well, they kind of just play whatever sport, but they don't really participate.

Each student in this way is located into different spaces depending on what sporting activity he is involved in. Understood through Foucault's (1995) notion of physical "partitioning" (p. 143), each individual within a space has his own place and each place its individual. Matthew and Ben draw attention to how they both find this process of picking what sport they like as contributing to their enjoyment of PE. Indeed, Mr Whyte also says that by allowing the students to pick from a range of different sporting activities they are "better able to cater for people's different interests". The physical partitioning of spaces can in this sense also be seen to determine who belongs to a space. The partitioned spaces of PE are performed through discourses and power relations that construct certain rules and boundaries. These boundaries, which are both social and spatial, define the inclusion or exclusion of boys from certain spaces (McDowell, 1999). For instance, Matthew's comment about how some boys as a result of this partitioning "don't really participate", is supported by one of the video clips (represented by the still images in Figure 4.8), in which several boys are seemingly just standing around shooting basketballs at a hoop while the rest of the class is playing a game of soccer.

The partitioning of spaces identified through the boys' experiences of PE occurs not only in a physical but also a psychological manner. One group of boys, for instance, talks about how they sometimes get grouped into ability groups or 'A' and 'B' teams depending on their sporting skills:

Figure 4.8 Spaces of Inclusion and Exclusion.

Adam: Well, yeah, sometimes when we play rugby and soccer and stuff we get into different games depending on how good we are.

Göran: Do you mean like ability groups?

Adam: Yeah, something like that.

James: Yeah, and then all the good ones play their own game and all the other ones play a different game.

Göran: What is that like?

James: Well, it is kind of like having A and B teams but makes it more fun for everyone, I think. You know, makes the games and teams more even.

When I ask one of the other teachers about putting the students into ability groups and teams, he says, "Well, by using that form of grouping, we think that more of them enjoy their PE since they get to play with people with similar ability levels, and it also makes it easier for us to follow their progress and give them more developmentally appropriate feedback". The boys' comments and this teacher's statement demonstrate that in order to enable the control and supervision of boys in PE, they are partitioned into both physical and psychological spaces within the general space of PE, such as the rugby field and 'A' and 'B' teams. The reason for this seems to be two-fold. Firstly, by locating boys in these defined physical places, as opposed to letting them freely roam the grounds of the school, it is easier to know where and how to locate individual boys during PE lessons, which also makes supervision easier (Foucault, 1995). Secondly, the locating of the boys into psychological spaces, such as ability groups, makes it easier for the teachers to track the boys' participation progress "to assess it, to judge it, to calculate its qualities or merits" (Foucault, 1995, p. 143). However, the locating of the boys into physically and psychologically partitioned spaces also has other consequences. Randy's visual imagery (represented by the still images in Figure 4.9 below) draws attention to how the performances of partitioned spaces in PE can be problematic for some boys:

Figure 4.9 Partitioned Spaces.

When I ask Randy to explain why he kept focusing the video camera on the lines of a rugby field he says:

Randy: Umm, well . . . within these damn lines, I always get tackled. . . . People get really aggressive.
Göran: Why?
Randy: Well, all the other boys like playing rough and tumble . . . but I don't really like sports like rugby. . . . They are too violent.
Göran: So what do you then?
Randy: Well, I guess me and some of the other boys, we kind of stay away from the game and hide in the corners and stuff. Especially when we are playing rugby.

In Randy's experience, the partitioned space of the rugby field becomes a space of (dis)pleasures where particular dominant masculine embodiments are privileged over others, which simultaneously puts boys into either dominant or subordinate positions. Randy's statement also provides an example of the "cellular" (Foucault, 1995, p. 143) nature of disciplinary and partitioned spaces. Foucault suggests that even if the compartments assigned through partitioning become purely 'ideal', the disciplinary spaces are always, basically, cellular. That is, the partitioned PE spaces, such as the rugby field, become divided into different 'areas' where different boys in turn lay claim to different cellular spaces within spaces. Whereas the 'sporty' boys are able to claim dominant spaces by occupying both social and physical space (Connell, 1983), some of the other boys, such as Randy, are subjugated to spaces away from the interaction of the other boys (Renold, 2004). Similar to Larsson, Fagrell and Redelius's (2009) findings, the teachers at this school also seem to be aware of how this partitioning often leads to both the dominance and subordination of boys in PE but believe that this is to be regarded as something 'normal' or 'natural' and something to be managed logistically rather than challenged. In particular, it appears that this way of partitioning space is a way to manage the boys in such a way that physical activity for the majority is promoted (Larsson et al., 2009).

Functional Spaces—Learning and Performing Sporting Skills

The allocation and distribution of the boys into different (sporting) spaces and spaces within these spaces brings us to how the boys' performances of gender and space in PE point to their functionality. The fact that spaces become "functional" spaces (Foucault, 1995, p. 145) in PE, where only certain activities, actions and movements can prevail, can be seen as a further producer of (dis)pleasures. For instance, in Randy's example above, he talks about the significance of being inside the lines of a rugby game. Within the functional space of the rugby field, you are expected to behave and follow the rules according to this particular space. The game of rugby itself in this example can be seen as an imposed 'relative' space (Harvey, 2006) because only within the confines of the game can the boys' actions be interpreted (Foucault, 1995). In other words, the boys are in this way disciplined into acting or performing in relation to this functional space.

Although the functionality of these disciplinary PE spaces can be seen as aimed at turning boys into docile, functional, sporting bodies associated with, for instance, playing rugby, the findings in my study also highlight these spaces as important products of and producers of pleasure. This example is taken from my logbook:

I watch as the boys get into their games of touch rugby, basketball and soccer. Immediately, I am struck by the sense of uniformity, all the boys seem to know what they are expected to do and it is like watching synchronised swimming. Boys kicking, running, tackling all at the same time and with great accuracy and success. The teacher is walking around watching the boys play and gives them both encouragement and feedback. The games carry on until the lesson ends.

Logbook entry 23/09/2010

This excerpt highlights how many of the boys in my study give the impression of constructing this homogenous unit of individuals doing the same thing and exactly what is 'expected' from them. Indeed, many of the boys describe this as both the purpose and one of the best things about PE; that is, "learning to work together as a team" (Sione, 14 years old, Māori, active in multiple team sports). The pleasures that the boys derive from these functional spaces of PE can be explained using Csikszentmihalyi's (1990) theory of 'flow'. From this perspective, the boys' pleasures stem from being so involved in the activities that they lose all sense of what is happening around them, and they find the activities so enjoyable that they keep doing them just for the pleasure of doing them. However, the extract above also illustrates how these functional spaces involve knowing the rules and learning the skills of different sports. The functional spaces created by this regime of practice in PE are therefore examples of boys learning the skills and the abilities needed to play different sports. From a Foucauldian perspective, the pleasures derived from these functional spaces stem from performing according to the discursively constructed functional spaces as 'sporting' spaces. That is, the pleasures derived from this functional space depend on having the skills and knowledge associated with particular sports. Drawing on Kretchmar's (2005) assertion that "playgrounds are made not found" (p. 152), it could be argued that the pleasures of functional spaces are only available to those boys who have the skills and knowledge needed to capitalise on these spaces.

In my study, I particularly found that this ability to capitalise on the functional and sporting spaces of PE is linked to boys' leisure time activities. This is in contrast to the boys in Azzarito and Sterling's (2010) study, who found PE as a "restrictive space" since "[In PE] you can't experience the same amount of competitiveness or the same amount of skill against you" (p. 214) as outside of school PE in organised sports. Boys such as Mitchell, who plays "rugby and soccer with the neighbours in the backyard", and Logan, who goes "down to the courts to play basketball", are able to turn PE spaces into pleasurable spaces more so than boys such as Joseph, who are "BMXing around my place". It seems that boys who are involved in team sports rather than individual sports are the ones who benefit the most from their leisure time activities during PE.

Conversely, those boys who are not able or willing to live up to the functional (sporting) spaces of PE have quite different experiences. As in Randy's case above, the functional space of the rugby field acts as a performative space where certain ideas of male identities and proper ways of acting manly are performed, enacted and displayed, through "rough and tumble". Not having the right body (a fit and athletic body) and not being able to perform gender that is congruent with these traditional and dominant discourses of masculinity, such as lacking the physique and skills in the traditional masculine sport of rugby, means that Randy is further alienated and positioned as the 'other' in PE. For him, the functional space of the rugby field (re)produces specific gender configurations that push him to the margins of the PE classes. Consequently, the boys' performance of functional spaces in PE, such as the rugby field, construct particular versions of masculinity comprising sporting ability, strength and competitiveness as productive and desirable.

Furthermore, what is interesting about the particular space of the rugby field is that there are three designated fields at this particular school that are often used for playing rugby and touch rugby during both PE and breaks. However, boys such as Joseph, who would rather do other things such as "BMXing" or "mountain biking", do not have existing spaces for their recreational use. That is, the higher 'ranking' (Foucault, 1995) of particular functional PE spaces such as the rugby fields further enables and restricts boys' performances of gender and pleasures at this particular school.

Ranked Spaces—The Provision (and Lack of) Spaces

Following Griffin (1985) and Kirk (1997), I was particularly interested in the ways in which the boys occupy and comport themselves in different spaces and how this linked with performances of gender and (dis)pleasures. For instance, despite ethical restrictions preventing video recordings of the boys outside of the PE lessons, it was often observed how the 'sporty' boys' use of space in the breaks coheres around contact sports and roaming playground games. The aim of these games does not seem to be related to keeping score or winning but rather to invade space through the use of physical bodies, verbal exchanges and gestures. Talking about what they get up to during breaks, Ben and Adam say:

Ben: Well, mostly we just play a bit of rugby or touch.
Adam: Yeah, especially after sitting down in the classroom, it's great to move around and stuff.
Göran: So what are these games of rugby and touch like?
Adam: Pretty relaxed. It's not like we keep score or anything.
Ben: Yeah, but it gets pretty nasty sometimes!
Adam: Yeah, people get dominated pretty badly sometimes.
Göran: What do you mean by dominated?
Adam: You know, tackled and stuff.
                [Laughter]

By engaging in these forms of competitive sporting activities during the breaks, 'sporty' boys such as Ben and Adam appear to derive pleasures by using their bodies in dominant and forceful, space-occupying ways (Pronger, 1999; Whitson, 1990). Indeed, rugby is an example of a sport in which the quest to forcefully take and maintain physical territory by bodily invasion is central to the game. These 'sporty' boys seem to construct a masculine identity based on physical size, muscularity, perceived strength, bodily actions and mannerisms, including occupation of space (Connell, 1983; Hickey, 2008). Connell (1983) points out that it is the use of the body to forcefully occupy space and manipulate objects that is valued about muscularity, rather than display. This observation reinforces the articulation between masculinity and action and suggests the mere display of muscle is less masculine than its use (Gorely, Holroyd, & Kirk, 2003). The concept of boys' bodies as productive and pleasurable (masculine) bodies is explored further in chapter six.

Conversely, the 'non-sporty' boys demonstrate alternative masculinities, and in their use of space, they are often sedentary and quiet. That is, there are not only gender-differentiated ways that males and females use space and their bodies (Nilges, 2000) but also differences within each gender. In particular, some boys recount the (dis)pleasures they experience by not having a space to "be active during school breaks" (Joseph). Indeed, Mr Whyte recognises that there are limited activities (sports) available at this school and that students who are interested in pursuing alternative sports either will have to do so in their spare time or choose another school. One particular activity that is not offered at Kea College is outdoor education, which is surprising since it is one of the key learning areas in the current New Zealand Curriculum (Ministry of Education, 2007). When asked about this, Mr Whyte quotes "limited resources" as one of the explanations. Many of the boys also quote the lack of school trips or camps as the "downsides" of being at Kea College:

Oliver: I like it, but we don't do anything outside of school like camps and school trips. Other schools got, like, ski groups and stuff.
Jack: No school trips, no camp because old-fashioned school.

Other activities that cannot be offered at Kea College are swimming and water polo, due to the lack of a school pool. William (15 years old, European/Pākehā, active in multiple team and individual sports) says:

William: I want a school pool [since] some of us play water polo. But it's not going to happen.

The ranking and provision of different spaces during PE and their connection with (dis)pleasures is also evident. For example, there is a clearly identifiable hierarchy in terms of the different playing fields or sporting spaces used in PE. In one of the focus groups, in which a series of video clips representing different sporting spaces in PE (represented by the still images in Figure 4.10) is played, the conversation ends up being about the sports and activities that the boys like doing in PE, and it is clear that a certain hierarchy exists:

Oliver: I love playing volleyball.
James: Yeah, me too, but we never get to do that.
Göran: Why do you think that is?
Oliver: Well, it is all about rugby, rugby and sometimes a little bit of soccer.
Dominic: Yeah, I wish we did get to play more volleyball and badminton.

Figure 4.10 Ranked Spaces.

James: Yeah, but whenever we get to choose sports, most people go for rugby and some soccer, so we never really get to play volleyball or badminton.

Oliver: Yeah, I wish we could do other sports and activities as well, like hockey, outdoor education and stuff.

Based on these findings, it appears that there is a dominant discourse associated with spaces such as the rugby field and the soccer field, which implies that this is what boys like doing and should be doing. The way in which school and PE spaces are presented and provided to these students reinforces ideas about what 'real' boys like doing (Armstrong, 2007; O'Donoghue, 2007) and in turn shapes boys' (dis)pleasures within those spaces. Just as the skiers in Stoddart's (2011) research, the boys in my study are inscribed with discourses of sport and masculinity in and through the spaces of PE. However, as demonstrated by the boys' comments above, this does not mean that all boys are willing to conform to these notions. Green (2004) therefore reminds us:

If, as seems to be the case, facilitating lifelong participation is viewed as a primary aim of the subject then PE needs to move with the prevailing tide of young people's leisure lifestyles by catering for their preferences for a wider range of activities [such as] the kinds of "option", recreational, lifestyle-oriented sports and physical activities that appear more likely to lead to the wide sporting repertoire.

(p. 73)

In summary, it can be argued that the disciplinary spaces associated with this school and PE classes are implicated both in boys' performances of gender and in (dis)pleasures. Although the disciplinary use of space has a significant effect on these boys by shaping their performances of gender (Venkatesh, 1997), the boys, to some extent, are also able to invest and construct their own unique meanings in these spaces as pleasurable spaces. That is, spaces are made or become meaningful when the boys ascribe qualities to the material and discursive spaces of PE. However, gender and pleasures are not somehow inherent in these PE spaces but rather "an ongoing practical and discursive production/imagining" (Gieryn, 2000, p. 472) or performative act of the people using them. The making or performing of pleasurable PE spaces in this context can be seen as heavily dependent on discourses of sport. The disciplinary (sporting) spaces of PE come to matter or become meaningful as pleasurable spaces when boys have the skills and knowledge required to capitalise on those spaces. The spaces of PE are in this way performative of the prevailing discourses of PE related to sport within this context, despite sport being only one of the components of the current New Zealand HPE curriculum (Ministry of Education, 2007). In the next chapter, I specifically turn my attention to the underpinning assumptions and associated teaching practices of PE at Kea College to explore the discourses that constitute and are constituted by boys' performances of gender and their articulations with (dis)pleasures.

References

Allen, L. (2008). Young people's 'agency' in sexuality research using visual methods. *Journal of Youth Studies, 11*(6), 565–577.

Allen, L. (2013). Behind the bike sheds: Sexual geographies of schooling. *British Journal of Sociology of Education, 34*(1), 56–75.

Armstrong, F. (2007). Disability, education and space: Some critical reflections. In K. N. Gulson & C. Symes (Eds.), *Spatial theories of education: Policy and geography matters* (pp. 95–110). New York: Routledge.

Atkinson, M., & Kehler, M. (2010). Boys, gyms, locker rooms and heterotopia. In M. Kehler & M. Atkinson (Eds.), *Boys' bodies: Speaking the unspoken* (pp. 73–90). New York: Peter Lang.

Azzarito, L., & Solmon, M. A. (2006). A feminist poststructuralist view on student bodies in physical education: Sites of compliance, resistance, and transformation. *Journal of Teaching in Physical Education, 25*(2), 200–225.

Azzarito, L., & Sterling, J. (2010). 'What it was in my eyes': Picturing youths' embodiment in 'real' spaces. *Qualitative Research in Sport and Exercise, 2*(2), 209–228.

Bale, J. (1996). Space, place and body culture: Yi-Fu Tuan and a geography of sport. *Geografiska Annaler: Series B, Human Geography, 78*(3), 163–171.

Bell, D., Binnie, J., Cream, J., & Valentine, G. (1994). All hyped up and no place to go. *Gender, Place and Culture, 1,* 31–48.

Burstyn, V. (1999). *The rites of men: Manhood, politics, and the culture of sport.* Toronto, Canada: University of Toronto Press.

Butler, J. (1997). *Excitable speech: A politics of the performative.* New York: Routledge.

Caudwell, J. (2006). *Sport, sexualities and queer/theory.* London, UK: Routledge.

Connell, R. W. (1983). *Which way is up? Essays on sex, class and culture.* Sydney: Allen & Urwin.

Connell, R. W. (2005). *Masculinities* (2nd ed.). Cambridge, UK: Polity Press.

Connell, R. W. (2008). Masculinity construction and sports in boys' education: A framework for thinking about the issue. *Sport, Education and Society, 13*(2), 131–145.

Coveney, J., & Bunton, R. (2003). In pursuit of the study of pleasure: Implications for health research and practice. *Health, 7*(2), 161–179.

Crang, M. (2005). Time: Space. In P. Cloke & R. Johnston (Eds.), *Space of geographical thought: Deconstructing human geography's binaries* (pp. 199–220). London, UK: Sage.

Csikszentmihalyi, M. (1990). *Flow: The psychology of optimal experience.* New York: Harper & Row.

Curry, T. J. (1991). Fraternal bonding in the locker room: A profeminist analysis of talk about competition and women. *Sociology of Sport Journal, 8,* 119–135.

De Visser, R. O., & McDonnell, E. J. (2013). 'Man Points': Masculine capital and young men's health. *Health Psychology, 23,* 5–14.

Eichberg, H. (1990). Race-track and labyrinth: The space of physical culture in Berlin. *The Journal of Sport History, 17*(2), 245–260.

Epstein, D., & Johnson, R. (1998). *Schooling sexualities.* Buckingham, UK: Open University Press.

Foucault, M. (1972). *The archaeology of knowledge and discourse on language* (1st American ed.). New York: Pantheon Books.

Foucault, M. (1978). *The History of Sexuality, Volume One.* Harmondsworth: Penguin.

Foucault, M. (1980). *Power/knowledge: Selected interviews and other writings, 1972–1977.* New York: Pantheon.

Foucault, M. (1995). *Discipline and punish: The birth of the prison.* Westminster, MD: Vintage.

Frosh, S., Phoenix, A., & Pattman, R. (2002). *Young masculinities: Understanding boys in contemporary society.* Hampshire and New York: Palgrave.

Gieryn, T. (2000). A space for place in sociology. *Annual Review of Sociology, 26,* 463–496.

Gilroy, P. (1993). *The black Atlantic modernity and double consciousness.* Cambridge, MA: Harvard University Press.

Gorely, T., Holroyd, R., & Kirk, D. (2003). Muscularity, the habitus and the social construction of gender: Towards a gender-relevant physical education. *British Journal of Sociology of Education, 24*(4), 429–448.

Green, K. (2004). Physical education, lifelong participation and 'the couch potato society'. *Physical Education & Sport Pedagogy, 9*(1), 73–86.

Gregson, N., & Rose, G. (2000). Taking Butler elsewhere: Performativities, spatialities and subjectivities. *Environment and Planning D: Society and Space, 18,* 422–452.

Griffin, P. (1985). Teachers' perceptions of and responses to sex equity problems in a middle school physical education program. *Research Quarterly for Exercise and Sport, 56,* 103–110.

Grosz, E. (1992). Bodies-cities. In B. Colomina (Ed.), *Sexuality and space* (pp. 241–253). New York: Princeton Architectural Press.

Gruenewald, D. A. (2003a). The best of both worlds: A critical pedagogy of place. *Educational Researcher, 32*(4), 3–12.

Gruenewald, D. A. (2003b). Foundations of place: A multidisciplinary framework for place-conscious education. *American Educational Researcher, 40*(3), 619–637.

Hardy, C., Palmer, I., & Phillips, N. (2000). Discourse as a strategic resource. *Human Relations, 53*(9), 1227–1248.

Harvey, D. (2006). *Spaces of global capitalism: Toward a theory of uneven economic development.* London, UK: Verso.

Hickey, C. (2008). Physical education, sport and hyper-masculinity in schools. *Sport, Education and Society, 13*(2), 147–161.

Hickey, C., Fitzclarence, I., & Matthews, R. (1998). *Where the boys are: Masculinity, sport and education.* Geelong: Deakin University Press.

Hunter, L. (2004). Bourdieu and the social space of the PE class: Reproduction of doxa through practice. *Sport, Education and Society, 9*(2), 175–192.

Kehily, M. J. (2002). *Sexuality, gender and schooling: Shifting agendas in social learning.* London, UK: Routledge Falmer.

Kehler, M., & Atkinson, M. (2010). *Boys' bodies: Speaking the unspoken.* New York: Peter Lang.

Kirk, D. (1997). Schooling bodies in new times: The reform of school physical education in high modernity. In J.-M. Fernandez-Balboa (Ed.), *Critical postmodernism in human movement, physical education and sport* (pp. 39–64). Albany, NY: State University of New York Press.

Kretchmar, R. S. (2005). *Practical philosophy of sport and physical activity.* Champaign, IL: Human Kinetics.

Larsson, H., Fagrell, B., & Redelius, K. (2009). Queering physical education. Between benevolence towards girls and a tribute to masculinity. *Physical Education and Sport Pedagogy, 14*(1), 1–17.

Mac an Ghaill, M. (1994). *The making of men: Masculinities, sexualities and schooling.* Buckingham, UK: Open University Press.

Markula, P. (2003). The technologies of the self: Sport, feminism, and Foucault. *Sociology of Sport Journal, 20*, 87–107.

Markula, P., & Pringle, R. (2006). *Foucault, sport and exercise: Power, knowledge and transforming the self.* New York: Routledge.

Markus, T. A. (1993). *Buildings and power: Freedom and control in the origin of modern building types.* London, UK: Routledge.

Martino, W. (1999). 'Cool boys', 'party animals', 'squids' and 'poofters': Interrogating the dynamics and politics of adolescent masculinities in school. *The British Journal of the Sociology of Education, 20*(2), 239–263.

Martino, W. (2000). Policing masculinities: Investigating the role of homophobia and heteronormativity in the lives of adolescent boys at school. *The Journal of Men's Studies, 8*(2), 213–236.

Martino, W., & Pallotta-Chiarolli, M. (2003). *So what's a boy? Addressing issues of masculinity and schooling.* Buckingham, UK: Open University Press.

Massey, D. (1994). *Space, place and gender.* Cambridge, UK: Polity Press.

Massey, D. (2005). *For space.* London, UK: Sage.

McDowell, L. (1999). *Gender, identity & place: Understanding feminist geographies.* Minneapolis, MN: University of Minnesota Press.

Messner, M. (1992). *Power at play: Sports and the problem of masculinity.* Boston, MA: Beacon Press.

Ministry of Education. (2007). *The New Zealand curriculum.* Wellington, NZ: Learning Media.

Mooney, A., & Hickey, C. (2012). Negotiating masculine hegemony: Female physical educators in an all-boys' school. *Asia-Pacific Journal of Health, Sport and Physical Education, 3*(3), 199–212.

Nilges, L. M. (2000). A nonverbal discourse analysis of gender in undergraduate educational gymnastics sequences using Laban effort analysis. *Journal of Teaching in Physical Education, 19*(3), 287–310.

O'Donoghue, D. (2007). 'James always hangs out here': Making space for place in studying masculinities at school. *Visual Studies, 22*(1), 62–73.

Payne, E., & Smith, M. (2013). LGBTQ kids, school safety, and missing the big picture: How the dominant bullying discourse prevents school professionals from thinking about systemic marginalization or . . . why we need to rethink LGBTQ bullying. *QED: A Journal of GLBTQ Worldmaking, 1*(1), 1–36.

Philips, R. (1997). *Mapping men and empire: A geography of adventure.* London, UK: Routledge.

Pink, S. (2011). From embodiment to emplacement: Re-thinking competing bodies, senses and spatialities. *Sport, Education and Society, 16*(3), 343–355.

Pronger, B. (1999). Outta my end zone: Sport and the territorial anus. *Sociology of Sport, 23*(4), 373–389.

Pronger, B. (2000). *Body fascism: Salvation in the technology of physical fitness.* Toronto, Canada: University of Toronto Press.

Raitz, K. (1995). *The theater of sport.* Baltimore, MD: Johns Hopkins University Press.

Rawlings, V., & Russell, K. (2012). Gender control: (Re) framing bullying, harassment and gender regulation. *University of Sydney Papers in Human Movement, Health and Coach Education, 1*(1), 17–27.

Renold, E. (1997). 'All they've got on their brains is football': Sport, masculinity and the gendered practices of playground relations. *Sport, Education and Society, 2*(1), 5–23.

Renold, E. (2004). 'Other' boys: Negotiating non-hegemonic masculinities in the primary school. *Gender and Education, 16*(2), 247–266.

Ringrose, J., & Renold, E. (2010). Normative cruelties and gender deviants: The performative effects of bully discourses for boys and girls in schools. *British Educational Research Journal, 36*(4), 573–596.

Rose, G. (1993). *Feminism and geography.* Minneapolis, MN: University of Minnesota Press.

Shropshire, J., Carroll, B., & Yim, S. (1997). Primary school children's attitudes to physical education: Gender differences. *European Journal of Physical Education, 2*(1), 23–38.

Stoddart, M. (2011). Constructing masculinized sportscapes: Skiing, gender and nature in British Columbia, Canada. *International Review for the Sociology of Sport, 46*(1), 108–124.

Swain, J. (2006). The role of sport in the construction of masculinities in an English independent Junior School. *Sport, Education and Society, 11*(4), 317–335.

Tinning, R. (2010). *Pedagogy and human movement: Theory, practice, research.* New York: Routledge.

Tuan, Y.-F. (1986). *The good life.* Madison, WI: University of Wisconsin Press.

Venkatesh, A. (1997). The social organisation street gang activity in an urban ghetto. *American Journal of Sociology, 103*, 82–111.

Webb, L., McCaughtry, N., & MacDonald, D. (2004). Surveillance as a technique of power in physical education. *Sport, Education and Society, 9*(2), 207–222.

Whitson, D. (1990). Sport in the social construction of masculinity. In M. Messner & D. Sabo (Eds.), *Sport, men and the gender order* (pp. 19–30). Champaign, IL: Human Kinetics.

Youdell, D. (2006). *Impossible bodies, impossible selves: Exclusions and student subjectivities.* Dordrecht, The Netherlands: Springer.

5 The Production of Masculine (dis)Pleasures in Boys' PE

This chapter investigates how discourses of PE articulate with boys' performances of gender and (dis)pleasures. It interrogates both the boys' and the teacher's overall understandings and experiences of PE, which, in the words of Mr Whyte, could be summed up as "a culture of everyone doing it" and "playing games". The word 'culture' (Hall, 1997) is used here in the sense of a set of social practices and relations, constituted by the discourses of PE operating in this setting. That is, discourses shape how individuals understand themselves and produce knowledge about the social, embodied individual and shared meanings, what we come to know as 'culture'. Hall (1997) also quoted Foucault, who argued that: "Each society has its regime of truth, its 'general politics' of truth: that is, the types of discourse which it accepts and makes function as true" (p. 49). The term 'regime of truth' makes clear a status of knowledge as power. Indeed, the way Mr Whyte and the boys talk about PE is shaped by the workings of discourses and power/knowledge relations.

I argue that these two PE 'cultures' of 'everyone doing it' and 'playing games' produce (dis)pleasures, as linked to the construction of masculinities and associated power relations. I demonstrate how these cultures—comprising discourses related to fitness, health, sport and masculinity—both enable and restrict boys' pleasurable experiences of PE. In particular, I draw attention to the fact that although these cultures/discourses are (eventually) productive for some boys, these power-induced pleasures end up having negative consequences/outcomes for those boys who are unable or unwilling to live up to (privileged) desirable masculinities within this context. That is, the pleasures of boys' PE that constitute and are constituted by the discourses operating in this context simultaneously produce (un)desirable masculinities. As this chapter unfolds, and by drawing on Foucault's notion of resistance as inseparable from discourse and power relations, I also start highlighting some boys' problematisations of the impact of power-induced (gendered) pleasures in PE (which is further explored in chapters six and seven).

'A Culture of Everyone Doing It'—Fitness, Health, Disciplinary Practices and Pleasure

One of my first observations about the boys' PE lessons at Kea College was that even before the lessons begin, most of the boys are eager to get started. As discussed in the previous chapter, some boys describe how they normally feel confined to "desks and chairs" throughout the other parts of the school day and how PE is the time when they are able to break free and move more freely. Their bodies are ready to go long before the lesson starts. On a number of occasions, the boys have already started playing a game of soccer or basketball before the start of the lesson (top image, Figure 5.1), which at times makes it hard for Mr Whyte to break up these games and get the actual lesson started (middle image, Figure 5.1). Even during the briefing, it is often difficult for Mr Whyte to contain the boys for long enough for him to explain the content and structure of the upcoming lesson (bottom image, Figure 5.1).

Figure 5.1 Before the PE Lesson Begins.

On other occasions, the boys' eagerness to free their bodies and get moving is demonstrated by their constant 'playfighting' that sometimes turns into 'proper' fights (Figure 5.2).

Even when leaving the lessons, the boys' enjoyment of PE is often evident, highlighted by their reluctance to move to the next class. At the end of one lesson, Logan and a couple of the other boys carry on playing soccer, not wanting to go the next class, and Mr Whyte has to call out, "Come on, Logan, hurry up, the bell's gone". The boys then slowly go from being active and cheering to walking with their heads down towards the changing rooms and their next class (Figure 5.3).

Figure 5.2 'Playfighting'.

Figure 5.3 After the PE Lesson.

My initial observation of the actual PE lessons is characterised by boys being completely caught up in doing an activity, playing a game, scoring, trying to win. Even the boys who are watching/bystanders are following every movement, action or shot (top image, Figure 5.4). One of the first things that Mr Whyte articulates about PE at Kea College is their focus on fighting what he calls "PE apathy", which he believes is a problem at other schools. He further states that at Kea College, "we make them all do it", and he refers to this as "a culture of everyone doing it". This 'culture of everyone doing it' also often translates into Mr Whyte involving himself in the lessons (bottom image, Figure 5.4). Mr Whyte's love and passion for PE (and in particular sport) is unmistakable throughout the entire study and, as asserted by Hawkins (2008), physical educationalists often enter this profession due to a "deep-seated love for the subject matter in and of itself" (p. 354).

Figure 5.4 During the PE Lesson.

The pleasure derived from 'everyone doing it' together is something that many of the boys also comment on. Marko (15 years old, European/Pākehā, active in multiple team sports) claims that "one of the best things about PE is that you always know what to do, it's much better than other subjects in that way . . . you know, everyone doing the same thing". The teacher is also an important source of this pleasure; for example, "The best thing about PE is the teachers" (Logan). The relaxed nature of the PE teacher(s), compared to other teachers, is noted; e.g., "Mr Whyte is pretty laid-back" (Mitchell). The "teachers are more free. . . . They don't force you to do something" (Dominic). Mr Whyte elaborates further on this 'culture of everyone doing it' by saying that "if the majority of students are able and willing to do it, then why stop the whole class from doing it just because some students show their reluctance". However, at the same time, he admits that some students therefore might "not get anything out of it [PE]".

In some of my early conversations and interviews probing the boys' overall attitudes and feelings towards PE, the majority of the 60 participating boys articulated positive feelings and experiences, expressed through phrases such as the "fun", "enjoyment" and "love" of PE. Although there is no homogeneous experience of PE as a whole, one of the most significant and meaningful aspects of participation for the boys is the opportunity that PE provides for friendship and sense of belonging. Lorenzo (14 years old, Asian, active in one individual sport) says, "I love PE . . . playing with friends and having fun", and Timothy similarly claims that "PE is fun and all your friends are there". "Mucking around with your friends" (Ben) and "time with your mates" (Joseph) are two other reasons for enjoying PE. However, this socialising and mucking around with friends is also questioned by some boys, who instead cite this as one of the negatives or (dis) pleasures of PE in that "some people muck around all the time" (Marko).

Related to socialising are issues of inclusion, whereby most boys experience their PE as an inclusive space within which "the good nature of it" means that "people get included" (Joseph). Being part of a group or a team is quoted as a significant source of enjoyment and motivation for engagement. For Ben, this is especially the case:

Ben: In PE, I'm part of a team, and we either win or lose, it's not just me. You know, we're all in the same uniform and stuff. Makes you feel good.

Ben's comment draws attention to the way in which team activities in PE place the boys in a social situation that is pleasurable ("makes you feel good"), despite the outcome of the contest and thus at odds with traditional discourses around performance. As Ben's comments also indicate, a part of the boys' sense of belonging to a group is associated with wearing the same PE uniform. Conversely, not wearing the PE uniform results in less pleasurable feelings, such as embarrassment. When William, during his individual interview, is asked what it is like seeing himself in one of the video clips, he says:

William: Weird! It is embarrassing.
Göran: Why is it embarrassing?
William: Because I look terrible!
           [Laughter]
Göran: What do you mean?
William: I forgot my PE gear so had to wear my normal t-shirt.

Not having your PE uniform on in some cases also means not being able to participate. For instance, in one of the video clips showing how Marko is not participating in the lesson, Mitchell is heard calling out: "Marko, why are you not doing PE?" and Marko replies, "I forgot my PE gear". The school rules stipulate that the Kea College PE uniform should be worn, but there is actually nothing stating that you cannot participate if for some reason you do not have it with you. Mr Whyte also says that spare PE uniforms are available for students who forget to bring them. In addition to the normal PE uniform, some boys instead wear their school sports uniforms to PE, with, for instance, Kea College 'rugby', 'soccer' or 'basketball' written on the front of the shirts. Dominic explains why:

Dominic: Yeah, I like wearing my soccer shirt, you know, it is pretty cool
           to be representing the school in soccer and stuff.
Göran: So do you ever wear it outside of school as well?
Dominic: Yeah, sometimes on the weekends. You know, I'm proud of
           going to this school and want other people to know that.

Dominic's statement signals that for some boys it is important, through the wearing of a uniform, to show your belonging to the school or a particular group or team. The boys' desire to be 'recognisable' (Butler, 2004) as a 'Kea College boy' can be seen as another significant discourse within which the boys' performances of gender and pleasures are constituted. Butler argues that desire is connected to recognition because it is through being recognised that we become "constituted as socially viable beings" (Butler, 2004, p. 2). That is, being included, belonging to and representing certain groups/teams at this school is important for boys such as Dominic, in terms of reaffirming privileged/desirable masculinities.

Although PE is seen as an 'inclusive' space by the majority of boys, some boys' feelings of being left out because they are "not the fittest one of the lot" (Timothy) also have other consequences (i.e., exclusion). However, boys being left out and excluded is questioned and problematised by Chris (15 years old, European/Pākehā, active in multiple team and individual sports). Chris claims that one of the main problems associated with his PE is that, as a group, the 'sporty' boys are often not interested in inclusiveness. Chris particularly suggests that commonly used excluding practices lead to some boys being positioned as "outsiders":

Chris: I think we are all like non-sporty and sporty at times. But I guess it is the sporty boys who are able to keep up the image of being sporty most of the time. It is like you have to constantly prove that you are one of the sporty ones by showing that you are not one of the non-sporty ones.

Göran: So how do you do that?

Chris: Well, I guess you kind of stick to the sporty group and don't involve the non-sporty boys in the games. It kind of sucks since it means some people always get left out, you know, like outsiders.

Chris's comments demonstrate the fluidity of performing masculine identities ("we are all like non-sporty and sporty at times") and the ongoing work required by the boys to negotiate and live up to desirable masculine identities ("keep up the image of being sporty"). However, Chris also draws attention to how belonging to this group of 'sporty' boys involves constantly maintaining a certain distance from the group of 'non-sporty' boys, proving that "you are one of the sporty ones by showing that you are not one of the non-sporty ones". One reading of this is that the techniques of power at work here help produce a problematic binary of 'sporty' and 'non-sporty' boys, where the 'non-sporty' ones are denied access to the realm of 'sporty' boys due to their lack of skills and abilities associated with privileged masculine sporting activities (Wright & Burrows, 2006). Being excluded from this peer group hinders these 'non-sporty' boys from confirming their privileged masculine status and may add to some of these boys' overall unhappy and negative experiences of PE (Hickey, 2008). That is, the notions of 'sporty' and 'non-sporty' boys as constitutive of discourses of sport and masculinity concurrently engender (dis)pleasures in boys' PE.

However, from another point of view, this can also be an example of the way that the techniques of power do not always work in male/female dualistic ways (Webb & Macdonald, 2007) because it has more to do with belonging to a sports club outside of school and thus having the skills and knowing the rules of these sports than to do with gender (see previous chapter on the functional spaces of PE). That is, the effects of the techniques of power are complex and multidirectional. Thinking about the capillary workings of power (Foucault, 1995) helps to explain the complex effects played out in these boys' lives. For instance, although part of the boys' experiences of (dis)pleasures in PE can be explained/understood by their performances of gender, it is also important to recognise the multiple and at times competing discourses that shape those differentiated experiences for different boys.

Nevertheless, through a self-reflexive process, Chris has started problematising the (dis)pleasures associated with practices that serve to include and exclude certain boys. In this sense, he has started questioning the ethics behind these actions and showing an awareness of the responsibility he has towards these 'outsiders' (Pringle & Hickey, 2010). What can be understood as Chris's 'mode of subjection' (Foucault, 1985) revolves around making PE more inclusive, which he importantly contrasts with sporting practices found outside of PE. As Chris explains:

Chris: What makes PE so good is that it can be so inclusive. It doesn't matter who you are, you can still enjoy it, get a lot out of it and contribute to a team, just like society. Whereas when playing sports outside of school, people get excluded all the time.

Göran: Why is that, do you think?

Chris: Well, you know, most sport is all about winning and having the best team on the field, that kind of thing. But I think PE should not be like that. It should be more about participating and having fun and learning about lots of different activities and games, which will help you live a healthier and more active life once you leave school.

Based on these comments, it seems as if Chris has started making an interesting shift from a PE based on a 'performance' discourse to a 'participatory' discourse (Tinning, 2010) since he claims that "what makes PE so good is that it can be so inclusive". Chris particularly points towards the role and purpose of PE as being participatory and inclusive in contrast with the competition and focus on winning associated with organised sports. He further argues that when sports are played "outside of school, people get excluded all the time". In this way, Chris's mode of subjection might be interpreted as involving the transformation of himself and others by asserting that the enjoyment and pleasures of PE are to be found through focusing on participation rather than performance. However, his mode of subjection could also be seen as transgressing the boundaries of the gendered pleasures produced within this context, insofar as he understands PE to offer opportunities for inclusion of people who might be judged as 'incompatible' by dominant male sporting discourses.

'Disciplining' and 'Working Them Hard'—Discourses of Fitness and Health

The culture of 'everyone doing it' in PE at Kea College is also closely linked to discourses of fitness and health. In particular, the fitness/health power/discourse nexus and its links with masculinity shape boys' performances of gender and their articulations with (dis)pleasures. Indeed, for nearly all the boys in this study, it seems that "a health/fitness discourse

[is] a central organising discourse" (Wright, O'Flynn, & MacDonald, 2006, p. 711). When talking about the role and purpose of PE, some of the boys say:

Logan: Be fit and healthy. . . . You can do a lot more stuff when you are fit and healthy.

Jacob: If we didn't have it, then people wouldn't be fit. . . . Fit and healthy not sitting down all day.

Daniel: Helps your body keep fit.

The fitness and exercise content is an important source of enjoyment in PE for many of the boys. Timothy says that "the best thing about PE is the exercise . . . you know, the fitness and stuff", and Alec (14 years old, Pacific Island, active in multiple team sports) similarly states that "PE is like a fitness time . . . exercise time". However, Miles (14 years old, European/ Pākehā, active in multiple team and individual sports) also questions this focus on improving fitness and health because "twice a week [of PE] is not that much". When asked why being fit and doing exercise is important, the boys say:

Matthew: Yeah, keeping in shape and stuff. Makes you healthier.

Peter: You don't get sick.

Campbell: To stay healthy.

Oliver: To live longer, I guess.

Marko: If you maintain your fitness, you live longer and enjoy life more.

The pleasures of PE articulated by these boys could be explained as 'instrumental' or 'developmental' pleasures (e.g., Pringle, 2009; Wright & Dewar, 1997) related to fitness/health (i.e., "don't get sick" and "live longer") and healthy bodies (i.e., "helps your body keep fit" and "keeping in shape"). In particular, these boys' comments can be seen as evidence of the global discourses of health that are circulating at the moment through which, at the international level, school PE is being 'called upon' to play a more significant role in the 'making' of 'healthy citizens' (McCuaig & Tinning, 2010). PE teachers are regarded as the 'front-line' workers for dealing with young people's presumed lower physical activity levels and the so-called 'obesity epidemic'. The instrumental/developmental pleasures that the boys refer to above can be seen as an important organising principle in neoliberal societies, where health discourses shape the pleasures boys derive from PE (Coveney & Bunton, 2003; Lupton, 1995). Coveney and Bunton (2003) further argue:

Pleasure and pleasure seeking is thus conceived as the weak link in the chain of command from authoritarian discourses of health governance to docile compliance for body maintenance. . . . The self-policing, or self-management, of health involves the fashioning and rationing of pleasure in ways that are highly socially situated.

(pp. 166–167)

Health discourses thus shape the way boys think and talk about pleasures. Various health discourses work as a form of 'bio-power' (Foucault, 1978) through which bodies are governed in specific socio-cultural contexts and in connection with pleasures. Prevailing fitness/health discourses in this setting both implicitly and explicitly 'teach' the boys the pleasure they should feel when engaging in regular and vigorous exercise. The personal pleasure and satisfaction they experience is derived from practices of 'self-policing' or 'self-management' that are meant to lead to self-transformation (i.e., avoiding obesity). As pointed out by Rose (1999), "In the new modes of regulating health, individuals are addressed on the assumption that they want to be healthy" (p. 86). This desire is evidenced above when the boys talk about the role and purpose of PE and why being fit and doing exercise is important and articulate that it is 'up to them', through participating in PE, to keep fit and stay healthy. That is, neoliberalism instils in these boys the desire to be responsible for their own health by promoting it as an individual responsibility that contributes to the greater good of society as a whole (Rose, 1999). In this way, neoliberalism encourages boys to give their lives a certain "entrepreneurial form" (Lemke, 2001, p. 202). Certainly, the boys' recognition of the importance and pleasures of exercise and fitness practices in PE can be interpreted as reifying global health discourses and neoliberalism. However, as I will discuss in chapter six, it could also be argued that this is related to the 'cult of the body' (Tinning & Glasby, 2002) in PE, where a sporty and muscly look helps reaffirm privileged/desirable (heterosexual) masculinities.

It is not only the boys who refer to the instrumental/developmental pleasures related to fitness and health. When Mr Whyte talks about the importance of fitness and health in PE at Kea College, he says that it is "all about *working them hard . . .* to keep *disciplining* them . . . otherwise, problems for me and everyone else" [emphasis added]. He also claims that the PE culture at this school is heavily influenced by the traditions and history of PE in New Zealand, back to the days of physical training for boys. Indeed, many times I felt that parts of the lessons, particularly the 'warm-ups' and 'fitness drills' (see below), could come straight out of the book with the title *Syllabus of Physical Training for Schools* published by Phillip Smithells in 1933. As pointed out by Kirk (2010) and Tinning (2004), contemporary versions of PE in boys' schools can still be considered to bear the historical trademark of 'masculinist' traditional pedagogies that position order, management and control as central to the teaching and learning process.

For instance, in the briefing before the lesson begins, Mr Whyte is always very clear about the rules/instructions, and during the lessons, he is often seen in a supervisory position (as demonstrated by the body language of

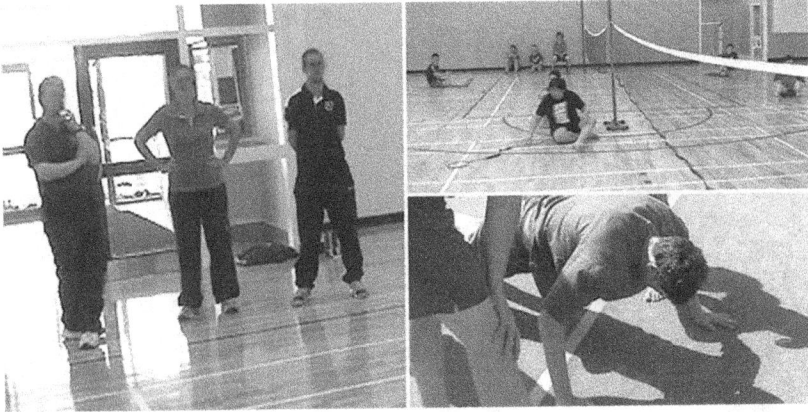

Figure 5.5 'Disciplining' and 'Working Them Hard'.

Mr Whyte and two student teachers in the left image, Figure 5.5), making sure the students are doing what they are supposed to do and thus ensuring the 'efficient use of time' (Foucault, 1991). During the lessons, Mr Whyte will often also sit the boys down to give them further instruction/feedback to make sure they are on track (top right image, Figure 5.5) and performing 'concise and precise exercises' (Foucault, 1995). The disciplining and working them hard motto sometimes also results in certain 'punishments', such as doing press-ups during a game for misbehaving (bottom right image, Figure 5.5). In another example, Zack (14 years old, Other, active in one team sport) is heard saying "Ben [one of the other students] was playing up so we had to do it again. . . . That was a bit harsh . . . unlucky" while watching a video clip of the boys doing some 'warm-ups' and 'fitness drills' (represented by the still image in Figure 5.6). However, these physical punishments can still be seen as simultaneously producing certain bodily pleasures because they provide (some) boys with an opportunity to display/demonstrate skilled and able (masculine) bodies (explored further in chapter six).

These warm-ups and fitness drills are the most common way the fitness/health discourse is translated into teaching practice. On many occasions, Mr Whyte talks quite openly about the lesson structure being warm-ups/fitness drills followed by games. Some of the explanations Mr Whyte provides for this particular lesson structure are that the "kids expect this structure" and that the warm-up/fitness drill segment is important because it gets the "students fitter and sweaty, ready to go and more involved in the lesson". Mr Whyte also believes that the students see this as something they have to "last through to play the games". Indeed, there is little or no questioning of these warm-ups/fitness drills. Instead, the boys' accounts of this practice vary from "it is good exercise" (James), "something you have to do to get better at sports" (Sione) and "they're worth it" (Ben) to "just something you have to do" (Logan), "you

Figure 5.6 Boys Doing 'Warm-Ups' and 'Fitness Drills'.

just have to get it done" (Dominic) and "the best part comes after [games]" (Steven, 14 years old, European/Pākehā, active in multiple team sports). Other boys draw on the 'kinaesthetic' or 'sensual' pleasures (Wright & Dewar, 1997) gained from vigorous physical activity to describe their experiences of (dis) pleasures when doing these warm-ups and fitness drills:

Adam: I love feeling stuffed at the end of the warm-up because you know it's good for you.
Thomas: I love all of it. I love training hard and sweating, like it's just part of it [PE].

Although this teaching practice can be seen in itself as somewhat painful, boring and something you have to last through, it also induces pleasures because of the benefits the boys derive from it in terms of getting fitter, stronger and better at/warmed up for the games/sporting activities that generally follow. These findings add to our understanding of how activities in PE that the students are 'made' or 'forced' to do at first might be seen/interpreted as less pleasurable, or even lacking in pleasure, but can be productive in terms of learning outcomes in PE. For example, students learn about how the body works, how to make it perform better/more efficiently, how to be more productive and how to avoid injuries.

As Pringle (2010) explains, that which is pursued for its own sake need not necessarily be pleasurable. Pleasurable or satisfying experiences may even include a measure of discomfort (Kretchmar, 2005), as evidenced by Adam's comment above ("I love feeling stuffed"). However, Thomas's statement also indicates how some boys derive pleasures *while* doing these exercises. That is, despite the 'intrinsic' pleasures of physical activity in PE being 'dampened' behind 'extrinsic' factors such as fitness/health and sporting performance (Booth, 2009), Thomas seemingly takes pleasure and satisfaction from pursuing these warm-ups and fitness drills for their own sake ("I love training hard and sweating").

In this manner, Locke (1996) and Pringle (2010) argue that rather than focusing on the instrumental/developmental pleasures related to fitness/health and producing 'healthy citizens', PE should put greater emphasis on the (movement) pleasures derived from actually doing an activity. Or, as Locke (1996) puts it: "Perhaps all of our knowledge about why exercise is good for people will turn out to be less valuable than our own love of sweat and games—and our consequent evangelical impulse" (p. 431, cited in Pringle, 2010). Focusing on movement pleasures rather than instrumental/developmental pleasures in PE can still be seen as productive because pleasurable experiences can indeed improve individuals' health/well-being (Esch & Stefano, 2004). That is, the health/well-being of individuals can be linked to happiness and pleasure (Vernon, 2008). However, Ereaut and Whiting (2008) remind us that even health/well-being is a social construct because "there are no uncontested biological, spiritual, social, economic or any other kind of markers for [health/]wellbeing" (p. 9). The discursively constructed pleasures that the boys find in and through their bodies will be explored further in chapter six.

Conversely, for some boys, the pleasures of these warm-ups/fitness drills are not found in conforming to this practice but rather, paradoxically, in its refusal. For instance, in the socio-cultural context of PE at Kea College, within which there is significant pressure for 'everyone to do it', there also exists a certain kind of pleasure derived from showing your resistance/reluctance to 'doing it'. For some boys in my study, this means 'forgetting' their PE gear or saying that they are sick/injured to avoid participating in certain parts of the lesson or taking part at all. Other boys show their resistance in a different way:

Ben: I hate the warm-ups fitness stuff. . . . I actually try and be last, but if I wanted to, I could probably be one of the first [to finish].

Ben's statement demonstrates that pleasures can be found not only in multiple but also competing ways from the same source (Bordo, 1993). This can also be seen to problematise the view that schools and PE are sites where particular masculinities are constantly reinforced as either hegemonic or subordinate (Parker, 1996) because the same performance can be read both as hegemonic and subordinate. In Ben's case, this means that his refusal to conform to the dominant discourses of fitness/health ("I hate the warm-ups fitness stuff") could be read as subordinate, whereas his refusal could also be seen as hegemonic due to his recognition of a performance/competition discourse related to this teaching practice ("if I wanted to I could probably be one of the first"). However, except for Ben and Jacob (15 years old, European/Pākehā, active in multiple team sports), who says, "you don't want to be last", none of the other boys associate these warm-ups/fitness drills with performance/competition but rather see them as something that you just have to participate in. As I will discuss in chapter six, this is in contrast to other common teaching practices at this school, such as the 'beep-test' and 'picking teams'. Nevertheless, the greatest pleasure derived from this teaching practice is what it is followed by, 'a culture of playing games'.

'A Culture of Playing Games'—Production of Masculine (dis)pleasures through Games

Mr Whyte claims that there is a strong tradition in PE at Kea College of playing games and calls it "a culture of playing games". Although, as will be illustrated in this section, he clearly supports such an approach to PE, on a couple of occasions he also critically reflects on this ideology. For instance, one day he 'indirectly' asks me if "they are a bit different in this regard compared to other schools?" On another occasion, he voices concerns over some of the other PE teachers at the school possibly using this approach as a way of making their jobs easier: "Well, sometimes the other teachers get a bit lazy, you know, organise a game and then sit down". Nevertheless, throughout my year in PE at Kea College, different games and sports (some of which are represented in Figure 5.7) were used in order to, in the words of Mr Whyte, "focus on different skills and provide for different people's interests".

This focus on 'games' can partly be explained by Kea College's focus on sport and the ambition of all students enjoying and finding pleasure in playing a sport to carry on with later in life, as discussed in the previous chapter. One of the underpinning philosophies of PE at this school can thus be related to notions of games and sports 'for their own sake'. Games and sports are seen as 'essential' activities linked to masculine identities, and the fostering of a 'culture of playing games' and becoming physically educated is dependent on boys learning to take pleasure in physical activity (Meier, 1980; Twietmeyer, 2012). From this point of view, PE teachers such as Mr Whyte need to 'teach' young boys (and girls) the importance and pleasures of games and sport (Rintala, 2009). In chapter two, I highlighted how the New Zealand Curriculum (Ministry of Education, 2007) actively supports 'movement' pleasures as a way of contributing to students' health/well-being. However, I also drew attention to how this focus on movement pleasures in PE can to some extent be related to the PE teachers' own pleasurable experiences

Figure 5.7 Some of the 'Games' Played Throughout the Year in PE at Kea College.

of (certain) games and sports (Pringle, 2010). Mr Whyte also comments on this when we are discussing the PE curriculum at Kea College. He says that there is "no or little room for individual sports . . . some golf and tennis, though" and that "physical activity for the majority" is of prime concern. The best way to fulfil the idea of physical activity for all, within the 'culture of everyone doing it', is through team games/sports. Mr Whyte also often cites the added "character-building" and fitness/health benefits that come with engagement in those activities. That is, games and sport are considered as 'intrinsically good' (Morgan, 2006; Rintala, 2009) masculine endeavours because they are understood to shape boys into moral, good, law-abiding, healthy and productive citizens.

When talking about the PE content, the majority of boys mention the games and sports basis of PE as one of the most pleasurable aspects of PE. Sports such as rugby, soccer, basketball, badminton, volleyball and dodgeball are all particularly popular among the boys. However, some also cite this as one of the main negatives of PE and something that restricts certain pleasures: "that it is all about sports" (Ben), "same sports all the time" (James) and "you get sick of sport" (Andrew, 14 years old, European/

Pākehā, not involved in any sport). Other boys, such as Emilo (14 years old, Pacific Island, active in one individual sport), critique the heavy focus on team sports and instead prefer individual sports:

Emilo: Don't really like the team sports . . . feel like letting them down. . . . No other people depend on you in individual sports.

This comment highlights some of the anxieties ("feel like letting them down" and "other people depend on you") experienced by boys such as Emilo when they are 'forced' into team sports as opposed to individual sports during PE. Louis (14 years old, European/Pākehā, active in multiple team sports) questions the way that sports are played during PE in a different manner and says it's "not really sports, just playing games". The inclusion of some sports, like badminton, is also critiqued, as it means "too much waiting around and not active enough" (Logan). Another boy (Jonathan, 14 years old, European/Pākehā, active in multiple team sports) claims that they used to do lots of contact sports in previous years of PE but that the focus now is more on racquet sports. He believes that this is possibly the result of the increasing number of Asian students at this school, based on the (mis)belief that "in Asia they don't really play rugby". Although these boys' accounts show how the inclusion/exclusion of certain sports restricts their pleasurable experiences of PE, it could also be argued that this provision of sports helps these boys' learning in PE and the construction of alternative (sporting) masculinities in PE, ranging from contact sports (i.e., rugby) to individual sports (i.e., badminton). The enabling and restricting of certain (sporting) pleasures in PE can be seen as a productive educational practice in terms of constructing more diverse physically educated masculinities.

Although sport is only one of seven learning areas in the current New Zealand Health and PE Curriculum (Ministry of Education, 2007), it seems as if at this school sport is closely associated with (Smithells & Cameron, 1962), or even the subject matter of, PE (Dewar, 1987). Despite clear messages about the importance of adopting a socially critical perspective in PE, a traditional notion of physical activity involving a shared passion for various sports (Rossi, Sirna, & Tinning, 2008) is a significant discourse among teachers and students at Kea College. One important aspect of being a normal or desirable boy in this context is thus associated with having the skills and knowing the rules needed to play different sports. The focus on the development and performance of bodily (sporting) skills and abilities in PE is discussed in the next chapter. However, some of the boys also talk about how they very rarely get taught how to play the different sports, that it is just assumed that as a boy you should be skilled at and know the rules of popular games like, for instance, rugby and cricket (Wright, 1993, 1996, 1997, 2000). Sam explains how this sometimes leads him to pretend that he knows the rules in order to avoid his identity as a normal or desirable sporty boy being brought into question:

Sam: I never ask the teacher to explain the rules of the games, and I don't really like asking any of the other boys either because then they will just laugh at me. You know, call me gay and stuff. So I just pretend, even though sometimes I have no clue what is going on. That way, I also get to be one of the popular sporty ones.

The technique of normalisation that is at work here is the aim for the individual to desire to be normal (i.e., being 'sporty') by avoiding punishment (i.e., being 'laughed at'). However, the techniques of normalisation rely on both a person's desire to be rewarded and his or her fear of punishment (Foucault, 1995). By pretending to know the rules, Sam reaps the rewards and pleasures of being considered as one of the sporty ones, as opposed to showing his peers and the teacher that he in fact does not know the rules and thereby running the risk of being 'punished' through ridicule. In this sense, disciplinary techniques such as normalisation can also be linked to discourses of pleasure (Markula & Pringle, 2006). That is, Sam wants to create himself in accordance to discursively constructed norms of boys, masculinity and sport in this particular context. Discourses also produce certain kinds of desires as normal and desirable (Turner, 1997), or what Rose (1999) refers to as 'technologies of desire', that boys such as Sam work to satisfy. For example, dominant understandings of the social and peer group status attained by sporty boys, along with the added fitness/health benefits, represent experiences/outcomes that are desirable for boys such as Sam. The fact that some boys perform dominant forms of masculinity in PE can in this way be related to their desire of (re)asserting privileged masculine identities, which involves having power or superiority over other boys who are not able or willing to live up to these masculine ideals. This exercise and experience of power can thus be seen as both productive and pleasurable (Foucault, 1980).

Furthermore, Sam's statement gives further evidence that for a boy to resist the values associated with team sports, or to show himself as 'unskilled' or 'uninformed' about a sport, is not only to identify himself as a poor or problem student but to bring into question his masculinity, his very identity as male (Wright, 2000). That is, discourses of pleasure are also about the desire to be 'normal', as related to gender, bodies, sexuality and so on. The strong emphasis on sport as inherently good and its close connection with PE can in this way be seen to restrict the ways in which boys find pleasure through participation in PE using their own bodies and performing masculine identities (Gard & Wright, 2001). These findings substantiate the need for PE teachers to teach according to the current New Zealand HPE curriculum and enable boys (and girls) to learn about themselves, others and their bodies in/through a broad range of health- and movement related contexts/activities (of which sport is also a part).

However, some boys also problematise dominant understandings of sport in PE. For instance, when talking about the difference between playing sports outside of school and doing sports in PE, two of the boys (Jacob and Zack) say:

Göran: So how is sport in school [PE] different?
Jacob: More relaxed.
Zack: Yeah, not so competitive.

Jacob and Zack seem to draw upon 'participation' rather than 'performance' discourses (Tinning, 2010) to articulate their sources of enjoyment and pleasure of playing sports in PE. That is, according to these boys, pleasure is derived from less pressure and focus on performances and competition in PE, compared to when engaged in organised sport outside of school. Indeed, resisting certain sporting practices and competition in PE as a way of producing pleasure is a common feature at this school. In one focus group, while watching a video clip representing a game of 'dodgeball', a popular ball game at this school, the following conversation takes place:

Dominic: No one is doing anything. Everyone is just standing there [laughter].
Logan: [Laughter] Look at Campbell. He is just bouncing the ball into the ground.
Göran: So why is no one doing anything?
Miles: We are just taunting each other [laughter].

Resisting the discourse of competition by not "doing anything", "just standing there" and making fun of or "taunting each other" is another source of enjoyment and pleasure. That is, sometimes physical activity contexts produce pleasurable sensations that at times transcend their social and cultural conceptualisation (Booth, 2009). This also provides an example of how pleasure may act not only as a neoliberal organising principle (Coveney & Bunton, 2003; Lupton, 1995) but also as a form of resistance. Further, the pleasure derived from the boys' resistance to dominant discourses of sport relating to competition can be seen as related to both the act itself and the subversive nature of it.

Some of the boys are not only resisting these sporting practices and competition but also questioning the (dis)pleasures constituted by this 'culture of playing games'. Adam, in particular, expresses concerns with the dominance of certain sports in their PE. When Adam asked one of the PE teachers if they could try some new activities in PE, he was told, "No, we don't do things like that in PE at this school". Adam's strategy was then to try and convince the rest of the class, whom he felt he had some influence over, to join his cause in trying to get the teacher to do some other activities in PE they had not tried before. Adam explains:

Adam: Well, you know, I don't believe PE is all about just playing various sports like rugby and stuff. I think it is more about learning the skills to live a healthy life once you leave school. And, I mean, how many of us are really going to play rugby for the rest of our lives? I mean, don't get me wrong, I like rugby, but I just think that PE should be more than just that.

Göran: So have you talked to your teacher about that?

Adam: Yep, and at first he was like, you know we do this and this in PE. That's the way it has always been. But when one of the student teachers was here last year, they did all this adventure-based learning stuff. You know, problem-solving, teamwork and communication activities, stuff like that. I think everyone loved it. You know, it was something different. So I sort of convinced the rest of the class to say to our teacher that we should do some more of that.

Göran: So have you?

Adam: Yeah, I mean, not that much yet. But I know the teachers are planning on doing more of that stuff later in the year. I really hope so.

Adam's frustration with the content and activities in PE is an example of the way classification and generalisation practices in PE have the effect of legitimating certain knowledges/skills (i.e., "playing various sports like rugby") and dismissing others (i.e., "adventure-based learning"). Adam in particular cites the power of teachers and of sporting discourses to assert what counts as 'facts' or 'truths' (Webb, McCaughtry, & MacDonald, 2004) when he recounts one of the teachers saying, "You know we do this and this in PE. That's the way it has always been". However, from a poststructural perspective, change comes about from unsettling dominant discourses and power relations and speaking into existence other ways of being (Webb & Macdonald, 2007), which is exactly what Adam's story gives evidence of. Through questioning the (dis)pleasures of the content offered in this PE context and suggesting alternative activities, Adam is to some extent able to challenge existing dominant discourses and power relations in this PE setting associated with certain sporting practices. Adam's 'telos' (Foucault, 1985) appears to revolve around a refusal to be disciplined by dominant and singular notions of what activities boys should and should not engage in during PE. Overtly and unapologetically competitive, sport is viewed by Adam as at odds with the inclusive and supportive environment he wants to foster in PE. In addition, Adam's contrasting of various sporting activities to "problem-solving, teamwork and communication activities" highlights the opposite ends of a continuum regarding the role that sport should play in the teaching of PE, with one end regarding sport as an essential, necessary experience, whereas the other end advocates a broad range of physical skills in a non-competitive environment (Stothart, 2000).

When talking about the overall content of PE during the individual interviews, Dominic tells a similar story to Adam's, which accounts for him and some of the other boys actively seeking to challenge the (dis)pleasures of the types of activities offered in their PE:

Dominic: I mean, not everyone likes the sports we are doing in PE. It doesn't mean that we are not sporty, it just means that we like other sports and activities. No wonder that some boys cannot compete with us rugby boys when some of them don't even play rugby outside of school. Sometimes I just think we play too much rugby and some other sports. I mean, don't get me wrong, I love rugby, but I just think it is not fair on other people if we don't also do other sports so they can show how good they are, you know.

Göran: So have you told your teacher what you think?

Dominic: Well, not at first because then I will just get mocked by all the other rugby boys who start calling you a fag and stuff. Some of them even tried stopping us from talking to the teachers about wanting to something different in PE. But eventually a couple of us had a meeting with the HOD [head of department] of PE and just said that we thought we were playing too much rugby and stuff and that we would like to do some other sports that some of the rest of us do.

Göran: Like?

Dominic: You know, badminton, tennis, lacrosse, etc.

Göran: And did you get to do that then?

Dominic: Yeah, we actually did do some of those sports for a while, but only a couple of times. We still play rugby and stuff most of the time. But hopefully we will do those other sports again. We might go and talk to the HOD again soon.

For Dominic, classifying some boys as 'non-sporty' because they do not like certain sports does not equal not being sporty or masculine; instead, he claims that "it just means that we like other sports and activities". In this sense, he is questioning dominant discourses of sport and rugby as being associated with ideal forms of masculinity. In fact, he is able to change the teaching practices, albeit for a short while. In achieving this, Dominic has a sense of the rugby boys' strong influence both at a wider school level and specifically within PE. However, he resists this by calling on the support of the head of department (HOD) and not giving in to the bullying of the rugby boys, which, for instance, involves being called a 'fag'. Dominic's story is therefore a good example of the multiple effects of power (Foucault, 1995). The 'rugby boys' try to exert power by attempting to prevent Dominic from voicing his concerns through tactics of domination such as bullying, but due to the advocacy of the HOD, Dominic and these other boys have some support. Dominic also has to have the confidence to challenge the intentions of the teachers and state what he and some of the other boys want to change about their PE. Dominic suggests that an important goal of transforming current practices in PE should be that gender stereotypes should not stop boys from being able to engage in a diversity and multiplicity of activities, games and sports as part of their PE. He concludes by stating what might be considered his 'telos':

Dominic: I believe that PE should teach us about using our bodies in as many ways as possible, you know, not just in boys' sports and stuff. I mean, I don't only want to learn how to kick and throw a ball and stuff. I would even not mind doing some dancing in PE [laughter].

In an attempt to rectify the lack of non-traditional activities that go against gender stereotypes, Adam and Dominic are engaging in 'ethical work' to transform the (dis)pleasures of current practices in PE via advocating for alternative activities. In order to do this, both Adam and Dominic use "parrhesia" (Foucault, 1999, p. 1) to influence others, which is an ancient Greek term Foucault (1999) uses to describe someone who attempts to tell the 'truth' or speak his mind within a particular discourse, without being worried about the consequences. However, as Markula and Pringle (2006) note, by using parrhesia, both Adam and Dominic are still exposing themselves to a certain degree of risk because they are speaking from a subordinated position with the aim of challenging a dominant discourse (e.g., the dominance of particular sports in the PE context or only learning "how to kick and throw a ball"). Through revealing their 'truth' about the (dis)pleasures of only including dominant sports in PE and focusing on developing certain skills, Adam and Dominic reveal a subjugated knowledge in the context of their PE, with the aim of encouraging alternative practices and pleasures.

The stories of Adam and Dominic illustrate how boys are not simply 'victims' of discourses. Rather, some boys are able to engage in the "double act of critique and self-stylization" (Markula & Pringle, 2006, p. 152), which to some extent shifts and re-articulates images and meanings of individual and collective boys. In so doing, Adam and Dominic provoke what Lloyd (1996) calls "a critical, querying reaction" (p. 258). That is, by problematising the (dis)pleasures of these activities and practices associated with their PE, Adam and Dominic have engaged in ethical conduct or practices of freedom and produced a space where gendered meanings, identities and (dis)pleasures can be contested and negotiated, which may in turn have an impact on power relations and the broader PE culture.

However, it is important to note that technologies of the self are always located within a socio-cultural context (Chapman, 1997). Although these alternative activities and practices in PE can act as a practice of freedom by expanding the limitations of boys' pleasures in PE, the dominant discourses of sport and gender in PE continue to hold strong. In other words, offering alternative activities and practices does not change the modes of domination

(Markula & Pringle, 2006). According to Foucault (1985), the strategic coordination of resistance is necessary to effect institutional changes; however, such changes will only ever shift existing power relations and not dissolve them (Markula, 2003). Thus, in this case, I draw on Foucault's notion of technologies of the self to highlight the agency and autonomy in these boys' stories, without suggesting that they are somehow able to perform gender free from the workings of discourse and relations of power operating within this setting.

Although many boys derive pleasure from performing dominant sporting masculinities but also resisting and questioning these practices associated with competition, some boys end up being positioned problematically within this discourse/power/pleasure arrangement. That is, power-induced pleasures reaffirm some boys' subordinated position in PE because of the way these pleasures are derived (from performing/conforming to stereotypical/dominant notions of sport and masculinity) while simultaneously producing some boys as the 'other'. This conversation takes place in another focus group while watching the same dodgeball video clip as referred to above (represented by the still images in Figure 5.8):

Figure 5.8 Boys Playing a Game of Dodgeball.

Matthew:	Ah, look at Kevin [top right image] sitting in the corner being afraid of getting hit!
	[Laughter]
Thomas:	Yeah, and look, there is a whole bunch of them [bottom right] doing nothing!
Matthew:	Yeah, they are like a bunch of girls . . . so gay!
Thomas:	Yeah, why don't they like playing dodgeball, I mean, all boys love dodgeball!
Matthew:	Not Kevin, he loves playing netball! What a girl!
Thomas:	Yeah, and they all throw the ball like a girl!
	[Laughter]
Thomas:	Yeah, they'd rather just talk to each other than play the game.

This conversation demonstrates the (dis)pleasures of how the boys represent and interpret different kinds of sporting activities in PE and how they engender themselves and others as gendered subjects of different kinds of sporting activities (Larsson, Fagrell, & Redelius, 2009). In this context, dodgeball is constructed as an activity for boys, which is then used by Matthew and Thomas to reaffirm their privileged/desirable masculine status. For instance, inflicting or receiving pain becomes normalised or is an expected part of the boys' dodgeball sporting experience (Markula & Pringle, 2006). It is worth noting that sometimes sport participants might take pleasure from bodily sensations conceptualised as 'positive' pain and that this need not necessarily be a 'bad thing' (Bridel, 2010). Conversely, netball is constructed as an activity for girls, which then instead puts Kevin's (15 years old, Asian, active in one individual sport) masculinity into question. In this way, different kinds of activities, notably different sports, seem to position individual boys and groups of boys in different ways depending on their performances of gender (Larsson et al., 2009). For example, boys such as Kevin, who through their performances display a lack of self-confidence and a reluctance to appear aggressive and competitive in connection with popular ball games such as dodgeball, represent 'undesirable' or 'abject' (Butler, 1990) masculine identities.

Rugby—The 'Glue' of Masculine (dis)Pleasures

Having spent only a couple of weeks at Kea College and engaging with its teachers and students, it was soon clear that it is not just how sport in general is constructed within this school but a particular sport, rugby, that plays a crucial role in the production of both masculine identities and (dis)pleasures. When asked to talk about Kea College, one of the first things Mr Whyte mentions is "just rugby . . . big rugby profile, and the principal Mr Andersson is well known for being the school's biggest 'rugby-head' ". Indeed, among the students, a form of 'pecking order' can be identified in which the rugby players are the ones with perceived higher social status and ability to exercise more power. In school assemblies and newsletters, the dominant sport of rugby seems to take up most of the time and space. Boys who are involved in other sporting activities such as soccer and basketball often find that their accomplishments are not recognised by the school and its teachers. Some boys, such as Joseph, even claim that the teachers, especially their PE teachers, treat them differently compared to how the rugby players are treated and revered, which leads them to not let their teachers know of their other sporting involvements. Joseph explains:

Joseph: If you don't play rugby, or aren't in any of the school teams, the teachers don't really notice you that much. All the school assemblies and newsletters are always about how the rugby team is doing. My PE teacher doesn't even know that I'm competing in mountain biking and stuff.

Thus, the polarity of 'sporty' and 'non-sporty' also constructs a dilemma for those boys caught in-between these definitions (Martino & Pallotta-Chiarolli, 2003). The status associated with playing certain sports, especially rugby, influences the boys' performances of gender, both for those who do and do not adhere to dominant notions. In a way, rugby can even be seen as one of the key discourses at this school, which has a direct implication on the "guiding rationalities whereby individuals and social structures regulate and police norms of thought and behaviour" (Foucault, 1991, p. 157). Understood through Foucault's (1991) notion of 'governmentality', the prevalence of this (rugby) sporting discourse shapes how these boys come to represent themselves as gendered. The idea proposed by Booth (2000) that rugby can in fact be seen as the 'glue' of masculine culture in New Zealand and something that functions as a kind of 'rite of passage' for boys on their way to becoming men, is also a recurring theme in the boys' visual representations and interpretations.

While watching a video clip of the boys playing a game of rugby in PE (represented by the still images in Figure 5.9) during one of the focus groups, the following conversation takes place:

Steven: Wow, what a pass, Mike! [Top left image]
Mike: Yeah, that was a mint pass, ay! But look at me getting tackled later! [Top right image]
Steven: And, wow, mean tackle, Bruce! Oh, that's gotta hurt Mike! [Laughter]
Mike: Yeah, but look at me getting up and getting my payback there! [Bottom left image]
Bruce: Yeah, you got me good there!

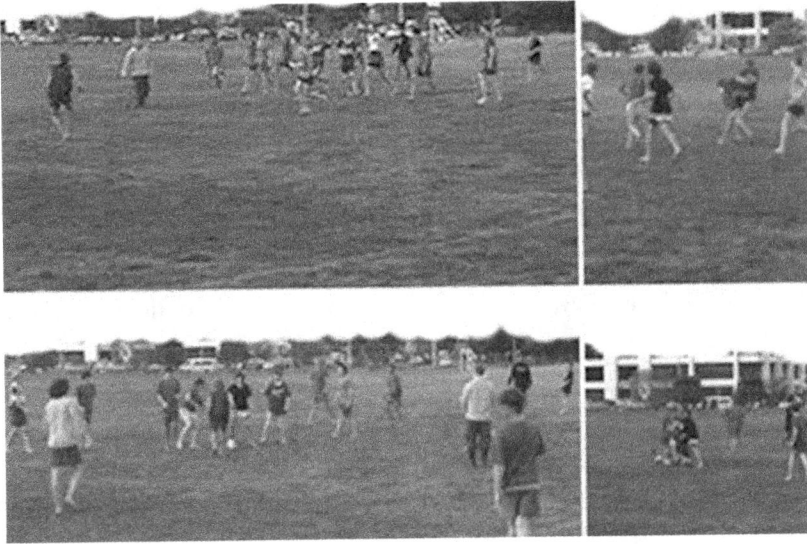

Figure 5.9 A Group of Boys Playing Rugby.

Steven: Awesome!
            [Laughter]
Steven: And, look, there's Duncan getting tackled too! [Bottom right image]
Mike: Yeah, but he is so weak, look he is not even getting up again!
Steven: What a loser!
Mike: Yeah, come on, don't be a poofter, be a man, Duncan!
            [Laughter]

This conversation demonstrates how rugby, as a sport commonly played by boys in New Zealand schools and during PE, can act as a strategic site for the production of multiple and competing masculinities (Pringle & Markula, 2005). The construction of rugby as a site where different types of masculinities are produced can be understood through the workings of sporting discourses. These discourses work to frame or construct knowledge, practices and facts about boys and masculinity. Steven's, Mike's and Bruce's (both 14 years old, European/Pākehā, active in multiple team sports) comments illustrate how some of these masculinities are related to demonstrating physical abilities/skills ("wow, what a pass"), aggression/physicality ("wow, mean tackle"), no fear of pain/injury ("look at me getting up") and heterosexuality ("don't be a poofter, be a man"). In this way, boys can be seen to be encouraged to engage in physicality in particular ways (Stoudt, 2006) that glorify "hard physical contact, in the capacity to both give and take it" (Fitzclarence & Hickey, 2001, p. 129). That is, a competitive sport such as rugby is seen as an important masculinising pursuit for boys because it "teaches them to transform any feelings of hurt, pain or sorrow into the more 'appropriately masculine' expressions of contained anger or stoic silence" (Messner, 2011, p. 163). This is further highlighted on a number of occasions when, for instance, one of the boys gets hit in the head with a ball and someone else asks if that person is okay; the person typically just walks away and sort of brushes it off as if to say, "Of course I am!" but then, when nobody is looking, he feels and checks his head to see if he really is okay.

"[A]s a contradictory and complex medium for masculinity making" (Fitzclarence & Hickey, 2001, p. 118), these boys' accounts of the sport of rugby and its role in the construction and performance of certain masculinities can also be understood in terms of pleasure. Boys are not simply 'taught' or 'forced' to use their bodies in physical ways (Edley & Wetherell, 1997; Heikkala, 1993; Light & Kirk, 2000) to construct a sporty, masculine identity (White & Gillett, 1994) but rather some boys, such as Steve, Mike and Bruce, find certain aspects of this pleasurable. Gard and Meyenn (2000) remind us that "just as pain and violence are embedded in the discourses of competitive sports, so too are bodily pleasures" (p. 30). The boys' conversation above seems to confirm Pringle's (2009) suggestion that some of the pleasures of rugby are derived from the sense of "mock battle", "friendships and teamwork," "development and display of skill, fitness and strategy", "physical contact and intimacy," and "affirming and/ or challenging gendered [sexual] identities" (p. 215). The discourses and normalising practices of historical descent associated with New Zealand's national sport of rugby not only allow for particular subject positions that enable various masculinities but also produce certain pleasures (pleasurable sporting/rugby masculinities). In this manner, Foucault (1980) viewed power as productive: "it traverses and produces things, it induces pleasure, forms of knowledge, produces discourses" (p. 119). The productive effect of power importantly highlights the boys as active (co-)producers of their own genders and pleasures, constrained, of course, by the discourses of sport, masculinity and pleasure and systems of meaning in circulation within this context.

Although sports such as rugby can be seen as producing multiple masculinities and pleasures, this school's promotion and organisation of rugby also contribute to the constitution of rugby as a 'technology of domination' (Foucault, 1973), which in turn (re)produces unequal power relations and certain (dis)pleasures. In other words, sports practices are not necessarily meritocratic or democratising and inherently 'good' (e.g., Burrows, 2005; Curry, 1993; Giulianotti, 2005; Kirk, 1992; Markula & Pringle, 2006). At the same time as sport produces desirable masculine behaviours and ideals, it also constructs that which can be seen as 'undesirable'. The boys' conversation above, for instance, demonstrates how the dominant sporting discourses of male toughness, aggressiveness and competition, often promoted through the school sport of rugby (Hickey,

2008; Light & Kirk, 2000), produce undesirable masculine behaviours such as an indifference to their own and other boys' physical pain ("Oh, that's gotta hurt". . . . "Yeah, but look at me getting up and getting my payback") and homophobia ("Don't be a poofter, be a man, Duncan"). In particular, this can be seen to (re)produce a hierarchy of masculinities in which boys are then assessed and hierarchically arranged based on how they live up to these masculine norms and ideals. In this sense, sports such as rugby can act as a "dividing practice" (Foucault, 1983, p. 208) by comparing, differentiating and hierarchising boys, subsequently producing particular relations of power that regulate and monitor the actions and behaviours of these boys. Hence, boys such as Duncan (15 years old, European/Pākehā, active in one individual sport), who are not able or are unwilling to live up to these masculine norms and ideals are judged as inferior or the 'other'. This 'other' is then (re) produced by the dominant sporting discourse as representing undesirable masculinities.

However, a number of boys in my study have started problematising some of the (dis)pleasures and unequal power relations induced by these discourses. While discussing his experiences of PE and sport during the individual interviews, Matthew tells me that he has become critically aware of the normalising practices associated with sports, and in particular rugby, at this school:

Matthew: I think as I have gotten older, I have started realising how important people think it is to be good at certain sports and PE, you know, to prove that you are man and stuff, but sometimes I think this also creates a lot of unnecessary pressure for us boys. You know, keeping up that whole image and stuff. Sometimes I find it really frustrating, you know.

Matthew problematises the connection between sporting ability and masculine identities by pointing towards the pressure involved in proving "that you are man" through this discourse, which he also cites as a source of discontent ("I find it really frustrating"). Matthew's comment illustrates Foucault's (1984) point that the ability of self-reflection opens up the opportunity to not only 'cope' with one's situation but also question the limitations of one's freedom:

Thought is not what inhabits a certain conduct and gives it its meaning; rather, it is what allows one to step back from this way of acting or reacting, to present it to oneself as an object of thought and question it as to its meaning, its conditions, and its goals. Thought is freedom in relation to what one does, the motion by which one detaches oneself from it, establishes it as an object, and reflects on it as a problem.

(p. 388)

This critical thought is the core of the ethical self-care that Foucault (1985) further conceptualised as "an exercise of oneself in the activity of thought" (p. 8). The critically self-aware individual therefore questions what seems "natural" and inevitable in their identity; through this interrogation of the limits of one's subjectivity emerges the "possibility of transgression" and with it the "potential for creating new types of subjective experiences" (Markula, 2003, p. 102).

Matthew's critical reflection of his own masculine identity as a 'rugby boy' has also led him to become aware of the greater attention and status granted to him as a rugby player compared to the 'non-rugby' and 'non-sporty' boys. He in particular accounts for how these other groups of boys often do not have the same ability to use specific discursive resources to help construct alternative privileged masculine identities (Markula & Pringle, 2006) and how this (re)produces a problematic positioning of boys:

Matthew: I really don't like how we as rugby players are sometimes seen as just rough and tough, I mean, don't get me wrong, I like playing rugby, but sometimes I wish we would not all be grouped into the same category. And I don't think it is fair how some of us think that other sports are girls' sports or for poofters. It is not like you are less of a man just because you don't play rugby. I mean, some still think like that, don't get me wrong, but I just don't like how some put other boys down for playing sports like soccer or badminton.

Göran: So what do you about that?

Matthew: Well, nothing really, but I wish I would stand up for some of those other boys more, but you kind of have to play along, otherwise the other rugby boys won't really like you. But like I said, I want to try and change that.

Göran: Change what?

Matthew: You know, stand up for the other boys and tell the other rugby boys to have more respect.

Matthew's experience of being one of the privileged rugby males demonstrates some of the aspects he finds troubling. He particularly points towards the derogatory statements used to label other boys ("poofters"). He also questions the way that some boys are positioned adversely through their participation in different sporting activities, given that some of these activities are objectified as feminine ("girls' sports") (Pringle & Hickey, 2010). Matthew also brings up one important aspect that relates to why ethical work needs to be undertaken. Through this self-reflexive process, focusing on the (dis)pleasures produced by discourses relating to sport and masculinities, Matthew recognises that he has a moral obligation towards some of the 'other' boys. His mode of subjection and thus the focus of his ethical work is to become someone who will stand up for these other boys and encourage himself and the other rugby boys to have more respect for other non-rugby playing boys. In this sense, Matthew is attempting to transform himself into an ethical masculine subject (Foucault, 1985). Matthew problematises the (dis)pleasures or (oppressive) effects of power associated with the social practices of rugby at this particular school and engages in some self-reflection, which in this case leads to the ethical use of pleasure/power (Foucault, 1985). In doing so, Matthew is, to some extent, minimising the effect of rugby as a 'technology of domination' (Foucault, 1973).

In summary, this chapter has shown how pleasures emerge within the discourses and relations of power of PE as constitutive of boys' performances of gender. The boys' performances of gender not only constitute and are constituted by this discursive formation but also produce and are a product of pleasure. The contextually specific discourses of PE at Kea College related to the cultures of 'everyone doing it' and 'playing games' shape, limit and constrain the way boys come to understand and experience pleasure. In particular, power-induced pleasure came to be recognisable through these two PE cultures related to fitness, health, sport and masculinity, which in turn regulated and elaborated boys' performances of gender. The findings in this chapter have highlighted how the way boys derive pleasures from the PE cultures of 'everyone doing it' and 'playing games' varies. Although some boys find pleasures from merely participating in PE (e.g., "time with your mates"), others seem to derive pleasures from instrumental/developmental goals based on discourses of fitness, health and sport (e.g., "getting fit", "being healthy" and "better at sport"). In particular, dominant understandings of the social and peer group status attained by the 'sporty' boys, along with the added fitness/health benefits, represent experiences/outcomes that are desirable for some boys. Others find pleasures in acts that are of a resistant and subversive nature by, for instance, resisting dominant understandings of sports and competition.

Based on these findings, it might be helpful to (re)conceptualise boys' performances of gender in PE by interpreting discursive practices related to fitness, health and sport not only as constrained and disciplined but also as engendering boys' agency/freedom and pleasure. My study adds to existing knowledge by demonstrating how both conforming to and disrupting discourses of PE can be both productive and pleasurable. I have also suggested that less pleasure (or even lack of pleasure) can be productive both in terms of learning outcomes and in the construction of alternative/more diverse masculinities in PE. In this sense, the enabling and restricting of certain (sporting) pleasures in boys' PE can be seen as a productive educational practice. However, the results presented in this chapter also warrant a continued concern for the discursive links between, for instance, dominant discourses of masculinity, toughness/ aggression, competition and (hetero)sexuality. That is, the discourses and relations of power in boys' PE that allow for particular subject positions and produce certain pleasures can at times also induce (dis)pleasures (e.g., exclusion pain, humiliation, embarrassment, harassment, bullying, homophobia). In this chapter, I have also shown how some boys have started problematising the (dis)pleasures induced by these discourses and articulating a desire to perform masculinities in more responsible, ethical and inclusive ways.

In the next chapter, I will turn my attention to the centrality of the body in the boys' performances of gender and (dis)pleasures by exploring the materialisation of pleasurable bodies in boys' PE.

References

Booth, D. (2000). Modern sport: Emergence and experiences. In C. Collins (Ed.), *Sport in New Zealand society* (pp. 45–63). Palmerston North, NZ: Dunmore Press.

Booth, D. (2009). Politics and pleasure: The philosophy of physical education revisited. *Quest, 61*(2), 133–153.

Bordo, S. (1993). *Weight, feminism, western culture, and the body.* Berkeley, CA: University of California Press.

Bridel, W. F. (2010). *'Finiswhatever it takes': Considering pain and pleasure in the ironman triathlon: A socio-cultural analysis* (Unpublished PhD thesis). Queen's University, Kingston, Ontario, Canada.

Burrows, L. (2005). Do the 'right' thing: Chewing the fat in physical education. *Journal of Physical Education New Zealand, 33*(1), 7–16.

Butler, J. (1990). *Gender trouble: Feminism and the subversion of identity.* London and New York: Routledge.

Butler, J. (2004). *Undoing gender.* New York: Routledge.

Chapman, G. E. (1997). Making weight: Lightweight rowing, technologies of power, and technologies of the self. *Sociology of Sport Journal, 14*, 205–223.

Coveney, J., & Bunton, R. (2003). In pursuit of the study of pleasure: Implications for health research and practice. *Health, 7*(2), 161–179.

Curry, T. J. (1993). A little pain never hurt anyone: Athletic career socialization and the normalization of sports injury. *Symbolic Interaction, 16*(3), 273–290.

Dewar, A. (1987). Knowledge and gender in physical education. In J. Gaskell & A. McLaren (Eds.), *Women and education: A Canadian perspective* (pp. 265–288). Calgary, Alberta: Detselig Enterprises.

Edley, N., & Wetherell, M. (1997). Jockeying for position: The construction of masculine identities. *Discourse & Society, 8*(2), 203–217.

Ereaut, G., & Whiting, R. (2008). *What do we mean by 'wellbeing'? And why might it matter?* Department for Children, Schools and Families, Research Report No DCSF-RW073, UK.

Esch, T., & Stefano, G. (2004). The neurobiology of pleasure, reward processes, addiction and their health implications. *Neuroendocrinology Letters, 25*(4), 235–251.

Fitzclarence, L., & Hickey, C. (2001). Real footballers don't eat quiche: Old narratives in new times. *Men and Masculinities, 4*, 118–139.

Foucault, M. (1973). *The birth of the clinic: An archaeology of medical perception.* London, UK: Tavistock.

Foucault, M. (1978). *The history of sexuality, volume one.* Harmondsworth, UK: Penguin.

Foucault, M. (1980). *Power/knowledge: Selected interviews and other writings, 1972–1977.* New York: Pantheon.

Foucault, M. (1983). Afterword: The subject and power. In H. L. Dreyfus & P. Rabinow (Eds.), *Michel Foucault: Beyond structuralism and hermeneutics* (2nd ed., pp. 208–226). Chicago, IL: University of Chicago Press.

Foucault, M. (1984). Polemics, politics, and problematizations. In P. Rabinow (Ed.), *Foucault reader* (pp. 381–390). New York: Pantheon Books.

Foucault, M. (1985). *The use of pleasure: The history of sexuality, volume 2.* London, UK: Penguin Books.

Foucault, M. (1991). *The Foucault effect: Studies in governmentality: With two lectures by and an interview with Michel Foucault.* London, UK: Harvester Wheatsheaf.

Foucault, M. (1995). *Discipline and punish: The birth of the prison.* Westminster, MD: Vintage.

Foucault, M. (1999). *Discourse and truth: The meaning of the word parrhesia* (lecture given by Michel Foucault at the University of California at Berkeley, October–November 1983). J Pearson (Ed.), compiled from tape-recordings and re-edited in 1999. Available at: http://foucault.info/documents/parrhesia/

Gard, M., & Meyenn, R. (2000). Boys, bodies, pleasure and pain: Interrogating contact sports in schools. *Sport, Education and Society, 5*(1), 19–34.

Gard, M., & Wright, J. (2001). Managing uncertainty: Obesity discourses and physical education in a risk society. *Studies in Philosophy and Education, 20*(6), 535–549.

Giulianotti, R. (2005). *Sport: A critical sociology.* Cambridge, UK: Polity Press.

Hall, S. (1997). *Representation: Cultural representations and signifying practices.* London, UK: Sage & Open University Press.

Hawkins, A. (2008). Pragmatism, purpose, and play: Struggle for the soul of physical education. *Quest, 60,* 345–356.

Heikkala, J. (1993). Discipline and excel: Techniques of the self and body and the logic of competing. *Sociology of Sport Journal, 10,* 397–412.

Hickey, C. (2008). Physical education, sport and hyper-masculinity in schools. *Sport, Education and Society, 13*(2), 147–161.

Kirk, D. (1992). *Defining physical education: The social construction of a school subject in postwar Britain.* London and Washington, DC: Falmer Press.

Kirk, D. (2010). *Physical education futures.* London, UK: Routledge.

Kretchmar, R. S. (2005). *Practical philosophy of sport and physical activity.* Champaign, IL: Human Kinetics.

Larsson, H., Fagrell, B., & Redelius, K. (2009). Queering physical education: Between benevolence towards girls and a tribute to masculinity. *Physical Education and Sport Pedagogy, 14*(1), 1–17.

Lemke, T. (2001). 'The birth of bio-politics': Michel Foucault's lecture at the College de France on neo-liberal governmentality. *Economy and Society, 30*(2), 190–207.

Light, R., & Kirk, D. (2000). High School Rugby, the body and the reproduction of hegemonic masculinity. *Sport, Education and Society, 5*(2), 163–176.

Lloyd, M. (1996). A feminist mapping of Foucauldian politics. In S. Hekman (Ed.), *Feminist interpretations of Michel Foucault* (pp. 241–264). University Park, PA: Pennsylvania State University Press.

Locke, L. (1996). Dr. Lewin's little liver patties: A parable about encouraging healthy lifestyles. *Quest, 48,* 422–431.

Lupton, D. (1995). *The imperative of health: Public health and the regulated body.* London, UK: Sage.

Markula, P. (2003). The technologies of the self: Sport, feminism, and Foucault. *Sociology of Sport Journal, 20,* 87–107.

Markula, P., & Pringle, R. (2006). *Foucault, sport and exercise: Power, knowledge and transforming the self.* New York: Routledge.

Martino, W., & Pallotta-Chiarolli, M. (2003). *So what's a boy? Addressing issues of masculinity and schooling.* Buckingham, UK: Open University Press.

McCuaig, L., & Tinning, R. (2010). HPE and the moral governance of p/leisurable bodies. *Sport, Education and Society, 15*(1), 39–61.

Meier, K. (1980). An affair of flutes: An appreciation of play. *Journal of the Philosophy of Sport, VII*, 24–45.

Messner, M. (2011). Gender ideologies, youth sports, and the production of soft essentialism. *Sociology of Sport Journal, 28*, 151–170.

Ministry of Education. (2007). *The New Zealand curriculum.* Wellington, NZ: Learning Media.

Morgan, W. (2006). Philosophy and physical education. In D. Kirk, M. O'Sullivan, & D. MacDonald (Eds.), *The handbook of research in sport and physical education* (pp. 97–108). Thousand Oaks, CA: Sage.

Parker, A. (1996). The construction of masculinity within boys' physical education. *Gender and Education, 8*(2), 141–158.

Pringle, R. (2009). Defamiliarizing heavy-contact sports: A critical examination of rugby, discipline, and pleasure. *Sociology of Sport Journal, 26*, 211–234.

Pringle, R. (2010). Finding pleasure in physical education: A critical examination of the educative value of positive movement affects. *Quest, 62*, 119–134.

Pringle, R., & Hickey, C. (2010). Negotiating masculinities via the moral problematization of sport. *Sociology of Sport Journal, 27*(2), 115–138.

Pringle, R., & Markula, P. (2005). No pain is sane after all: A Foucauldian analysis of masculinities and men's rugby experiences. *Sociology of Sport Journal, 22*(4), 472–497.

Rintala, J. (2009). It's all about the -ing. *Quest, 61*(3), 279–288.

Rose, N. (1999). *Powers of freedom: Reframing political thought.* Cambridge, UK: Cambridge University Press.

Rossi, T., Sirna, K., & Tinning, R. (2008). Becoming a health and physical education (HPE) teacher: Student teacher 'performances' in the physical education subject department office. *Teacher and Teaching Education, 24*, 1029–1040.

Smithells, P., & Cameron, P. E. (1962). *Principles of evaluation in physical education.* New York: Harper.

Stothart, B. (2000). Pegs in the ground: Landmarks in the history of New Zealand physical education. *Journal of Physical Education New Zealand, 33*(2), 5–15.

Stoudt, B. (2006). 'You're either in or you're out': School violence, peer discipline, and the (re)production of hegemonic masculinity. *Men and Masculinities, 8*, 273–287.

Tinning, R. (2004). Rethinking the preparation of HPE teachers: Ruminations on knowledge, identity, and ways of thinking. *Asia-Pacific Journal of Teacher Education, 32*(3), 241–253.

Tinning, R. (2010). *Pedagogy and human movement: Theory, practice, research.* New York: Routledge.

Tinning, R., & Glasby, T. (2002). Pedagogical work and the "cult of the body': Considering the role of HPE in the context of the 'new public health'. *Sport, Education and Society, 7*(2), 109–119.

Turner, B. S. (1997). From governmentality to risk: Some reflections on Foucault's contribution to medical sociology. In A. Petersen & R. Bunton (Eds.), *Foucault, health, and medicine* (pp. xi–xxi). London, UK: Routledge.

Twietmeyer, G. (2012). The merits and demerits of pleasure in kinesiology. *Quest, 64*(3), 177–186.

Vernon, M. (2008). *Wellbeing.* Stocksfield, UK: Acumen.

Webb, L., & MacDonald, D. (2007). Dualing with gender: Teachers' work, careers and leadership in physical education. *Gender and Education, 19*(4), 491–512.

Webb, L., McCaughtry, N., & MacDonald, D. (2004). Surveillance as a technique of power in physical education. *Sport, Education and Society, 9*(2), 207–222.

White, P. G., & Gillett, J. (1994). Reading the muscular body: A critical decoding of advertisements in Flex Magazine. *Sociology of Sport Journal, 11*, 18–39.

Wright, J. (1993). Regulation and resistance: The physical education lesson as speech genre. *Social Semiotics, 3*(1), 23–56.

Wright, J. (1996). Mapping the discourses in physical education. *Journal of Curriculum Studies, 28*(3), 331–351.

Wright, J. (1997). The construction of gendered contexts in single sex and coeducational physical education lessons. *Sport, Education and Society, 2*(1), 55–72.

Wright, J. (2000). Reconstructing gender in sport and physical education. In C. Hickey, L. Fitzclarence, & R. Matthews (Eds.), *Where the boys are: Masculinity, sport and education* (pp. 13–26). Geelong: Deakin University Press.

Wright, J., & Burrows, L. (2006). Re-conceiving ability in physical education: A social analysis. *Sport, Education and Society, 11*(3), 275–291.

Wright, J., & Dewar, A. (1997). On pleasure and pain: Women speak out about physical activity. In G. Clarke & B. Humberstone (Eds.), *Researching women and sport* (pp. 80–95). London, UK: Macmillan.

Wright, J., O'Flynn, G., & MacDonald, D. (2006). Being fit and looking healthy: Young women's and men's constructions of health and fitness. *Sex Roles, 54*(9), 707–716.

6 'Sporty', 'Fit' and 'Healthy'

The Materialisation of Pleasurable Bodies in Boys' PE

This chapter considers the role of the body in boys' performances of gender in PE. In particular, I explore how boys not only have bodies and learn about their bodies in particular gendered ways but how they are also productive and 'pleasurable' bodies—bodies as producers and the product of pleasure. Although the findings reiterate the results of previous studies in terms of boys competing to achieve idealised masculine bodies related to fitness, health and sport, they also draw attention to the fact that it is through the boys' use of their bodies in PE that bodies come to matter. That is, seen through a pleasure lens, the boys' desire to discipline/train their bodies in particular ways is more related to the performance than the display of the body in which the body is the vehicle or "the material condition" (Grosz, 1995, p. 103) for enabling pleasurable experiences. By elucidating the discursive practices of PE in this setting and employing Butler's (1993) concept of 'materialisation', I demonstrate how boys' bodies materialise as pleasurable bodies through the focus on: disciplining/training the body, the development/performance of bodily (sporting) skills/abilities and the ongoing evaluation/examination procedures related to those bodies. I argue that the discursive practices in this context, the disciplining, training, development, performance and examination of bodily (sporting) skills/abilities, produce masculine (bodily) (dis)pleasures in PE that simultaneously are productive/destructive for boys, depending on how successful they are at living up to these masculine body ideals. I conclude by suggesting that boys' bodies are integral, as it is by means of the body that masculinities, (dis)pleasures and spaces are perceived, lived and performed in PE.

The Disciplining and Training of Boys' Bodies into Productive and Pleasurable Bodies

As a way of introducing how the discursive practices of PE not only control and discipline but also materialise boys' bodies as productive and pleasurable bodies, I begin by including an extract from my logbook:

At the start of the lesson, one of the boys asks the teacher, "What are we doing today, sir?" and another one yells out, "Dodgeball, sir, please sir!" Mr Whyte replies, "Yes, dodgeball", and it seems like the whole gym erupts from boys calling out, "Yes!" Then Mr Whyte calls out, "Okay, boys, let's get moving!" The boys start lining up against one of the walls while some boys are still getting changed. Mr Whyte looks at them and says, "Hurry up you lazy bums!" . . . Mr Whyte then calls out, "Okay, go!" All of the sudden, all the boys start doing this warm-up/ fitness drill involving running back and forwards between the lines and stopping at times to do a number of push-ups and sit-ups. They seem to do this every time at the start of the PE class since everyone knows exactly what to do. The teacher hardly has to intervene at all; however, every now and then, he calls out, "Come on, you lot, faster, faster!" Some of the boys start chanting and singing military style songs while running and doing their push-ups and sit-ups. About 10–15 minutes later, they all line up against the wall again, and Mr Whyte calls out, "You and you, you are team captains". Two of the boys step away from the wall and turn around and face the rest of the group. They then start calling out the names of the other boys to come and join their teams. The boys who get picked stand up and walk proudly with their heads up high towards their team captain, with some of them high-fiving them as they walk past. By the time the last few boys get picked, the other boys have already started playing with the balls. . . . The game of dodge-ball starts, and the gym is filled with loud noises from balls bouncing everywhere; no one is safe, including myself and the boys who are not participating. . . . The game goes on right until the end of the class, and I have no idea if anyone won the game or if they were even keeping some kind of score. Right before the end, Mr Whyte calls out, "Okay, that's it for today, boys!" A final burst of noise and grunts is heard, and the boys rush over to the side of the gym to get changed back into their school uniforms. As the boys start leaving the gym, I overhear one of the boys saying, "Man, I love dodgeball, we should just do that every time in PE!"

Logbook entry 21/08/2010

Firstly, this logbook entry demonstrates how most PE classes at Kea College are broken down into two main segments: warm-up and physical activity, typically involving warm-ups/fitness drills for 5–10 minutes, followed by a popular ball game like dodgeball or rugby for the remainder of the lesson. Regardless of PE being inside or outside, this sequence is adhered to the majority of the time. This structure seems to be used in order to provide fitness benefits for the boys in the best possible way within the time that is given to them. Indeed, Foucault (1995) notes that timetabled activities such as PE classes are often broken down into smaller elements to increase the effectiveness of the time used and consequently the control of the bodies involved. The PE teachers at Kea College often would comment that "there is never enough time", which then in turn requires more 'effective' use of time (Foucault, 1995). The only exceptions to this structure include when the boys are being assessed, for instance when doing fitness tests such as the 'beep-test'. The lesson format also typically involves the teacher, Mr Whyte, nominating two or more team captains, who are then responsible for picking the teams. The common perception of PE at Kea College, as discussed in chapter four and five, revolves around making sure the boys are active as much as possible, and the use of various fitness regimes and sporting activities are assumed as the best way of achieving this. In the words of one of the other PE teachers, "It's all about getting them active for as long as possible". This focus on the accumulation of physical activity as opposed to other educational objectives can be seen as further evidence of prevailing obesity epidemic discourses in PE (e.g., Burrows, 2005; Gard & Wright, 2005; Pringle & Pringle, 2012).

One of the outwardly 'sporty' boys (James), who appears to love everything about sport and PE, talks about the warm-ups/fitness drills (Figure 6.1) at the beginning of the lessons in his individual interview:

James: I love the fitness stuff we do as a warm-up at the start of the lessons.
Göran: How come?
James: You know, getting sweaty and stuff. Gets the adrenaline going. And, you know, we kind of do the same things every time. Like running, push-ups and sit-ups, you know, to make us faster and stronger.
Göran: And does it work?
James: Yeah, totally, I mean, maybe not for everyone. But most of us like, you know, are able to do more and more push-ups and sit-ups every

Figure 6.1 A Group of Boys Doing 'Warm-Ups/Fitness Drills'.

time we do it. You know, we get stronger and stuff. It's also great having Mr Whyte yelling at us, it kind of motivates us.

Göran: Do you think everyone feels that way?

James: Well, I guess it can be quite hard for some of the boys who are not that fit and stuff. They usually don't have time to finish their exercises before we start playing games. So I guess it is a bit of a fitness test really.

James's comments highlight how this warm-up/fitness regime involves several different segments ("running", "push-ups" and "sit-ups"), which progressively over time involves more repetitions and increased durations (Foucault, 1995). The warm-up/fitness drills are organised into various durations revolving around either time or repetitions and located into a particular order. Separate exercises, such as running between the lines, push-ups and sit-ups, are then combined and progressively increase in intensity over time to include more repetitions and last for longer as the boys get older. Throughout the year spent with these two PE classes, I observed how the boys are expected to carry out more repetitions within the same time frame, thus ensuring progression ("make us faster and stronger").

Furthermore, all the boys follow the teacher's instructions ("it's also great having Mr Whyte yelling at us, it kind of motivates us") so that each separate exercise unit is performed in a concise and precise manner, making it similar to how exercises are performed in the army. The use of military style warm-ups and fitness drills, which are organised as a combination and progression, and the focus on the concise and precise use of the body throughout these activities, can be seen as aimed at the disciplining and training of the boys' bodies into certain 'fit' and 'healthy' masculine bodies (Foucault, 1995).

Incidentally, James's feeling of being 'tested' while doing these warm-ups/fitness drills draws attention to the role of examination in disciplinary practices (Foucault, 1995). The way examination practices in PE afford the boys the opportunity to display/perform bodily skills/abilities will be explored in the next section in relation to two common 'examination' practices in this setting, 'picking teams' and the 'beep-test'.

Boys' Bodies as Pleasure Machines

One frequent theme is how the boys talk about using their bodies as a 'machine' (Messner, 1992), which reinforces the Cartesian notion that the mind and body are separate. In this dichotomy, the mind is positioned as rational, logical and in control of the body but ultimately not physical. The body, conversely, is the location of desire, feeling and irrationality. As Arnold (1979) argues, this dualism is hierarchical, with the lower-order, instinctual and non-intellectual human traits defined as physical and positioned in the body, whereas higher-order, academic and spiritual development are mental and inhabit the mind.

This dualistic thinking is evident when one of the boys (Dominic) says to the teacher, "I have got a headache, sir", and Mr Whyte replies, "Running will be oaky, will not affect [the] mind, you don't need your mind for running". The mind/body split is also evident by how 'physical' pleasures in PE, according to the boys, are derived from "training and stuff" (Logan), "not just sitting there doing nothing, actually doing stuff" (Dominic), "more interesting running around than sitting in the classroom" (Sam), using the "physical instead of mental side" (Louis). From these accounts, it is demonstrated how PE is enjoyed by contrasting it to other subjects, where the "physical side" of this subject is compared to the "other subjects' quite mental side" (Louis). These physical pleasures also appear to induce certain 'sensual' pleasures. Timothy says that in PE, "you can, like, release the stress [whereas] in other classes you have to work hard". Other boys similarly articulate the best thing about PE being "letting off energy", "releasing all the energy", "stress relief".

According to Foucault (1995), the cumulative result of successful disciplinary training is the production of not only a docile but also an "efficient machine" (p. 164). That is, bodies should not only be docile but also functional bodies that can be used in productive and pleasurable ways. The boys' embodied performances of gender give evidence of how bodies are to a large extent treated as 'machines', a 'thing' that needs to be disciplined and trained to carry out specific tasks/skills needed to, for instance, play different sports. Many of the boys express feelings of pleasures in relation to these bodily practices, and some even claim this to be the role and purpose of PE, to make the body as efficient as possible by going to the gym, doing fitness drills, etc. Thus, the body is seen as an important vehicle or "the material condition" (Grosz, 1995, p. 103) for performing privileged/desirable masculinities. Indeed, the boys often referred to, as Thomas did, "training my body" as a way of being better at sports but also as a way of building self-confidence and self-esteem by "being muscly and not fat":

Thomas: I need to train my body hard to be able to go all out at sports. . . . You know, being muscly and not fat. You don't want to be fat because then you are not able to compete with the other boys and stuff. Then you get picked on. Called fat and stuff.
Göran: It that something you worry about, being called fat?
Thomas: Yeah, that is one of the main reasons why I always want to do sports and PE and stuff.
Göran: So do you feel pressured into doing sports and PE, then, to avoid being overweight?
Thomas: Yeah, I guess it can be quite difficult at times since sometimes you just want to lie on the couch and watch TV and eat chips [laughter].

Thomas's comments can be seen to give further evidence of how boys police and discipline themselves, through the workings of disciplinary power (Foucault, 1995), to achieve or maintain a specific shape, size and muscularity. Thomas's experiences of the pressures involved in living up to these cultural and social expectations of masculine bodies particularly draw attention to Foucault's conceptualisation of self-surveillance as also importantly involving the recognition that practices of self-policing are normal and not reserved for those people who are perceived as 'abnormal'. Understood through Foucault's (1978) principle of (self-)surveillance, boys such as Thomas can be seen as being 'trained' in monitoring and participating in particular normalising bodily practices.

However, Thomas's account of his bodily experiences in PE can also be understood through a pleasure lens, which suggests that the desire of boys like himself to train their bodies is related to the performance rather than the display of the body. By training their bodies, they are able to "go all out" and perform and "compete better with the other boys" when engaged in various PE (sporting) activities. In this sense, the body is not only an important vehicle for displaying or performing privileged/desirable masculinities but also in enabling pleasurable experiences.

In finding pleasures in and control over their bodies, boys such as James and Thomas embody an understanding of themselves that supports ongoing engagement in physical activity by conforming to many of the dominant and productive discourses related to fitness, health, sport and masculinity. In this sense, the disciplining and training of the body can be seen as a source of masculine (or feminine) bodily pleasures. Or, in other words, boys' bodies materialise as pleasurable bodies in PE through discursive practices related to the disciplining and training of the masculine body. These findings draw attention to the centrality of the body in the performances of gender and how boys' bodies are performed through pleasurable physical/bodily experiences. The intersection of bodies, pleasures and gender is therefore useful in terms of gaining an understanding of boys' bodily experience in PE and the potential of different bodily performances to produce pleasures.

The boys also draw attention to the multiple and competing understandings and experiences of bodily (dis)pleasures in PE. These findings importantly remind us that pleasure/displeasure is not to be seen as a rigid binary (see chapter one). For instance, some boys experience sensual (dis)pleasures through being physically active. Peter (15 years old, Asian, not involved in any sport), in contrast to James above, does not like PE when they do too much running: "I hate sweating . . . when [I] start sweating, [it] doesn't feel very good". Other bodily (dis)pleasures are related to pain and the body. Jonathan said, "I don't like rugby and volleyball. . . . It kind of hurts my hand, and rugby [is] too much contact . . . not enjoyable". Conversely, bodily pleasures are also derived through pain, from inflicting or being in pain. In the video clip represented by the still image in Figure 6.2, one of the boys laughs and says, "Ahhh, Joseph, that's on camera!"

Bodily (dis)pleasures are not something inherent in physical activities or experienced the same in our bodies because pleasure, like displeasure, is shaped by discourse and relations of power (Foucault, 1978, 1985; Pringle, 2010; Pronger, 2000). The boys' accounts related to their bodies as

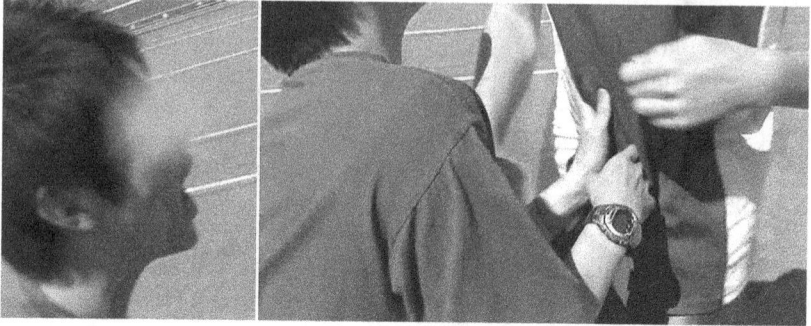

Figure 6.2 Bodily (dis)pleasures—Inflicting and Being in Pain.

machines highlight the blurring between (bodily) (dis)pleasures because the same activities and the bodily responses that ensue are experienced and interpreted differently. Some boys derive pleasure from, for instance, being in pain or sweating, whereas others find this experience less pleasurable.

Although all the boys have bodies that experience both pain and pleasures, the way these experiences are understood or come to matter is both multiply and discursively constructed (Butler, 1993). For instance, when it comes to inflicting and being in pain, some boys, as discussed in chapter five, through discourse of sport and masculinity, see this as a natural part of learning how to play contact sports such as rugby, whereas other boys, such as Jonathan (above), find this focus on hard, and at times painful, physical contact less enjoyable. For some boys, such as James (above), sweating is interpreted through discourses of fitness/health as a desirable response from the body because it means the body is working hard and getting fitter/healthier. Such understandings of sweating can be seen as the result of the workings of bio-power and governmentality (Foucault, 1991) related to neoliberal ideas about the importance and the individual's responsibility of achieving a 'fit' and 'healthy' population (Markula & Pringle, 2006; McDermott, 2007; Rose, 1999). However, for others, such as Peter, this bodily response is undesirable because it makes him feel uncomfortable. From an educational viewpoint, it would have been interesting to discuss this further with Peter and unpack why he does not feel good when sweating because understanding the role of sweating as a 'natural' response to the body being in movement for an extended period of time can be seen as an important learning outcome for students in PE. On the other hand, the reason for Peter sweating could also be related to other factors such as being nervous/anxious about being on display in front of the other boys, who he might feel are much fitter than him. In chapter seven, I address further the (dis)pleasures boys (and girls) derive through certain activities in PE.

In the next two sections, I focus on how the discursive practices of PE in this setting, related to the development/performance and examination of bodily (sporting) skills and abilities, shape boys' embodied performances of gender and their articulations with (dis)pleasures.

The Development and Performance of Bodily (Sporting) Skills/Abilities

One way in which the boys' bodies come to matter or materialise as pleasurable bodies in this PE setting is through a focus on the development and performance of bodily (sporting) skills/abilities. Indeed, one of the most common articulations of PE coheres around the development of bodily (sporting) skills and abilities to enhance performance. Fun and pleasure is closely associated with this 'performance' discourse (Tinning, 2010). In fact, sporting practices dominate talk of pleasurable bodily experiences within PE at Kea College, where the public display of the body and skill in a competitive environment (Garrett, 2004) is particularly significant.

For instance, one frequent observation is how the PE lessons revolve around working on developing different sporting skills (i.e., 'digging' in volleyball). It is not just the teacher who is helping the boys (left image, Figure 6.3), but the boys themselves are also often seen helping each other (right image, Figure 6.3).

During one of the focus groups, when watching the video clip of the boys practicing their volleyball skills (represented by the still images in Figure 6.3), Sam says, "It's great how we always help each other get better and stuff". Sam's comment about how 'great' it is that the boys help each other develop bodily (sporting) skills/abilities supports Kretchmar's (2005) assertion that satisfaction or pleasures also can be found through

Figure 6.3 Helping Each Other Working on Bodily (Sporting) Skills/Abilities.

helping others. The boys are often seen or heard praising each other for their efforts, such as "Ah, that was a mean ball, Adan!" (Dominic) and "Ah, good shot, Joseph!" (Matthew). Developing skill/ability is also seen as a natural progression over time. For instance, when I ask the boys during the focus groups what it is like having PE with the older boys, Jacob says, "Oh, it's more fun because they are better than us, so we can play tougher".

Furthermore, for a number of the boys in my study, PE provides an opportunity to display physical competency, which often translates into elevated/heightened confidence and peer group status. That is, it helps them give evidence of the public display of skill/ability and the physical competence needed. Pleasures in particular seem to be derived through the experience of personal competency. This finding resonates with other studies that link skilful action to the pleasures of 'flow' (O'Reilly, Tompkins, & Gallant, 2001). For those boys like Ben, pleasures are gained from presenting physical skills/abilities: "I don't know, it's just something that I can do, so that's why I like doing it". For others, like Matthew, pleasures are derived through a sense of bodily strength, control and discipline, where boys conform to traditional constructions of masculinity as fit and strong: "I feel strong, you know, in control and stuff" (Matthew). This is further highlighted by the dialogue below, between a group of boys watching a video clip of a penalty shoot-out in a game of indoor soccer (represented by the still images in Figure 6.4). Dominant discourses surrounding the masculine body play an important role in these boys' constructions of privileged/desirable masculinities in this context:

Ryan: Wow, look at Matthew, he kicks the ball so hard! [Top image]
Scott: Yeah, he is awesome at soccer.
Ryan: Yeah, he is pretty awesome at all sports. He is definitely one of the sporty ones!
Scott: I went and watched one of his games and, man, there were so many hot girls there cheering on him.
Scott: Not that I am one of the non-sporty ones, but, man, I wish I was more like Matthew.
Ryan: Yeah, me too.

In this focus group, Matthew's high status as a successful soccer player and someone who is embodying the athletic and skilled sporting body is highlighted. One way of interpreting this conversation is that these boys construct meanings about the ideal boy's body by identifying a variety of body types, such as muscular, strong, athletic and skilled bodies. For instance, when asked to elaborate on boy's body ideals, one of the boys from the focus group above (Scott, 14 years old, European/Pākehā, active in multiple team and individual sports) says:

Scott: Well, I think guys should be like muscular but also toned, you know. Being able to do lots of different sports, you need to have the right body and stuff. You know, being able to be aggressive and competitive in the games. Then I guess you become more popular, as well, with the girls since they like guys like that. I guess it is a combination of having the right body size, being muscly and sporty.

Size, muscularity and athletic physicality are fundamental masculine features, providing a high status and popular form of masculinity among boys in the school culture (Renold, 2004). What Tinning and Glasby (2002) call the 'cult of the body' is thus clearly linked to privileged masculinities at this school. Scott also draws attention to the convergence of gender, biological sex and sexuality in which heterosexual masculinities are closely aligned

Figure 6.4 A Penalty Shoot-Out in a Game of Indoor Soccer.

with particular bodily appearances (Nayak & Kehily, 1996). In particular, Scott's observation that "they like guys like that" can be linked to the production of masculine and feminine bodies in a heteronormative process (Disch & Kane, 1996). Some boys, in their quest to conform to the 'normal' body, aim to develop muscularity by engaging in athletics or fitness exercise. Being able to embody the 'sporty' boy who is seen as tough and competitive reaffirms a privileged status both in terms of masculinity and heterosexuality. The particular 'truth' that is being constructed here through the workings of discourse is that the ideal masculine body is a body that is athletic, skilful and desirable, in front of both the other boys and the opposite sex.

On the other hand, another way of interpreting this statement is that boys such as Ryan (14 years old, European/Pākehā, active in multiple team and individual sports) and Scott identify the necessity of physical competence to sporting ability and see that possessing this physical competence means that you are able to use this as a way of gaining social acceptance and status. The productive side of the boys' masculine identities is related to the physical skills/abilities (experiences) of their bodies (Gilroy, 1989). That is, the performances in and through the boys' bodies is inextricably linked to their performances of gender (Grosz, 1992). As a significant space for the development of physical (sporting) skills and abilities, PE then becomes a crucial site for boys to develop their physical potential (Gilroy, 1997) or physicality (Garrett, 2004), as linked to the performance of confident, skilled and able masculine bodies. Through PE experiences that afford the boys with opportunities to experience themselves as physically 'skilled' or 'able' by developing bodily skills/abilities, strength and muscularity, the space of PE materialises as a productive and pleasurable space for some boys.

However, other boys are unsure and find it difficult to express the source of their attraction to the development and performance of bodily (sporting) abilities and skills. When discussing his own performance in some of the video clips, one of the boys (Zack) says:

Zack: Oh no, I keep stuffing up!
Göran: What do you mean?
Zack: I keep hitting the ball out! [shows me what he is doing wrong]

Some boys' frustration with their lack of bodily skills/abilities is also shown in the visual data, such as in Figure 6.5, where Joseph (left image) has just played a 'bad' shot in badminton.

When realising that he is being filmed by one of the other boys, Joseph says to the boy behind the camera, "Why are you filming me, I am useless at badminton?" Showing 'lack' of bodily skills/abilities by, for instance, missing the ball in front of peers and teachers is a particularly embarrassing and less pleasurable (displeasurable) experience. When I ask Andrew (the boy in the right image, Figure 6.5) about this, he says:

Figure 6.5 Lack of Bodily Skills/Abilities.

Andrew: It was so embarrassing.
Göran: What do you mean?
Andrew: You know, completely missing the shot like that and on top of
            that in front of one of the [student] teachers.

Indeed, comparing a certain performance with that of others is also a common feature of the boys' PE lessons. For instance, while watching a video clip of the boys doing warm-ups/fitness drills, Lorenzo says, "I'm doing it twice, but I'm still doing it faster than you, Joseph [laughter]", and in some other video clips, the boys are heard saying, "Caleb, are you dominating?" and "Oh, Dominic, you must be the worst goalie in history". In this sense, the boys' development and performance of bodily (sporting) skills/abilities are also evaluated and ranked. The language used by these boys can be seen to sort out the hierarchy between the boys and their bodily performances. However, the competing and comparing of bodily (sporting) skills/abilities is not necessarily seen as something problematic for the boys. For instance, in one of the video clips showing the boys playing badminton (represented by the still image in Figure 6.6), Dominic (the boy in the right corner of the image) calls out:

Dominic: This is what happens when you verse [Xavier] in badminton
             [laughter].

The boy referred to here is Xavier (14 years old, Asian, active in one individual sport), who is really good at badminton (at the time ranked highly in New Zealand for his age-group). What I remember from this particular scenario is that although the other boys acknowledged Xavier's skills and experience in this game, they also took great pleasure from challenging him even though they were likely to lose. When I ask Dominic what it is like playing against Xavier he says:

Figure 6.6 Playing Someone 'Mean at Badminton'.

Dominic: Well, he is pretty mean at badminton and stuff, but I like the challenge.
Göran: Why is that?
Dominic: Makes you better, and you are also not too worried about losing since in PE it is just about having fun, you know.

In this way, PE can be seen as a safe environment where boys can challenge each other without all the pressures of competitive sport. Indeed, the fact that "PE is more relaxed and less competitive than organised sports" (Thomas) is also a recurring theme in the boys' accounts of their PE experiences. Dominic's comment is also further substantiated by how most of the video clips recorded by the boys in my study portray boys who are particularly good at different sports, and very few represent boys in a derogatory way.

Despite PE being seen as less competitive than organised sport, the pleasures the boys derive from, for instance, scoring a point in badminton (left image, Figure 6.7) or the joint celebration that often comes afterwards (right image, Figure 6.7) in the form of hugging and touching is another frequent theme in the visual data.

Figure 6.7 Boys 'Celebrating'.

However, for some boys, these pleasures are derived from resisting dominant competitive sporting practices such as scoring and winning. For instance, when talking about playing volleyball in one of the focus groups, the following conversation takes place:

Göran: How important is the scoring?
Jacob: No, not really. If we have some good rallies, it feels like we have actually achieved something. It seems a bit harder to keep the ball in the air rather than slamming it into the ground.
Timothy: Yeah, the three shot rule is good, when you have to pass the ball around three times first . . . then you have more rallies.

Jacob's and Timothy's comments can be seen to give further evidence of how the boys gain pleasures from demonstrating (sporting) skill/ability. Their comments also draw attention to how it is the process (having 'good/more' rallies) rather than the outcome (i.e., scoring/winning) that is important. Jacob's comment in particular highlights the pleasures derived from "actually [having] achieved something" since it is "harder to keep the ball in the air rather than slamming it into the ground". That is, whereas some boys derive pleasures from conforming/adhering to notions of competition and performance in PE, other boys find pleasures through engagement in and/or accomplishment/fulfilment of the activity itself in a way that is more satisfying/rewarding than, for instance, scoring and winning. These findings highlight how the materialisation of pleasurable bodies through the development and performance of (bodily) sporting skills and abilities in PE is a complex process. Pleasures are found in multiple and at times competing ways through the same practices/activities in PE.

The development, performance, competing and comparing of bodily (sporting) skills and abilities in this PE setting also translated into two common teaching practices, 'picking teams' and the 'beep-test'.

The Examination of Pleasurable Masculine Bodies

The common teaching practices of picking teams and the beep-test are two important practices in this PE context through which boys' embodied performances of gender articulate with (dis)pleasures. Through 'picking teams' and the 'beep-test', boys' bodies materialise as pleasurable bodies because these two discursive practices provide the boys with particular public (and pleasurable) opportunities to present and construct themselves as having the 'right' or desirable masculine bodies (i.e., fit, skilled, able bodies). Conversely, other boys' inability or unwillingness to conform to or live up to skilful, able (productive) masculine bodies induced certain bodily (dis)pleasures. Indeed, I would argue that both 'picking teams' and the 'beep-test' can be seen as representing questionable or even 'poor' PE practice. Denzin (2010) stresses the importance of identifying key moments in which the 'sting of memories' is felt and, indeed, some of the boys in my study express the discomfort they experience through these two teaching practices. In this sense, these two practices can also be seen as technologies of 'examination' (Foucault, 1995), which serve as evidence of how (un)successful the boys have been at developing/performing the desirable bodily (sporting) skills/abilities described earlier in the chapter.

'Picking Teams'

While watching a video clip of the boys picking teams for a game of indoor soccer (represented by the still images in Figure 6.8), one of the boys (Campbell) says:

Figure 6.8 Boys 'Picking Teams' for a Game of Indoor Soccer.

Campbell: Look how when we are picking teams how everyone good gets
            picked first.
Göran: And that is okay?
Campbell: Yeah, makes the teams more fair than if you go 1,2,1,2 . . . fair
            teams are important.

Campbell's (14 years old, European/Pākehā, active in multiple team and individual sports) account of this teaching practice highlights how 'picking teams' "makes the teams more fair". Making 'fair teams' is important to the boys, and their enjoyment of the PE lessons is partly dependent on this. This observation is further substantiated when the picking of teams is contrasted with other ways of getting into teams, such as using numbering (e.g., '1,2,1,2'). One of the boys (Zack) explains, "I like the captain picking better because, like, otherwise you might have all the good people in one team and all the bad people in one team . . . so you can get fair teams". However, other boys, such as Timothy, think differently: "I prefer numbers since I usually get picked last and that kind of stinks . . . and he [Mr Whyte] can make the teams even too". That is, for some boys, the picking of teams is important because of the pleasures induced from having fair/equal teams, whereas for boys such as Timothy, this practice is linked to the less pleasurable experience of being picked last and, thus, constructed as undesirable within this context. This teaching practice can be seen as one of those highly gendered 'high stakes' moments in PE in which boys are picked according to bodily (sporting) skills and abilities, where traditional masculine (bodily) values are sought after and constructed as desirable. The 'sporty', 'fit' and 'skilled/able' desirable boys are picked before the 'non-sporty', 'unfit' and 'less skilled/able' undesirable boys. When the same video clip as above is shown in one of the other focus groups, the following conversation takes place:

Mitchell: Ah, look, I'm zooming in on all the nerds who are being picked
            last!
            [Laughter]
Göran: What do you mean?
Mitchell: Well, look at them, they are just sitting there! [He demonstrates
            how the boys who are being picked last sit with their arms
            crossed, leaning against the wall of the gym and with their heads
            facing the ground]. No one wants them on their team because
            they don't really care about PE, they'd rather be doing their
            homework.
Göran: So who gets picked first then?
Mitchell: All the popular ones, you know, the sporty ones.
Duncan: Yeah, the ones who are the fittest and strongest.

Even though the process of picking teams in this manner can be related to the contemporary 'performance discourse' in PE (Tinning, 2010), in which team captains are simply tactically choosing players with the aim of securing the best possible team, this practice can also be interpreted through a gendered lens. Through the picking of teams, boys' bodies materialise as producers and the product of pleasures when their performances of gender articulate with the discourses of PE in this setting related to fitness, health, sport and masculinity. In particular, it could be argued that this practice adds to the ongoing process of evaluating masculine identities and pleasures through the body.

Mitchell and Duncan, who can both be described as belonging to the popular sporty group and therefore among the first boys to be picked regardless of sport, for instance, draw attention to the hierarchising of boys and their bodies associated with picking teams. Mitchell's and Duncan's statements in particular highlight how those boys who are picked last are publicly displayed as the less physically competent and less popular boys because of their bodies being perceived as 'weaker' and 'less fit' masculine bodies (Davison, 2000). There is also little these boys can do to escape from this humiliating position. Indeed, the gendered distribution of bodies in space (Webb & Macdonald, 2007) is also evident in this scenario. The sporty able bodies are standing up tall and occupying space, whereas the non-sporty less able bodies are low to the ground and taking up a minimal amount of space. Mark (15 years old, European/Pākehā, not involved in any sport), who has developed a rather negative body image and a feeling of being physically deficient, also comments on this:

Mark: I just don't know why the team captains always have to stand up and the rest of us sit down. I mean, then when all the good ones get picked first and they get to stand up as well, the rest of us are stuck sitting down on the floor. It is so embarrassing, and you feel like you are useless. Sometimes I just want to run away and hide.

Techniques of power are therefore evident also in this situation through the gendered placement of the boys' bodies in certain positions during the procedure of picking teams. Mark went on to describe how these kinds of experiences often discouraged him from participating in PE. Consequently, consideration of the effects of the examination and distribution of bodies may help in understanding why some boys are pushed into marginal positions in PE.

However, some boys do not simply conform to this practice but in different ways seek to resist it. For instance, James tells me about his way of resisting the way picking teams ends up sorting skilled/able (desirable) and less skilled/able (undesirable) masculine sporting bodies into different teams:

James: Well, I always try to pick teams differently from some of the other boys. I think it is really unfair how some people always get picked last.
Göran: So how do you pick teams?

James: Well, I usually try to pick teams so that we get a team that works together well. Because that is more important than picking all the best people, you know, the sporty ones. If you have too many like that, people just don't work as a team. Too many people trying to show off their strength and skills and stuff.

Göran: Can you explain more?

James: Well, you know, it is better having people that have different skills. And, I mean, just because you don't look all strong and fit and stuff doesn't mean you can't be good at stuff. Like one of the guys who always gets picked last because he is overweight is, like, super good with coming up with strategies and stuff for the team. I always pick him first.

In this interview, James states that he picks "teams differently from some of the other boys" and indicates that there are other things that matter more when picking teams than bodily attributes and skills/abilities. James's 'mode of subjection' can be seen as being made up of the belief that it is crucial for him to start recognising and working to include different people in his team. He suggests that having a team consisting of a mixture of people with unique skills and talents often results in a more successful team. In this way, he proposes that the success of a team is dependent on the recognition of differences within the team. Picking "a team that works together well", in James's view, trumps picking people solely based on sporting ability associated with, for instance, the strong and skilled sporting body. James in particular draws attention to how bodily characteristics do not always determine skill/ability in the context of PE and sport. Other skills and abilities, such as strategical awareness, can be more important and crucial to a well-functioning team. James questions the association between bodies and sporting skills/abilities, where in particular the archetypical sporting masculine body can lead to negative consequences for a team, such as people being egocentric and "trying to show off".

The 'telos', or broad existential goal, of James seems to be a desire to show respect, regardless of bodily appearance and skills/abilities or, in the words of Foucault (1988, cited in Pringle & Hickey, 2010), to "allow the games of power to be played with a minimum of domination" (p. 130). That is, in this exercise of power, and by being one of the privileged/desirable sporty boys, James uses this power to minimise the effect that dominant discourses of the masculine sporting body have on those less privileged/undesirable non-sporty boys. In this sense, he can be seen to perform gender not only differently but also more "ethical masculinities" (Pringle & Hickey, 2010, p. 133), which in turn challenges dominant notions of desirable masculine identities and bodies in this particular PE context. James's comments can also be seen to support the argument that diversity and multiplicity should be acknowledged and accepted as important parts of sports and PE (Hickey & Fitzclarence, 1999; Hickey, Fitzclarence, & Matthews, 1998).

The 'Beep-Test'

Fitness testing, such as the commonly used 'beep-test' at Kea College, can be seen to provide the boys with a space and context in which knowledge and learning about bodies, fitness and health is constructed (Wrench & Garrett, 2008). This assessment technique, which ranks people's fitness performances in relation to a standardised scale, is also in keeping with Foucault's (1973) notion of the use of statistical norms against which to measure people's behaviour in order to determine normalcy or deviancy. Foucault (1995) suggests that on almost every occasion, disciplinary practices are often adopted in response to particular needs, such as a "renewed outbreak of certain epidemic diseases" (p. 138). In terms of what is taught in school-based PE, Burrows (2005) argues that New Zealand educators appear to be particularly influenced by a widespread set of concerns about the youth, such as the 'obesity epidemic'. This focus on improving fitness levels based on discourses of the obesity epidemic enhances pressures to succeed and transforms boys' embodied performances of gender into a form of bodily test or display. The boys' responses draw attention to how the testing of bodily skills and abilities brings with it feelings, experiences and expressions of masculine bodily (dis)pleasures in PE.

While watching a video clip of the boys doing the beep-test (represented by the still image in Figure 6.9) during the focus groups, one of the boys (Mitchell) explains:

Mitchell: I quite like tests like the beep-test because I know I am pretty good at it. However, if I wasn't fit enough, I don't think I would like doing it.

Göran: Why is that?

Mitchell: Well, you know, when I do the beep-test, I feel really good about myself, you know, having a fit body and stuff, which makes you more popular and stuff, but if I wasn't [fit] it would be quite embarrassing, I think.

Figure 6.9 A Group of Boys Lined up for the 'Beep-Test'.

For participants in my study such as Mitchell, the structure of the testing environment is a significant factor in defining their pleasurable bodily experiences. Being fit and doing well at the beep-test allows Mitchell to experience his body in positive and pleasurable ways, which also importantly serves as a high status marker among the peer group. For boys such as Mitchell, who experience success, the 'beep-test' provides yet another particular pleasurable and public opportunity to present and construct themselves as having the 'right' or desirable masculine body.

One of the other boys, Zack, who describes himself as 'overweight', talks about how his teachers were initially supportive of his willingness to improve his fitness and lose weight by requesting that the class spend more time on fitness testing/assessments such as the 'beep-test'. However, over time, he has become aware that he is something of a 'problem' student in relation to both his 'failure' to make any significant changes to his fitness/body weight and his refusal to participate fully in the PE lessons:

Zack: Since I never seemed to get any fitter or lose any weight, my teachers would kind of shake their heads at me or just sigh. I think they sort of saw me as a bit of a problem. I have kind of given up on ever getting a better body, and I don't really like PE anymore since it keeps reminding me of this failure.

Göran: So have you stopped wanting to do more beep-tests then?

Zack: Yeah, whenever we do tests like that in PE, I now make sure I bring a note from my dad saying that I can't participate in PE on that day.

Göran: So how do you feel about PE now then?

Zack: Well, I still like it, but it is hard sometimes because it makes me feel a bit left out, and I guess I have lost a bit of self-confidence altogether but especially in PE.

Zack's experiences of the beep-test highlight how those boys who are not able to live up to desirable images of masculine bodies when engaged in examination practices such as the beep-test are significantly affected in more negative ways. For instance, the teachers' shaking of their heads and sighs importantly serve as an indication to Zack that he has failed to make any real changes to his fitness and body weight. The shaking heads and sighs are also examples of how techniques of normalisation in the Foucauldian sense occur in everyday life. The message of getting fit and losing weight is presented as a form of 'common sense' in the context of PE, where it is about 'doing what's best for your own good' (Foucault, 1995). Zack's story is also one that demonstrates how certain discursive practices such as the beep-test may actually contribute to or underpin diminishing interest in PE in particular and physical activity in general (Cale & Harris, 2005). The dislike and humiliation experienced by Zack during the beep-test has resulted in him adopting particular avoidance practices (e.g., the note from his dad).

Other boys are also bothered by the public display in which their performances and the standards they achieved are painfully evident and deemed to be lacking. Through the panoptic gaze, they internalised a deep sense of inadequacy that contributed to a construction of themselves as physically deficient. Mark, another boy who, like Zack, appears to struggle with his physical self-confidence, tells me a similar story of his less pleasurable experiences of the beep-test in PE:

Mark: I always feel like crap when doing the beep-test since so many of the other boys are fitter than me. I find it really hard that everyone is watching you, you know, all that pressure to keep going. If you stop too early, you feel like a loser. Stopping first is like being in hell.

Mark's statement draws attention to the fact that dropping out early or even first seems to be particularly humiliating and a public demonstration of an 'unfit' and undesirable masculine body. As Burrows (2000, 2005) points out, some boys experience clear disadvantages because of prevalent attitudes and beliefs about the importance of fit, healthy and sporty bodies in PE. Discourses of fitness, health and sport, through techniques of normalisation, (re)produce notions of the 'normal' and 'abnormal' masculine body in PE, which contributes to a hierarchy of masculine bodies and unequal power relations. On top of that, some boys, such as Zack and Mark, have additional self-esteem and confidence issues related to their body image to deal with (Drummond, 2003; Grogan & Richards, 2002). Zack's and Mark's bodily inadequacies or (dis)pleasures are therefore related to having a body that deviates from the 'archetypical' male body (Drummond, 2003). At the same time as some boys derive pleasures in and through the body and spaces of PE, for others this discursive practice materialises their bodies as undesirable or less pleasurable (displeasurable) masculine bodies.

These combined effects can have severe long-term consequences for how Zack, Mark and other boys view themselves as embodied, masculine, physical educated beings (Macdonald & Tinning, 2003; McCuaig & Tinning, 2010) because 'unfit' and 'overweight' bodies can be seen as representing/embodying 'failed' masculine identities (Mosher, 2001). The way that Zack's and Mark's bodies materialise through the discursive practice of the beep-test in this setting highlights the sensitivity of boys' bodily experiences in PE and how the effects of power are experienced at the most intimate level of self (Grosz, 1994). That is, the lived experiences of their bodies through the beep-test as lacking in physical corporeality have consequences for their embodied masculine subjectivity.

Focusing on improving fitness levels and attendant fitness through fitness testing is a problematic concept, especially because multi-stage tests like the beep-test were originally designed for use with adults and elite athletes (Cale & Harris, 2005). Two of the boys (Chris and James) explain to me how they are actively involved in seeking to challenge fitness testing and examination procedures in their PE, such as the beep-test. Chris and James in particular speak about advocating for alternative ways of doing the beep-test:

Göran: What do you think of fitness tests like the beep-test?

Chris: Well, I think most of us really hate it. I mean, some might like it, like the ones who get the highest score. But, I mean, why do we have to do this test?

James: Yeah, I don't understand that either, I guess we get a bit fitter and stuff, but not really because we never really do anything to improve our running and stamina and stuff. It is only people who do this at sports who get better and fitter.

Chris: I think it would be better if we all got to do it by ourselves without everyone else looking, and then we would just try and improve our own score every time. That way, it would be less of a competition, and people wouldn't have to feel so bad about stopping early.

James: Yeah, and I think we should do other fitness tests as well that help us improve in lots of different ways.

Göran: What do you mean?

Chris: I mean the beep-test is only good for running and stuff, but I think we should include other things like, you know, being able to jump, run, do rolls, flips, hand-stands and that sort of stuff.

James: Yeah, so more people can show what they are good at. Just because you are not good at the beep-test doesn't mean you can't do lots of other things.

Göran: But so you all think that various tests are still good then?

Chris: Yeah, they kind of motivate you a bit, I guess. But they shouldn't be a competition between us but more a way for everyone to improve. You know, for themselves. It should be more an individual thing, I guess, where people can set their own goals and stuff. I think PE should be more like that.

What is particularly interesting about this conversation is that Chris and James seem to acknowledge the importance of various testing regimes but believe that this should be done as "an individual thing" instead of as a competition and collectively. The boys state that testing "kind of motivates" them but only if the boys themselves are able to set goals and be responsible for achieving these. In this sense, they question both the normalising and examination nature of discursive practices such as the beep-test since they are pointing towards the need for recognising the diversity or multiplicity of physicalities in PE that excludes the ranking and ordering of boys and their bodies (Wrench & Garrett, 2008).

Bodily (Sporting) Skills/Abilities and (dis)Pleasures

The pleasures derived from the disciplining, training, development, performance and examination of bodily (sporting) skills and abilities can be read in different ways. For instance, Gard (2008) argues that proficiency and pleasure are two different things and that, contrary to commonly held beliefs, it is often proficiency (socially defined) that precedes physical pleasure. He gives the example of how a tall child may decide that he enjoys basketball once he has discovered that his height gives him a competitive advantage and access to the prestige that accrues from sporting prowess in our society. Many of the boys in my study, as evidenced above, offer examples of this because the source of their pleasures is mainly derived from being able to display/show off their bodily (sporting) skills and abilities.

Although I agree with Wright (2004), who asserts that mastery as well as enjoyment are both necessary and complimentary in terms of the focus on skills in PE, I also wonder what the interrelationship of these two is. For instance, there is the risk of complacency among PE teachers, as it is easy to forget that the activities they teach need to be experienced positively in the first place, or conditions need to be provided so that they can be experienced positively (Wellard, 2012). The findings presented in this chapter draw attention to how the discursive practices of PE simultaneously produce experiences of bodily (dis)pleasures. Indeed, Pringle (2010) claims that "many students are not currently gaining a love for movement in their PE experiences" (p. 130). For instance, some boys (as discussed in the previous chapter) comment that they do not spend a lot of time developing and practicing their bodily (sporting) skills/abilities in PE but that they are assumed to already possess a certain proficiency level in this regard due to stereotypical assumptions of boys as inherently 'sporty'. However, taking into consideration the importance of the development and performance of bodily skills and abilities that the boys signal in this chapter, it could be claimed that PE can and should contribute significantly to the materialisation of pleasurable bodies in PE.

Based on these findings, it could be argued that it is the development and performance of bodily skills/abilities that are significant factors for boys' enjoyment and pleasurable experiences in PE. That is, the boys' accounts of pleasurable bodily experiences in PE draw attention to how the materialisation of pleasurable bodies in this context is dependent on the teaching/ practices of bodily skills/abilities or 'kinaesthetic' skills (Stothart, 2005). Stothart (2005) argues that "the raw pleasure of physical skill learning (sometimes referred to as 'skill thrill') moving towards mastery . . . is the home turf of the physical educator, the basic building blocks of a balanced physical education programme" (pp. 98–99). Just as I discussed in relation to space in chapter four, boys need to learn how to enjoy their bodies. In other words, bodily pleasures need to be 'cultivated' (Vernon, 2008) through the practices of PE.

Twietmeyer (2012) argues that "although play, games, and sport are not magical founts of automatic pleasure production, they do contain the seeds of pleasure" (p. 183). Based on the boys' accounts above, I am inclined to agree with Twietmeyer (2012), who further argues:

> The joys of soccer are only open to those initiates who have rubbed shoulders with the rules, skills, institutions, and traditions that maintain the game. One cannot find pleasure in "a diving header" or a beautifully crossed "corner kick" unless one has been taught the necessary skills. In turn, skill development relies upon a vibrant soccer culture. As such, the inherent pleasures of soccer are fragile.
>
> (p. 18)

Similarly, I would argue that the 'inherent' pleasures of boys' PE are fragile and that unless boys already possess the skills needed to fully engage with whatever the content of PE might be, they need to be taught them. Based on these findings, it seems that making the teaching of bodily skills/abilities (rather than, for instance, fighting obesity) a priority again might enable more boys (and girls) to experience pleasures or the 'skill thrill' in PE. Although as discussed in the previous chapter, the focus on learning skills through repetition/practice might be seen by the students as restricting pleasures, it can still be productive in terms of enabling and giving them access to pleasurable experiences in the future.

Just as Gard (2008) talks about how a tall child starts enjoying basketball, the boys in my study draw attention to how the disciplining and training of their bodies are important in terms of enabling/giving access to discursively constructed pleasures. The boys' bodies can in this way be seen as a condition of possibility, the material condition of subjectivity (Grosz, 1995), or what Foucault (1972) refers to as 'a surface of emergence' of discourses about the masculine body and pleasures prevailing in this PE setting.

The space of PE can also be seen as an important condition of possibility for these boys. The fact that, as discussed in chapter four, this setting is largely constructed and produced as sporting space means that the boys' embodied performances of gender and the pleasures they derive from these are influenced by the material features of the PE spaces, such as the old gym, the new gym, the rugby field, the soccer field and the multipurpose sports field. The architecture of these spaces, as undeniably designed and constructed based on the spaces and lines needed for sports such as rugby, volleyball, tennis, badminton and soccer, shape what kind of performances of gender and bodies are constructed/produced as privileged, productive and pleasurable. That is, in analysing the processes of materialisation, we need to account for both human and non-human bodies (Butler, 1993; Massey, 1994). It could be argued that it is the spaces of PE, along with the discourses/discursive practices operating within this particular setting, that are influential in the materialisation of pleasurable bodies in boys' PE.

The simultaneous and relational (Grosz, 1994) or mutually articulated (Massey, 1994) nature of pleasures, spaces and bodies is a complex issue. Further theoretical advancements based on the lived experiences of people are needed in order to better our understanding of this complex interrelationship and its consequences for understanding the co-construction of gender, pleasures, spaces and bodies in PE. (This will be further explored in the next chapter.)

In summary, this chapter has shown how boys' bodies become meaningful or start to matter through the discursive practices of PE. In particular, the findings highlight how the productive effects of power related to the discursive practices in this PE setting not only produce certain bodies but also the pleasures of those bodies (Foucault, 1980). The discursive practices described in this chapter, the disciplining, training, development, performance and examination of bodily (sporting) skills and abilities, enable/produce masculine bodily pleasures in PE. Although the findings presented in this chapter demonstrate how PE can be seen as a disciplinary 'machine', which influences how boys inhabit and experience their bodies in different ways by progressively exercising/shaping boys into docile and functional bodies (Foucault, 1995) that above all are fit, healthy and sporty masculine bodies, I argue that the same discursive practices also materialise boys' bodies as productive and pleasurable bodies. Boys' bodies are not only inscribed with (gendered/ sexualised) knowledge (Gard, 2008; McLaren, 1991), but they are also productive bodies that contribute to boys' participation in and enjoyment of PE. I suggest that the body is integral, as it is by means of the body that masculinities, pleasures and spaces are perceived, lived and performed in PE.

Conversely, some boys articulate anxieties and feelings of inadequacy in relation to bodily skills and abilities. In particular, they give evidence of the (dis)pleasures involved in not having a skilled/able (sporting) body and the failures they have experienced in trying to live up to these masculine body ideals. However, others resist these masculine body ideals by questioning the role/purpose of PE and the impact of certain (discursive) teaching practices. In particular, they articulate a desire that finding pleasures in, about and through movement cannot exclusively be about attaining the ideal masculine (sporting) body and that laying the foundations for a life full of diverse movement pleasures needs to be at the forefront in PE.

The findings presented in this chapter draw further attention to complexities surrounding gender, (dis)pleasures, bodies and spaces because the way these are performed/embodied and understood/experienced varies greatly, even when discussed/analysed in relation to the same setting/practice/activity. I therefore conclude this chapter by reasserting the need for recognising the multiple and competing understandings and experiences of both gender and (dis)pleasures in PE. In the next chapter, I consider the effects power-induced (gendered) pleasures have on teaching and learning in PE but also the pedagogical possibilities of opening up spaces for different gendered performances and pleasures in the (re)production of pleasurable physically educated (masculine) identities and bodies in PE.

References

Arnold, P. J. (1979). *Meaning in movement, sport and physical education*. London, UK: Heinemann.

Burrows, L. (2000). Old games in new rompers? Gender issues in New Zealand physical education. *Journal of Physical Education New Zealand, 33*(2), 30–41.

Burrows, L. (2005). Do the 'right' thing: Chewing the fat in physical education. *Journal of Physical Education New Zealand, 33*(1), 7–16.

Butler, J. (1993). *Bodies that matter: On the discursive limits of 'sex'*. New York: Routledge.

Cale, L., & Harris, J. (2005). *Exercise and young people: Issues, implications and initiatives*. Houndmills, UK: Palgrave MacMillan.

Davison, K. G. (2000). Boys' bodies in school: Physical education. *The Journal of Men's Studies, 8*(2), 255–266.

Denzin, N. K. (2010). *A critical performance ethnography that matters*. Paper presented at the Contemporary Ethnography across the Disciplines, 17–19/11, 2010, Hamilton, NZ.

Disch, L., & Kane, M. J. (1996). When a looker is really a bitch: Lisa Olson, sport, and the heterosexual matrix. In R. E. Joeres & B. Laslett (Eds.), *The second sings reader* (pp. 326–356). Chicago, IL: University of Chicago Press.

Drummond, M. (2003). The meaning of boys' bodies in physical education. *The Journal of Men's Studies, 11*(2), 131–143.

Foucault, M. (1972). *The archaeology of knowledge and discourse on language* (1st American ed.). New York: Pantheon Books.

Foucault, M. (1973). *The birth of the clinic: An archaeology of medical perception*. London, UK: Tavistock.

Foucault, M. (1978). *The history of sexuality, volume one*. Harmondsworth, UK: Penguin.

Foucault, M. (1980). *Power/knowledge: Selected interviews and other writings, 1972–1977*. New York: Pantheon.

Foucault, M. (1985). *The use of pleasure: The history of sexuality, volume 2*. London, UK: Penguin Books.

Foucault, M. (1991). *The Foucault effect: Studies in governmentality: With two lectures by and an interview with Michel Foucault*. London, UK: Harvester Wheatsheaf.

Foucault, M. (1995). *Discipline and punish: The birth of the prison*. Westminster, MD: Vintage.

Gard, M. (2008). When a boy's gotta dance: New masculinities, old pleasures. *Sport, Education and Society, 13*(2), 181–193.

Gard, M., & Wright, J. (2005). *The 'obesity epidemic': Science, ideology and morality*. London, UK: Routledge.

Garrett, R. (2004). Negotiating a physical identity: Girls, bodies and physical education. *Sport, Education and Society, 9*(2), 223–237.

Gilroy, S. (1989). The embodiment of power: Gender and physical activity. *Leisure Studies, 8*(2), 163–172.

Gilroy, S. (1997). Working on the body: Links between physical activity and social power. In G. Clarke & B. Humberstone (Eds.), *Researching women and sport* (pp. 96–112). London, UK: Macmillan.

Grogan, S., & Richards, H. (2002). Body image: Focus groups with boys and men. *Men and Masculinities, 4*(3), 219–232.

Grosz, E. (1992). Bodies-cities. In B. Colomina (Ed.), *Sexuality and space* (pp. 241–253). New York: Princeton Architectural Press.

Grosz, E. (1994). *Volatile bodies: Toward a corporeal feminism*. Bloomington, IN: Indiana University Press.

Grosz, E. (1995). *Space, time, and perversion: Essays on the politics of bodies.* New York: Routledge.

Hickey, C., & Fitzclarence, L. (1999). Educating boys in sport and physical education: Using narrative methods to develop pedagogies of responsibility. *Sport, Education and Society,* 4(1), 51–62.

Hickey, C., Fitzclarence, I., & Matthews, R. (1998). *Where the boys are: Masculinity, sport and education.* Geelong: Deakin University Press.

Kretchmar, R. S. (2005). *Practical philosophy of sport and physical activity.* Champaign, IL: Human Kinetics.

MacDonald, D., & Tinning, R. (2003). Reflective practice goes public: Reflection, governmentality and postmodernity. In A. Laker (Ed.), *The future of physical education: Building a new pedagogy* (pp. 82–101). London and New York: Routledge.

Markula, P., & Pringle, R. (2006). *Foucault, sport and exercise: Power, knowledge and transforming the self.* New York: Routledge.

Massey, D. (1994). *Space, place and gender.* Cambridge, UK: Polity Press.

McCuaig, L., & Tinning, R. (2010). HPE and the moral governance of p/leisurable bodies. *Sport, Education and Society,* 15(1), 39–61.

McDermott, L. (2007). A governmental analysis of children 'at risk' in a world of physical inactivity and obesity epidemics. *Sociology of Sport Journal,* 24, 302–324.

McLaren, P. (1991). Schooling the postmodern body: Critical pedagogy and the politics of enfleshment. In H. Giroux (Ed.), *Postmodernism, feminism and cultural politics* (pp. 144–173). Albany, NY: State University of New York Press.

Messner, M. (1992). *Power at play: Sports and the problem of masculinity.* Boston, MA: Beacon Press.

Mosher, J. (2001). Setting free the bears: Refiguring fat men in television. In J. E. Braziel & K. LeBasco (Eds.), *Bodies out of bounds: Fatness and transgression* (pp. 166–193). Berkley, CA: University of California Press.

Nayak, A., & Kehily, M. J. (1996). Playing it straight: Masculinities, homophobias and schooling. *Journal of Gender Studies,* 5(2), 211–230.

O'Reilly, E., Tompkins, J., & Gallant, M. (2001). 'They ought to enjoy physical activity you know?': Struggling with fun in physical education. *Sport, Education and Society,* 6(2), 211–221.

Pringle, R. (2010). Finding pleasure in physical education: A critical examination of the educative value of positive movement affects. *Quest,* 62, 119–134.

Pringle, R., & Hickey, C. (2010). Negotiating masculinities via the moral problematization of sport. *Sociology of Sport Journal,* 27(2), 115–138.

Pringle, R., & Pringle, D. (2012). Competing obesity discourses and critical challenges for health and physical educators. *Sport, Education and Society,* 17(2), 143–161.

Pronger, B. (2000). *Body fascism: Salvation in the technology of physical fitness.* Toronto, Canada: University of Toronto Press.

Renold, E. (2004). 'Other' boys: Negotiating non-hegemonic masculinities in the primary school. *Gender and Education,* 16(2), 247–266.

Rose, N. (1999). *Powers of freedom: Reframing political thought.* Cambridge, UK: Cambridge University Press.

Stothart, B. (2005). Nine strikes and you're out: New Zealand physical education in crisis? *Journal of Physical Education New Zealand,* 38(1), 95–102.

Tinning, R. (2010). *Pedagogy and human movement: Theory, practice, research.* New York: Routledge.

Tinning, R., & Glasby, T. (2002). Pedagogical work and the 'cult of the body': Considering the role of HPE in the context of the 'new public health'. *Sport, Education and Society,* 7(2), 109–119.

Twietmeyer, G. (2012). The merits and demerits of pleasure in kinesiology. *Quest*, 64(3), 177–186.

Vernon, M. (2008). *Wellbeing*. Stocksfield, UK: Acumen.

Webb, L., & MacDonald, D. (2007). Dualing with gender: Teachers' work, careers and leadership in physical education. *Gender and Education, 19*(4), 491–512.

Wellard, I. (2012). Body-reflexive pleasures: Exploring bodily experiences within the context of sport and physical activity. *Sport, Education and Society, 17*(1), 21–33.

Wrench, A., & Garrett, R. (2008). Pleasure and pain: Experiences of fitness testing. *European Physical Education Review, 14*(3), 325–346.

Wright, J. (2004). Post-structural methodologies: The body, schooling and health. In J. Evans, B. Davies, & J. Wright (Eds.), *Body knowledge and control: Studies in the sociology of physical education and health* (pp. 19–31). London, UK: Routledge.

7   The (dis)Pleasures of Learning in, through and about Movement

In this concluding chapter, I summarise the key findings presented in the previous three chapters in relation to my research questions. I also bring together some of the key theories and empirical findings discussed in this book and explore the implications for future PE practice/research. In the first sections of this chapter, I provide an overview of the main research findings and discuss their implications with respect to previous literature, the relationships between PE and gender, the use of Foucauldian theorising and what these might offer to the understanding of boys' performances of gender in PE in the future. I draw attention to pleasures as an educational, productive practice in boys' PE, while at the same time critiquing such pleasurable moments within this context. In doing so, I provide some tentative suggestions for the implications of my study for PE teachers, educators and researchers, not as a logical set of findings but as a set of questions or tensions that teachers might consider in their own settings. Towards the end of the chapter, I reflect on the research design/methods used, including their limitations and possibilities for future research. I suggest that combining participatory visual research approaches with Foucauldian theoretical frameworks can be fruitful in terms of enabling students to critically examine the (gendered) (dis)pleasures of learning in, through and about movement in PE.

The Co-Construction of Gender, Spaces, Pleasures and Bodies in PE

In chapter one, I outlined the background to this study and began addressing the issue of researching boys, gender and PE and why this is of importance. To further our understanding of boys as gendered subjects in PE, this book has attempted to examine how boys' performances of gender articulate with pleasures, as shaped by the workings of discourse and relations of power. In chapter two, I argued that such an examination was particularly justified due to the absence of empirical investigations of pleasure in PE. The issue of pleasure can be seen as particularly relevant in the New Zealand context because both the current and previous curricula have been critiqued for marginalising movement pleasure (Pringle, 2010; Stothart, 2005). This focus was developed further because themes relating to bodily pleasures, fun and enjoyment as factors in PE participation appeared both in the verbal and visual data. In contrast to previous research on pleasures in PE, which has mainly drawn on psychological models, I wanted to challenge the idea of 'inherent' pleasures in this context and highlight the discursive nature of pleasure. Consequently, this book has explored the importance of acknowledging pleasure in boys' PE as more than just an intrinsic, subjective, highly individual experience. I proposed that there was a need to examine how pleasures articulate with and/or produce relations of power that simultaneously enable and restrict boys' performances of gender. I suggested that examining pleasure from a Foucauldian perspective could better our understanding of how boys' pleasures constitute, and are constituted by, their performances of gender at the intersection of bodies and space.

To help narrow the focus of examination, I formulated my prime research questions, which asked: *(i) How do boys' performances of gender in Physical Education articulate with (dis)pleasures? (ii) How are spaces and bodies implicated in these performances?* I addressed these research questions by conducting an ethnographic account of two boys' PE classes, involving observations, interviews and video recordings. Data was analysed using Foucault's discourse/power/pleasure combination to make meanings and understand the boys as gendered subjects and in relation to Foucault's (1972, 1978) assertion that discourses, as contextually specific systems of meanings, are both constituting and constitutive of social realities, subjectivities and power relations. I followed Foucault's assertion that my aim as a researcher was not to discover the 'truth' but to understand how discursive practices/formations bring forth various 'truths' in particular ways. In this manner, I explored how the "games of power" (Foucault, 1988a, p. 18) associated with boys, gender, pleasures, spaces and bodies in PE were played out. Indeed, power-induced pleasures were identified through the discursive practices/formations of PE related to fitness/health, sport and masculinity that regulated and elaborated boys' performances of gender during my fieldwork at Kea College.

Using Foucauldian thinking, I have shown how the boys in this study are immersed in a power/discourse nexus (Markula, 2003) that simultaneously enables/restricts both performances of gender and pleasures. Based on the findings in this book, it seems that the current power/discourse nexus in this particular school and PE context is responsible for subjecting boys to disciplinary power and hence producing fixed gendered selves such as 'fit', 'healthy' and 'sporty' boys. Previous research both into gender in schools in general (e.g., Bain, 1985, 1990; Bradbury, 1989; Fernandez-Balboa, 1993; Mac an Ghaill, 1994; Skelton, 1997) and in PE (e.g., Drummond, 2003; Hickey, 2008; Parker, 1996) has shown how schools and PE, through both the official and hidden curriculum, reproduce dominant discourses of gender, making only certain gender identities available to the students

(Skelton & Francis, 2003). However, the examples provided throughout this book illustrate how disciplinary power (Foucault, 1995) not only works to normalise boys' performances of gender by subjecting them to power relations within certain discursive practices/formations but also produces pleasures. A Foucauldian analysis here offers a different reading of the workings of discourse and relations of power that support boys' participation in and enjoyment of PE.

Based on these findings, it is suggested that boys' performances of gender in PE need to be understood as a co-construction of pleasures, spaces and bodies. Each depends on the other; that is, they are reciprocally constituted. Any critical engagement with boys' performances of gender needs to take into account these three interrelated factors.

Spaces

Chapter four explored how space is implicated in the boys' performances of gender and pleasures in PE. To do this, I used Gregson and Rose's (2000) concept of 'performative space', an extension of Butler's notion of performativity, to illustrate how the pre-existing spaces of PE come to matter or become meaningful through the boys' performances with/in those spaces. In particular, I suggested that the boys' performances of both gender and space need to be understood as produced by the discourses and relations of power associated with sport and their discursive links with masculinity. Drawing on Foucauldian understandings of power, I further argued that the boys derive pleasures as the productive effect of the power articulated in and through the spaces of PE. I demonstrated how the boys, through their performances of gender, as shaped by discourses and relations of power associated with sport and masculinity, capitalise on the spaces of PE to highlight these as not only disciplinary but also productive spaces.

I also argued that spaces of PE come to matter or become meaningful as pleasurable spaces when boys have the skills and knowledge required to capitalise on them. That is, boys enter the spaces of PE with different experiences regarding engagement in physical activities. Some boys are unable to compete on equal terms if they have been 'disadvantaged' by their previous experiences in developing the kind of skills, knowledge and understanding necessary for participating in and enjoying particular (sporting) activities in PE. For instance, the differences in leisure time activities that encourage some boys to develop dominant masculine identities privileged in sports, such as physical power, speed and strength, give those boys an advantage in those physical activities that predominantly require the display of qualities associated with dominant forms of sporting masculinity (Piotrowski, 2000). In my study, it was particularly boys who were experienced and skilled at team sporting activities, rather than individual sporting activities, who were able to turn PE into pleasurable spaces.

However, the findings presented in chapter four also highlighted how boys' performances of gender within the spaces of PE both conform with and disrupt dominant discourses of sport and masculinity. In particular, the boys' changing room was identified as an 'unauthorised' space (Epstein & Johnson, 1998; Kehily, 2002), somewhat removed from the surveilling gaze of the teachers, which enabled some boys to (re)negotiate this 'hyper-masculine' 'heterotopic scapeland' space (Atkinson & Kehler, 2010) into a safe, caring and sensitive masculine space. These findings draw further attention to the unstable and fluid nature of both gender and spaces.

Pleasures

Chapter five was an exploration of the discourses of PE at Kea College that produce (dis)pleasures. Based on the cultures of 'everyone doing it' and 'playing games', as coined by the teacher, Mr Whyte, I demonstrated how discourses of fitness/health and sport and their discursive links with masculinity enable pleasures in a variety of ways. For instance, some boys derive pleasures from performing gender that conforms with instrumental/developmental goals related to fitness/health and sport.

Dominant understandings of the social and peer group status attained by the 'sporty' boys, along with the added fitness/health benefits, represent experiences/outcomes that are desirable for some boys. One particular idea that was homogenised in this PE context was boys as inherently sporty, fit and healthy. That is, dominating discourses of masculinities also articulated with sporting and fitness/health discourses. However, other boys found pleasures in performances that were of a subversive nature (i.e., resisting the role of competition) or simply by participating in PE. These findings indicate that boys' performances of gender and feelings of pleasures can vary greatly even when derived from within the same source/space. This further demonstrates the complexity of genders, pleasures and spaces. My main argument in this chapter was that discursive practices in PE related to fitness, health and sport are not only constraining and disciplining but also engendering of boys' agency/freedom and pleasures.

Findings in chapter five also drew attention to the important role that the sport of rugby plays in the production of both masculinities and pleasures. Although rugby can be seen to subject boys to a set of normalising practices that contribute to the broad disciplining of boys and their bodies (Pringle, 2003) by encouraging them to engage in a form of physicality that, for instance, glorifies hard physical contact (Fitzclarence & Hickey, 2001; Stoudt, 2006), it also enables the boys certain (masculine) pleasures. Some of these, as previously suggested by Pringle (2009), cohered around "mock battle", "friendships and teamwork", "development and display of skill, fitness and strategy", "physical contact and intimacy", and "affirming and/or challenging gendered [sexual] identities" (p. 215). In this sense, the national sport of rugby can be seen as the 'glue' of masculine pleasures in New Zealand schools and PE.

My findings also suggested that the dominance of rugby at this school and during PE acts as a dividing practice that contributes to the development of both privileged and subjugated masculinities. I agree with Pringle (2003) that the sport of rugby should not be considered as 'the social problem' but concern should be directed towards the discursive articulations that help constitute rugby's current state of dominance. The sometimes problematic construction of masculinities and pleasures associated with rugby stem from the dominating discourses that position rugby as the national sport of New Zealand and as a 'rite of passage' for boys becoming men (Drummond, 2003). The boys' responses, for instance, highlighted how the sport of rugby constructs/produces undesirable masculine behaviours and (dis) pleasures, such as an indifference to their own and other boys' physical pain and heterosexism/homophobia.

Bodies

In chapter six, I demonstrated the materialisation of boys' bodies in ways that produce (dis)pleasures within the contextually specific social and spatial context of boys' PE. More specifically, in an examination of the discursive practices of PE, I pointed towards the vital role that the body plays and suggested that the workings of discourses related to fitness/health and sport that serve to discipline and normalise the body in PE create not only gendered and docile bodies (as related to particular masculinities and masculine body ideals) but also productive and pleasurable bodies. In this sense, PE not only 'teaches' boys to inhabit and experience their bodies in different ways (Davison, 2000) but also produces the pleasures of those bodies.

I argued that it is through discursive practices that focus on disciplining/training the body, along with the development/performance of bodily (sporting) skills/abilities and the ongoing evaluation/examination procedures related to those bodies, that boys' bodies materialise as pleasurable bodies because they are able to perform gender in a way that enables them to capitalise on the pleasurable spaces of PE. In this sense, the body is integral, as it is by means of the body that masculinities, pleasures and spaces are perceived, lived and performed in PE.

I further suggested that the boys' bodies also shape the discursively constructed masculine and pleasurable body (Grosz, 1994; Malson, 1997). As a material condition of subjectivity, I drew attention to the importance of the teaching and learning of bodily (sporting) skills and abilities for boys (and girls) to perform and embody privileged and desirable masculinities. I argued that making skill development a priority again might enable more boys (and girls) to enjoy their bodies and experience (bodily) pleasures in PE.

The Game of Truth/Pleasure Games in Boys' PE—Being/ Performing Kea College Boy

The pleasures that boys derive from the discursive practices/formations operating within school and PE at Kea College related to co-construction of gender, spaces, pleasures and bodies can be seen as linked to performing and conforming to dominant notions of being a boy at Kea College. Indeed, the boys' desire to become 'recognisable' (Butler, 2004) was a significant act in the discourse of being a boy at Kea College. The freedom and power to refuse to "break with culture" (Barthes, 1975, p. 14) and to choose to present themselves as someone 'recognisable' (Butler, 2004) to their peers was both related to feeling normal and a source of pleasures. Butler argues that being recognisable is an important site of power because who becomes recognised, and by whom, is determined by social norms (discourses). Butler further suggests that choosing to be recognised or not within those social norms (discourses) points towards the agency of individuals in the performances of gender. This idea of recognition and its connections to pleasures and power in boys' school PE is significant. There are all sorts of ways that the boys could be recognised in their performances of gender, whether conscious or not.

As I have illustrated in this book, including pleasures in the analysis of discourses and relations of power reveals the different ways in which the boys' gendered selves are performed that might otherwise go unnoticed. Boys' performances of gender and their articulations with pleasures demonstrate how they attempt to make themselves viable or recognisable within the social norms or the discourses of schooling and PE at Kea College. In this sense, the social norms or the discourses of schooling and PE in this setting produce a range of options and constraints for the boys. Within this book, I have shown how the discursive articulations between masculinities, fitness/health, sport and PE are influential in shaping the boys' experiences of schooling and PE and the production of both masculinities and pleasures. Pleasures emerged within discourses and relations of power at Kea College to render the boys recognisable (Butler, 2004) as, for instance, fit, healthy and sporty boys.

The social norms and discourses centred around fitness/health and sports can be seen to act as 'incitements' for the boys to enter into the 'game of truth' (Markula & Pringle, 2006) and form themselves as a Kea College boy within relations of power. As pointed out by Whelen (2011) in his ethnography of boys' schooling, and drawing on Foucault and Butler, "Becoming such a subject [a Kea College boy] . . . requires not only that the subject be performatively constituted within a discursive frame, but that subjects repeatedly draw on (or cite) the rules or conventions of the discourse" (p. 19). Within this discourse/power/pleasure arrangement, boys then need to engage in particular disciplinary practices to (re)affirm privileged and desirable masculinities. To sustain such an image, the boys must engage in constant self-surveillance that enables them to live up to the dominant notions of masculinity and masculine appearances at this school. While this also requires the boys to be active agents in some of these practices, the reason for taking part in them is to conform, to become 'normal' and successful and gain popularity within their own peer group, as defined by this specific power/discourse nexus (Markula, 2003; Markula & Pringle, 2006). In this sense, these practices of the self are productive for boys. That is, the boys enter this game of truth or pleasure game to reaffirm certain privileged and desirable masculinities within this context.

However, the findings in this book have also shown how those boys who are unable or unwilling to play these power games or this game of truth related to gender and pleasures experience school and PE more negatively. The results also warrant a continued concern for the discursive links between, for instance, dominant discourses of masculinity, toughness/aggression, competition and (hetero)sexuality. The discourses and relations of power in boys' PE that allow for particular subject positions and produce certain pleasures can at times also induce (dis)pleasures (e.g., exclusion pain, humiliation, embarrassment, harassment, bullying, homophobia). In chapter four, I highlighted how the performative and pleasurable sporting and masculinising spaces of PE (re)produce unequal power relations, where boys experience the space of PE as uncomfortable and where they are kept in 'enclosed' and 'public' spaces leading to the displeasures of being on display and showing themselves as 'inferior' and 'inadequate' in front of their peers. In addition, chapter four's findings drew attention to how boys' pleasures are restricted with the provision and lack of certain spaces, as shaped by dominant discourses of sport and masculinity. In chapter six, I highlighted some boys' anxieties and feelings of inadequacy in relation to not having a skilled/able (sporting) body and the failures they have experienced in trying to live up to masculine body ideals. That is, power-induced pleasures in PE related to performances of gender and the game of truth in PE not only restrict certain pleasures but end up having negative consequences/outcomes for those boys who are unable or unwilling to live up to or perform privileged/desirable masculinities within this context. Based on the findings in this book, the argument I progress is that it is perhaps pleasures that are the 'glue' that (re)produces 'traditional' forms of PE and existing (unequal) power relations between boys. Returning to Jackson's (1996) question about how it ended up this way, I would suggest that it is pleasure as co-constitutive of boys' performances of gender that (re)constructs certain masculinities as productive and privileged/desirable within PE.

Any real attempt to challenge the normalisation of gender in PE therefore needs to include an attempt to challenge dominant forms of pleasures as well. In particular, there is a need to challenge the prevalence of dominant discourses of gender and pleasures by "detaching the power of truth from the forms of hegemony, social, economic and cultural, within which it operates at the present time" (Foucault, 1980, p. 133). By addressing normalising technologies of power, there is a further need to scrutinise the gendered pleasures of PE.

However, before discussing the impact and role of (dis)pleasures in PE, I will discuss how some of the boys in my study problematised the way performances of gender articulate with (dis)pleasures in boys' PE and expressed a desire to perform gender or construct masculine identities in more responsible, ethical and inclusive ways.

Boys' Problematisations of (Gendered) (dis)Pleasures in PE

The boys' problematisations of how power-induced (gendered) pleasures lead to the (re)production of 'traditional' forms of PE and existing unequal power relations between boys draws attention to how they are not purely docile bodies who exclusively allow the dominant discourses of gender and pleasures that circulate in this PE context to constitute their subjectivities. Conversely, as active agents within this discourse/power/pleasure arrangement, they are also able to critically reflect on and problematise these discourses. However, mere critical thinking does not transform these discursive constructions, which is why it is also important to consider how this critique works in practice (Markula & Pringle, 2006). Although many of the participating boys in this study articulated a critical awareness and problematisation of the discursive practices of PE, this was primarily performed 'quietly', and the majority simply adopted "coping mechanisms" (Markula, 2003, p. 103). To preserve their enjoyment of PE, many ignored these problematic practices. Yet for a small group of boys, this critique promoted an active response through investing themselves in a "double trajectory of critique and ethically informed practice" (Thorpe, 2008, p. 210). Their critical reflection and active problematisation can be seen as an example of how a socio-critical curriculum in PE might function in practice.

In order to explore these boys' problematisations of gendered pleasures in PE, I drew on Foucault's (1988a) 'technologies of the self' and in particular his framework for understanding the process of forming oneself as dependent on the four "modes of subjectivation" (Foucault, 1985, p. 28) (see chapter two). I focused on the stories of individual boys and groups of boys who during the time I spent with them were particularly engaged in questioning, challenging and problematising aspects of their own gendered identities in PE. It is worth pointing out, however, that at times these boys were not always necessarily employing technologies of the self with the sole focus on changing or transforming the self but that, through this process, they were also targeting other people or the practices around them. Despite the broad connections to gender issues, some of the boys typically identified their 'ethical substance' in relation to particular feelings, desires or actions rather than as an aspect of their masculine identity (Pringle & Hickey, 2010). Through retelling the boys' stories, I aimed to demonstrate how their problematisation of dominant social practices in their PE still led to a critical self-reflection of their own performances of gender and the pleasures derived from these. In particular, the findings in this book related to boys' problematisation of gender and pleasures have further demonstrated that PE can be understood as a context of competing discourses that produce a diversity of gendered identities and pleasures, which, at times, leads to ethical dilemmas and identity tensions (Pringle & Markula, 2005). Such knowledge might also have important pedagogical implications for future teaching practices in PE because it could be used as a critical pedagogical tool to challenge and transform gendered expectations.

For example, in chapter five, I illustrated how Adam and Dominic were primarily concerned with dominant modes of aggression, competitiveness and subordination of 'non-sporty' boys associated with sporting practices in PE and how Chris questioned practices related to exclusion. Chapter six described how Chris and James problematised masculine body ideals by questioning the role/purpose of PE and the impact of certain (discursive) teaching practices. They articulated a desire (their 'telos') that finding pleasure in, through and about movement (Arnold, 1979) cannot exclusively be about attaining the ideal masculine (sporting) body and that laying the foundations for a life full of diverse movement pleasures needs to be at the forefront in PE. Through considering these tensions, the boys scrutinised their own performances of gender and experiences of pleasures by reflecting on these as connected with certain moral/ethical dilemmas, problematic gendered identities and unequal power relations (Pringle & Hickey, 2010). This process of self-reflection resulted in a desire to change various 'practices of self', that of others and the discursive practices associated with their school and PE, 'the mode of subjection'. In particular, the ethical work performed by these boys is a useful example of boys' critical engagement (Lloyd, 1996) with dominant discourses of gender and pleasures in PE, which might have, indeed, challenged both the teachers' and the other boys' way of thinking.

Indeed, when I caught up with Mr Whyte at the later stages of writing up the findings of this study, when the boys in my study were in Year 13, he talked about how the PE subject is about to undergo some major changes. Prompted by me sharing some of my findings and conclusions, he talked about "revamping the curriculum". He referred to "changes in teaching styles and assessment through Year 7–10 to improve NCEA[1] results [by] introducing three grade levels". This, he believed, would "motivate the students to do more, to achieve merit and excellence certificates", which are important for university entrance. "All of the sudden, PE is seen as a subject that could help some boys make it into university degrees" (Mr Whyte). In order to do so, one aspect that Mr Whyte believed needed to change/ improve is to include and "cooperate" with the NZ HPE curriculum more/ further. However, at the same time, he said that was going to be "hard with boys". Is it that the (re)production of gender and pleasures in boys' PE somehow is at odds with the learning objectives and outcomes in the curriculum? Is the ongoing marginalisation of (movement) pleasures in current and past HPE curricula (Pringle, 2010; Stothart, 2005) the reason why the educational goals of PE are not fully realised in settings such as Kea College? Would a greater focus on pleasure in its many forms make PE 'a better place' for more boys (and girls)?

Critical physical educators assert that PE can be a space of critical engagement, enjoyment and learning, that it can potentially be a space where narrow gendered norms can be exposed and challenged. Azzarito (2009) argues that "physical education settings can become sites of transformation . . .

[and] resistance . . . conceivably safe learning spaces in physical education can destabilise oppositional and hierarchical gendered constructions of the body" (p. 35). What might these kinds of PE lessons look like? How can PE be a site of transformation that destabilises dominant understandings of gender and pleasures? The stories of boys' problematisation of some discourses of PE highlight the possibilities of transformative practices in this context. Such practices of self-open up a space for challenging regulatory norms of boy, gender and pleasures and PE. As Butler (1993) points out, although gendered discourses and categories of sex and sexuality are powerful, "bodies never quite comply with the norms" (p. 62). She argues that the gap between the "regulatory ideal" of bodies and their material existence creates a space for constant reiteration of norms, which in turn "call into question the hegemonic force of that very regulatory law" (p. 62). From the standpoint of the technology of the self (Foucault, 1988a), it can be further suggested that these boys are continuously in the process of turning themselves into ethical beings, capable not only of determining their own behaviours but also able to challenge and resist dominant discourses of PE related to boys, gender and pleasures. In particular, by raising awareness of those aspects of PE that contribute to the alienation of some boys, it is possible that these boys contributed to an alternative discourse of PE that creates spaces and opportunities for the production of more ethical and diverse masculinities and pleasures.

My intention of highlighting the boys' problematisation of the gendered pleasures of PE was not to somehow downplay the effect of the workings of discourse and imply that the boys are somehow able to freely create gendered selves as they please. Even the boys who actively problematised understandings and experiences of gender and pleasures in PE could be seen as employing "a certain number of tricks" (Foucault, 1988b, p. 12) that were unlikely to radically transform existing discursive practices in this PE setting. That is, although these boys problematised discursive practices in PE, it did not necessarily change this regime of practice. These boys' problematisation also suggested that this regime of practice in PE and its links with gender and pleasures were also under some form of scrutiny. Technologies of the self are thus not practices that individuals can use to radically transform discourses and allow them to change social practices without being constrained by the workings of dominant discourses and disciplinary power (Markula & Pringle, 2006). Indeed, Markula (2003) observed that Foucault did not envisage technologies of the self as akin to strategies of resistance. In this book, I wanted to draw attention to the fact that discourses and disciplinary technologies do not act as sovereign forms of power that have a 'divine-like' authority. I point instead towards the relationship between discourse/power/pleasure and gendered subjects as co-constitutive.

With only a few boys in my study engaging in problematisations related to dominant understandings of gender and pleasures in PE (from a pedagogical point of view), it is worth considering who are the most likely to do so because this is an important feature of the current HPE curriculum in New Zealand. Markula and Pringle (2006) asked a similar question in their study of the fitness industry. Following Foucault (1988a), who rejected the notion of individuals "possessing an innate ability to problematise their identities and to develop practices to change it" (Markula & Pringle, 2006, p. 170), Markula and Pringle (2006) located "critical awareness of discursive practices" and the drive toward "alternative practices" in "knowledge and experience" of one's immediate world (p. 170). This also seemed to be the case in my PE context. Not all boys had an equal opportunity to move freely within these discourses and power relations. Marginalised and subordinated boys (i.e., the 'non-sporty' boys) were less likely to have any influence, whereas privileged and dominant boys (i.e., the 'sporty' 'rugby' boys) had more opportunities to do so. However, as mentioned above, not all boys with this opportunity were willing to do so. Markula (2004) suggests that possibilities of resistance and transgression are created when physical activity practices are accompanied by critical awareness, a 'tuning into one's self'. PE practices themselves are neither liberating nor oppressive. Rather, it is the individual's awareness of their agency in negotiating dominant discourses that makes transformation possible. The key factors here are therefore both critical awareness and position, within the power/discourse nexus (Markula & Pringle, 2006). That being said, I believe that PE teachers hold the key and have both the knowledge and experience to facilitate such critical pedagogical learning environments. In the next section, I will suggest that interrogating the impact and role of (dis)pleasures in PE could be a good starting point.

The Impact and Role of (dis)Pleasures in PE

So, if power-induced pleasure can be seen as both an educational productive practice and also as responsible for (re)producing 'traditional' forms of PE and existing (unequal) power relations between boys, what role should pleasures play in PE? The importance of recognising pleasures in PE has been acknowledged for a long time (e.g., Booth, 2009; Burrows, 2005; Hawkins, 2008; Locke, 1996; Morgan, 2006; Pringle, 2010; Rintala, 2009; Stothart, 2005), with Booth (2009) even stating that pleasures could act as a "potential pillar of disciplinary coherence in physical education" (p. 133). Similarly, Morgan (2006) argues that a 'legitimate' educational goal of PE could be to allow students to experience movement pleasures in a meaningful manner, whereas Gard (2008) takes a slightly different approach by suggesting that experiences of (dis)pleasures should be at the forefront of PE, rather than 'dry' formal educational objectives. The findings in this book show how the boys' performances of gender conform to fitness, health and sport discourses to derive pleasures in and through the spaces and bodies in PE.

I want to draw attention to pleasure as an educational productive practice but also critically reflect on the impact and role of (dis)pleasure in PE. I am particularly concerned about simplistic readings of pleasures that suggest that participation in certain games/activities automatically results in experiences of pleasure. As pointed out by Pringle (2010), the focus on (certain) pleasures in PE can also be seen as an example of how PE teachers' own favourable relationships with (certain) games and sports have influenced their views of movement pleasures. Rintala (2009), for instance, argues that the responsibility of physical educators "is to provide opportunities for people to move in many ways so that they find some of the satisfactions and meanings that we ourselves have experienced" (p. 284). Indeed, Gard (2008) also reminds us that in enabling our students to explore the pleasures of various movement experiences, we need to recognise how these pleasurable experiences are always contextually situated/specific. Pleasures, like performances of gender, constitute and are constituted by surrounding discourses. That is, PE teachers need to be aware that they are not only enabling boys' (and girls') gendered experiences of pleasures through, for instance, fitness, health and sport, but that they are also influential in shaping their understandings about the gendered (dis)pleasures of these movement experiences. Drawing on Foucault's idea that pleasure has no passport, Allen and Carmody (2012) argue that teachers in this way can be seen as 'border protection officers' who monitor and regulate the pleasures students derive from certain (physical or sexual) activities. However, by reminding ourselves that Foucault (1983) argues that no one really knows what pleasure is and understanding pleasure as having no passport, we can conclude that there is also hope for creating new understandings and experiences of pleasure in PE that are less restricted by dominant discourses of fitness, health, sport and masculinity.

I therefore believe that there is much more that can be said about PE as a space of pleasure. In considering the impact and role of pleasures in PE, we need to scrutinise why boys (and girls) find certain movement experiences desirable/pleasurable. My suggestion in this book is that we need to look at the discourses of gender, and masculinity in particular, in PE through the lens of pleasure. In other words, we need to explore pleasure and gender simultaneously. The fact that the boys' pleasures in my study relied so heavily on instrumental/developmental goals signals the need to further scrutinise the way pleasure is constructed/produced in dominant fitness/health, sport and masculinity discourses.

Since gender and pleasure are embodied in and through movement, any attempt to challenge the pervasive/traditional culture of PE teaching would have to carefully consider which kinds of activities to include in the PE curriculum and to make it possible for the students to move in new ways. Such a strategy would include a critically reflexive approach among PE teachers towards conventional perceptions of what activities are 'for boys' and 'not for boys' or 'for girls', involving an emphasis on exploring how individual boys and girls experience different physical activities as enjoyable or not. Indeed, when talking about the activities and programmes offered in PE, many of the boys in this study indicated that there might be a need to scrutinise the type of activities and games that are traditionally associated with PE. In this sense, PE is identified as an important site for changing and reforming gendered regimes of practice. How then would it be possible to challenge pervasive/traditional gendered practices in PE? One of the boys in this study (Dominic) might have an answer:

Dominic: I wish we would experiment more with new and different activities in PE. We always do the same old things, rugby for one term, then badminton/volleyball the next one and so on. Why can't we come up with completely new activities that we have never done before, things that no one is good at? You know, so we are all beginners, then we can create our own games and activities that everyone would like, so no one has to just stand there and watch.

Göran: What kinds of activities would that be?

Dominic: You know, anything that is not for boys or for gay boys or for girls and stuff. But, like, games that everyone can do where we can just be ourselves.

What Dominic is saying is that we need to experiment more with new and different activities in PE, activities that are "not for boys or for gay boys or for girls" but "games that everyone can do". These comments by Dominic draw attention to the fact that in order to deal with enduring issues of gender stereotypes, we need to make changes in the way PE programmes are organised and implemented. Coakley (1994) argues that the real challenge in addressing enduring issues of gender in PE lies in transforming the way people think about boy/girl and masculinity/femininity and developing alternative activities that are constructed according to the values and experiences of boys and girls who do not see themselves in terms of dominant definitions of masculinity/femininity.

However, I do not believe that this should be achieved by, for instance, "increased opportunities to participate in less gendered physical activities, such as the kind of more neutrally gendered outdoor and adventure activities", or the students "having greater access to physical activities which challenge traditional conceptions of masculinity and femininity (for example, greater access to dance for boys; rugby for females)" (Piotrowski, 2000, p. 44) because this would most likely reinforce entrenched binary notions of gender. Instead, this might involve, as Dominic suggests, creating alternative activities and programmes that are based on the belief that PE is something that everyone, regardless of age, gender, sexuality, class and ethnicity, should be able to participate in and experience as enjoyable. That is, creating activities and programmes that challenge the normalisation of gender and pleasure, that recognise the multiplicities of masculinity/femininity and pleasure and that make PE a more inclusive space for all (Clarke, 2006). The task for the future PE teacher would then be to help the students participate in new, and perhaps different and unaccustomed, activities and games, which would enable boys and girls to perform gender differently and allow for the creation of new and unforeseeable gendered identities and pleasures. In my last meeting with Mr Whyte, the conversation cohered around the future of PE at Kea College. Mr Whyte talked about letting the students be more involved in the creation of different games and activities in PE. Like Dominic, he talked about creating and providing different types of games and activities in PE: "Greater focus on non-traditional games . . . make field more even [but also] a game-making approach [where] they create their own games".

The findings in this book have also highlighted how the (dis)pleasures associated with PE exist in "multiple and competing forms" (Pringle, 2010, p. 132). My study demonstrates that within PE there are multiple discourses circulating, which work in different ways to produce masculinities and pleasures. Foucault (1978) suggests that we operate in a "multiplicity of discursive elements that can come into play in various strategies" (p. 100). The ways that the boys in my study talked about their understandings and experiences of PE give further evidence that they made sense of their experiences of PE, and the meaning they make of it in their lives, in multiple and competing ways. Although many of the boys took pleasures out of performing and conforming to discourses of fitness/health, sport and masculinity, others derived pleasure from simply participating in PE. As stated by Gard (2008), "Many of us derive pleasure from physical activity at which we are not particularly proficient" (p. 186). He also reminds us that it is not uncommon for people to stop deriving pleasure from forms of physical activity at which they are still (at least compared to other people) extremely skilled (e.g., the story told by former professional tennis player Andre Agassi in his autobiography). Consequently, it is important not to, just as with gender, homogenise boys' pleasures (Gard, 2008) but instead recognise the range of pleasures experienced/performed by boys in PE. PE practices should allow for multiple physical identities and multiple ways of being physical as well as challenging narrow and limiting conceptions of gender and pleasure. I agree with Pringle (2009) and Wellard (2012), who argue that we need to escape from simplistic readings of pleasure and recognise the range of pleasures available in sport and physical activity in order to be able to promote, encourage and enable positive, meaningful and pleasurable experiences for boys (and girls).

The findings in my study also importantly demonstrate how (dis)pleasures can be productive. As pointed out by my main doctoral supervisor, Louisa Allen, "For instance, there is much (dis)pleasure in being a PhD student who has to keep revising a chapter they thought they had completed. In terms of learning outcomes, though, this might be quite productive". That is, pleasure and displeasure are not rigid binaries. The same person's (dis)pleasure is also their pleasure or there might (eventually) be pleasure in (dis)pleasure. Such (dis)pleasure can also be productive in terms of learning in PE and/or the construction of diverse masculinities. Indeed, in chapter six, I demonstrated how the disciplining and training of the body as a machine is by some boys seen as less pleasurable (displeasurable) but also productive in terms of the pleasurable experiences it enables/gives access to (i.e., getting fitter and better at games/sports that follow). Exposing boys to what for some is linked to (dis)pleasures, such as Gard's (2001, 2003) work on dance education, can be important in terms of learning in, through and about movement in different ways and learning about the body and bodily expressions in new ways, which can also help in the production/legitimation of diverse masculinities within PE. Gard's (2001, 2003) work in particular focuses on the:

> possibilities that dance education offers for "disruptive and discomforting experiences", as well as pleasurable ones, for students in schools and universities, more specifically, exhuming the taken-for-grantedness of gendered male bodies and heterosexual embodiment.
>
> (p. 211)

In this way, the binary of positive/pleasurable and negative/displeasurable experiences in PE might be reworked and help construct a more nuanced understanding of the impact and role of (dis)pleasures in PE.

However, although certain (dis)pleasures can be seen as productive, some, as indicated in this book, can be oppressive (e.g., exclusion, harassment, bullying, heterosexism/homophobia, etc.) and therefore needs to be further scrutinised/challenged. As pointed out by Allen and Carmody (2012), pleasurable experiences can quickly turn into displeasurable experiences. All of this demonstrates the messiness of gender and (dis)pleasures and the multiple readings/interpretations of such performances.

When talking about change and reforming the PE curriculum, Kirk (2010) suggests:

> We need then to apply a broader range of scholarship of the highest standard to the task of securing the conditions for radical reform in physical education, drawing on evidence from a scholarship of discovery, imagining new possibilities through a scholarship of integration, testing these ideas through a scholarship of application, and transmitting them through a scholarship of teaching.
>
> (p. 144)

Based on Kirk's suggestions and the findings in this book, I would suggest that we put pleasures at the forefront of further examinations and development of PE practice. We need to know more about the types of activities that boys and girls find pleasurable and how these pleasures are produced.

Although my book contributes to this knowledge, I contend that we need more research that combines lived experience and discourse analysis in order to understand the pleasurable movement experiences in PE and the meanings that boys and girls make of them in their own lives. In particular, I agree with Rintala (2009), who argues that we need to know more about "how our own teaching and scholarship may help bring people to the joy of the experience of moving" (p. 287).

We need to develop critical pedagogical frameworks that enable boys and girls to reflect on the pleasures of certain movement experiences. Boys and girls need to experience a range of movement experiences in order to be able to make distinctions about what is considered pleasurable for them (Wellard, 2012). In agreement with Allen and Carmody (2012), who draw on Fine (1988) in their discussion on the impact and role of pleasure in sexuality education, I call for a similar focus on students' exploration of pleasure in PE: "what feels good and bad, desirable and undesirable, grounded in experience, needs and limits" (p. 33). That is, it is not about just providing the opportunity for students to 'have a go' in order to comply with curriculum directives related to movement pleasures in PE. It is about providing opportunities for young people to experience activities and make assessments about when, where and how an activity is pleasurable. That is, pleasures need to be recognised, unpacked and reflected upon (Booth, 2009) by the students so that they can "establish which are likely to lead to the greatest happiness, and therefore which are the best to cultivate" (Vernon, 2008, p. 19).

As pointed out by Davison (2000), PE classes are positioned within young people's social, physical and educational sphere and may offer the possibility to broaden the way they think about gender and bodies. Specifically, in New Zealand, the coupling of health education with PE not only provides a space but also urgently requires more resources for examining the relationship between gender, the body and health from a critical socio-cultural perspective (Fitzpatrick, 2013). Based on the findings in my study, I would argue that this also needs to include an examination of how pleasure is influential in shaping boys' (and girls') performances of gender. This is of particular pertinence because the results from my study indicate how power-induced pleasures seem to support both mechanisms of inclusion and exclusion within the boys' peer groups. For some students, PE (re)produces experiences of (dis)pleasure (e.g., pain, humiliation, embarrassment, boredom, frustration). The long-term outcome for these students, who continually experience such (dis)pleasures, is the likely withdrawal from any movement context. For instance, in chapter six, I demonstrated how Zack's and Mark's experiences of the 'beep-test' not only induced (dis)pleasures but also led to the avoidance of PE and physical activity in general.

Finally, we need to view pleasure as both an educationally productive practice and also something that needs to be understood as (re)producing certain gendered identities, bodies and spaces in PE and the pleasures of those identities/bodies/spaces. This book has demonstrated, following others before (Booth, 2009; Gard, 2008; Pringle, 2010), that in order to change the social construction of dominant masculinities in PE, we need to interrogate the discourses of pleasures in PE. The educational opportunities of the HPE curriculum may not be fulfilled because of the pleasures boys continue to derive from dominant discourses of fitness/health and sport and their discursive links with masculinity. By focusing on how and why the students experience certain movement experiences as pleasurable or less pleasurable (displeasurable), we might discover new ways of implementing and transforming the HPE curriculum. This may lead to more young people experiencing the excitement of learning in, through and about movement and thus help lay the foundation for a lifelong participation in—and enjoyment of—various movement pleasures. I agree with Pringle (2010), who argues that exploring the production of pleasure in PE is a difficult but vital task.

In the next section, I reflect on the limitations and possibilities of this research project and of future research before exploring the pedagogical spaces of opportunity provided by boys' (and girls') visual representations and interpretations.

Reflecting on my Visual Ethnography of Boys' PE

This study focused entirely on boys' experiences of PE and did not include girls. Numerous studies on girls and PE have been conducted, and fewer studies to date have investigated boys' performances of gender in PE. This study adds to what Connell (2005) describes as the "ever-growing library of descriptive studies, which provide important understandings of specific settings and problems" (p. xvii).

While the stories and accounts I offer deal with individual lives, which are not necessarily generalisable to other places or people, I claim that this research can be considered in terms of what Cammarota and Fine (2008) call "theoretical and provocative generalisability", which requires researchers to "understand the long reach of injustice and resistance over time and place" (p. 5). While this is just one study, in a particular time and place, it contributes to the pantheon of research stories of which the ethnographies of Drummond (2003), Hickey (2008), Mac an Ghaill (1994), Parker (1996) and Willis (1977) are also a part.

This study hopefully adds to our understanding of boys' performances of gender in PE and how these influence their experiences of this curriculum subject. This increased awareness may encourage physical educators to produce new ideas about how to (re)assure that (more) boys (and girls) experience PE as something both enjoyable and meaningful.

In particular, this book offers a different reading of the workings of discourse in PE, which adds to our understanding of the techniques (or effects) of power that support boys' participation in and enjoyment of PE. More broadly, it also adds to the field of sociology of education by demonstrating how pleasures are produced within an educational setting. However, I have also suggested that it is possible that pleasures are the 'glue' that reproduces stereotypical notions of masculine identities, spaces and bodies in PE, due to the pleasures boys continue to derive from performing and capitalising on these. Indeed, the results presented in this book also warrant a continued concern for the discursive links between, for instance, dominant discourses of masculinity, toughness/aggression, competition and (hetero)sexuality. In particular, the findings highlight how power-induced pleasures in PE end up having negative consequences for those boys who are unable or unwilling to live up to or perform privileged and desirable masculinities within this context. That is, the discourses and relations of power in boys' PE that allow for particular subject positions and produce certain pleasures can at times also induce (dis)pleasures (e.g., exclusion pain, humiliation, embarrassment, harassment, bullying, homophobia).

I have also shown how some boys demonstrate resistance/agency by problematising dominant understandings of gender and pleasures in PE (through the use of technologies of the self). By retelling their stories, I attempted to demonstrate boys as active subjects in negotiating the working of discourses and relations of power. These findings might offer alternative discursive resources and opportunities for helping deconstruct and reconstruct dominant ways of knowing boys, gender and pleasure in PE. Nonetheless, most boys in this study did not engage in such critical reflections/practices, which highlights the need to teach the current HPE curriculum. That is, the outcome of this study becomes grounds for actually teaching and further attempting to deliver the socio-critical perspective upon which the current New Zealand HPE curriculum is built.

The teachers and the HPE curriculum were not used as main data sources in my study, although they inevitably were included as an important part of the discussion and analysis of the findings. I did not focus on examining or critiquing the teachers' practice, and this will need to be examined in future research projects. The limited amount of teaching experience of the researcher may have influenced the way the study was designed and carried out. More experienced teachers and other researchers who have conducted similar studies were therefore approached and asked to discuss the design and the results of the study.

This research project was carried out at a school with students from similar socio-economic and cultural backgrounds, which might have affected the type and diversity of data collected. Future studies should therefore include research participants from a wide range of socio-economic and cultural backgrounds. I have not focused on how gender intersects with issues of sexuality, race, ethnicity and socio-economic class (Azzarito & Solomon, 2005), and this should also be further addressed in future studies.

The inability to incorporate video material is another limitation because the format of the (conventional) book does not allow for the easy inclusion of video. It is not possible to explore the very rich nature of this data, nor conduct an in-depth analysis of it, because the boys' movements it demonstrates/represents cannot be easily conveyed by written text. In the presentation of findings, I only used narratives and still images to represent the video material being discussed/analysed. Although the scope of this research and the limitations of the book format did not allow me to include video data/analysis, I plan to do so in future projects, drawing in particular on the works of Sarah Pink (2007) and Gillian Rose (2007).

In chapter one, I defined gender as something that can be performed in multiple ways and not exclusively linked to the sexed male or female body, which means that an analysis of boys' gendered identities needs to extend beyond their sexed bodies. For my study, this meant that I attempted to explore both masculinity and femininity as relating to boys' performances of gender. However, in contrast to Pascoe's (2007) study, I found no real evidence to support the contention that masculinity and femininity are made up of various practices and discourses that both boys and girls may perform and embody in different ways and to different degrees (Pascoe, 2007). This might need to be more closely scrutinised in future research into boys' performances of gender in PE.

Future studies also need to more fruitfully illustrate that gender performances are always blurred and that existing theoretical tools that work on an understanding of a gender binary are problematic as they help reinforce this binary. We need to explore how we can study gender by going beyond the gender binary. In particular, I suggest that Foucauldian thinking could help analyse and deconstruct entrenched binary oppositions in order to uncover the way they manufacture hierarchical tables of value that often arbitrarily privileges one set over others (Wright, 2004). Future studies could employ Derrida's (1976) notion of deconstruction in an attempt to deconstruct the boys' performances of gender, not only to explore what might represent the constitutive outside and other (Butler, 1990) in this context but also to reveal possible 'unforeseeable' (Derrida, 1996) gender identities and performances of gender that we do not expect to find.

In attempting to deconstruct gender binaries, deconstruction is something more powerful than simply undoing gender binaries since it would offer a way to move beyond the present and the given to think outside of gender binaries and to unsettle meaning. This might open up new analytical possibilities that move beyond and transcend rigid gender binaries and that make visible parts of the boys' gendered identities previously not visible. Such research should be guided by Butler's (2004) assertion that:

> to assume that gender always and exclusively means the matrix of "masculine" and "feminine" is precisely to miss the critical point that the production of that coherent binary is contingent, that it comes at a cost and that those permutations of gender which do not fit the binary are as much a part of the gender normative.

(p. 42)

Although Foucauldian approaches may offer new perspectives on the performance of gender, some critics (e.g., Knoppers & McDonald, 2010) propose that we need to move beyond typical gender, race and class analyses. For instance, combining with other approaches, such as post-colonial understandings (Jamieson, 2003), can lead to new insights about boys' performances of gender that move beyond these traditional categories (Francis, 2010).

In chapter three, I discussed how throughout this research project I wanted to actively involve the boys themselves in the research process and attempt to bridge the gap between the researcher and the researched because, through a poststructural lens, reality is a co-construction, a 'fusion of horizons'. I identified visual methodologies as a way of allowing the boys to reflect on their own participation in PE rather than me introducing predetermined themes. I therefore discussed why visual representations, together with focus groups and individual interviews, were deemed an important method in my study and emphasised that as a researcher, I cannot attempt to understand boys' performances of gender without including their own voices and interpretations. In my research, I did not know what was personally important to the boys who participated, and I therefore took extra care in enabling the boys to speak for themselves in meaningful ways by employing visual research methods. I suggested that this might contribute to the 'polyvocality' in PE research by offering "new forms of interpretation and insight" (Sparkes, 1991, p. 127). Of equal importance to the study was that the participating boys were actively involved in the research process.

The still image in Figure 7.1, captured from one of the video clips, symbolises to me what visual methodologies have to offer as a research instrument. To me, it is the corporeality and bodies moving through spaces and time that visual methodologies allow us to capture. Just by having a quick glance at this image, there are so many things we can pick up on: me, the researcher, in front of the camera, fully engaged in this game of volleyball just like the other students, everyone having their eyes fixed on the ball (or is there even a ball?), the very distinct body languages of the students, the variation of clothing, the material aspects that make it easy to identify the space as a school gym, etc. But an image like this also raises so many questions: Who is behind the camera? (Or is there no one behind the camera?) Where is the teacher? Where are all the other students? Who is winning? (Or are we even scoring?)

Based on the findings in my study, I argue that my participatory visual research approach provided the participating boys with a medium through which they were able to think about, reflect, articulate and reason their experiences in PE and their relationships with their peers and, more importantly, themselves. Using visual research methods, and in particular participatory visual methods, can help identify gendered identity issues that are seen as important to the students themselves. O'Donoghue (2007) argues that participatory visual research methods can help "open up spaces where we can engage meaningfully with issues of power, surveillance, segregation,

Figure 7.1 Myself and a Group of Boys Playing Volleyball.

isolation, dominance and subordination; places where we can situate these issues" (p. 66). It creates a space for the students to address issues of gendered performances and the fluidity of creating the self through PE, which might help highlight and challenge narrow conceptions of gendered selves still inherent in this subject. But it also, as discussed and displayed in relation to the image above, allows an exploration of students' enjoyment and pleasurable experiences when involved in PE. It can help us identify those important moments when the PE classroom is turned into a fun and enjoyable space, where students are experiencing the excitement of learning about their embodied (gendered) selves in, about and through movement. It also allows us to 'look at the bigger picture' and add to our understanding of the co-constructed nature of boys (and girls), gender, pleasures, spaces and bodies in PE.

Looking back, I realise that my research approach/methodology could have been 'critical' to a greater extent. I spent a year with these boys, and although establishing a critical visual participatory research project would have taken more time, it could have generated some additional interesting findings. Despite my attempt to consciously reject the ethnographic tradition of 'observation' and, as demonstrated by the image in Figure 7.1, actively participate in the PE classes and the lives of these boys, I also held back aspects of my own criticality. Could I have involved these boys even more, as a form of critical co-researchers? Cammarota and Fine (2008) suggest that participatory research approaches can achieve this by combining "the acquisition of knowledge on injustice as well as the skills of speaking back and organising change [with] establishing key research questions and methods to answer them" (p. 5). Wright (2004) further suggests that in order to "be active participants in a world characterised by social and cultural diversity, people need to be able to critically engage with that world" (p. 6). Azzarito (2009) argues that teachers can employ PE contexts for this purpose "to resist not only the control of the body, but also the control of the soul, the suppression of consciousness" (p. 36). Nonetheless, some boys in this study did have their own critical engagement and response to the workings of dominant discourses of gender and disciplinary power in their PE setting. While they did not fully reject PE, they certainly problematised and challenged aspects of it. In this critical task, they employed particular technologies of self to achieve this.

I also struggled throughout this project with ideas of representation. It was evident during both the observations and interviews that the majority of my participating boys derived great joy/enjoyment/pleasure from their participation in PE. For many, their involvement tied to their social networks/peer groups and to their sense of (a masculine) identity beyond school and PE. Their excitement about the games and activities engaged in during PE challenged me to think about my own negativity directed at PE, following what I had read in much of the existing literature on boys, masculinities and PE and based on some of my own teaching experiences/observations. It also, more importantly, resulted in me revising the prime research question to include a focus on pleasure. Reflecting on this, as I am making my final revisions to the book before publication, I strongly believe that it was the boys' own representations/interpretations of their PE pleasures and agency as co-researchers, through the use of participatory visual research approaches, that inevitably led me down that path—a path that I am determined to continue on in future research projects.

I suggest that participatory (visual) research approaches could fruitfully be combined with Foucault's theoretical framework of technologies of the self to provide PE teachers, educators and researchers with a critical pedagogical tool to engage students in socio-critical analyses of their participation in, through and about movement, as promoted by the current HPE curriculum in New Zealand (along with other countries such as Australia and Sweden). A spatially oriented visual analysis can be seen as of particular importance because if we think of space in terms of the ever-shifting geometry of social/power relations, then the spatial is both open to and a necessary element in politics, in the broadest sense of the word (Massey, 1994). As McGregor (2004) points out, "As spatiality is made and remade there is openness for change, finding spaces for a more critical pedagogy and democratic relationship" (p. 368). That is, conducting a spatial analysis may also provide "an active and empowering epistemological tool for challenging existing knowledge/power structures" (Price-Chalita, 1994, p. 236). This, in turn, leads to the capacity of spaces to describe and promote social change. Therein also lies the potential of spatial analyses to "progressively transform the process of creating new knowledges—not just its content or theoretical underpinnings" (Johnson, 2008, p. 568). Indeed, the findings in my study make visible the importance of considering space in sociological inquiries into boys and performances of gender in PE. As a PE researcher, I am therefore interested in the physical spaces that are produced and presented to our boys (and girls), and in accordance with O'Donoghue (2007), I call for further inquiries into what these spaces say about learning and where it occurs and how it occurs. I continue to be interested in devising visual research methods based on Foucault and Butler's work on power and gender, which can lead to research designs that can offer boys and girls more opportunities to critically examine their conditions of (im)possible gender identities. The use of such research approaches might have the potential to improve educative outcomes in PE and serve the public good by enabling more boys (and girls) to experience the excitement of participating in a range of health and movement related contexts and become active and critical consumers of physical culture in our society.

In general, my research supports Andrews's (2000) supposition that "Foucauldian theorizing" (p. 125) is a particularly useful framework for understanding the complex relationships between gender, pleasures, spaces, bodies, subjectivities, lived experiences and power. I believe that Foucauldian thinking can help us continue to reflect on various social practices by raising critical awareness, which may ultimately lead to a transformation of discourses of gender and pleasures in PE. This may enable even more young boys (and girls) to experience the excitement of learning in, through and about movement in PE.

Note

1   New Zealand's National Certificates of Educational Achievement (NCEA) are national qualifications for senior secondary school students.

References

Allen, L., & Carmody, M. (2012). 'Pleasure has no passport': Re-visiting the potential of pleasure in sexuality education. *Sex Education: Sexuality, Society and Learning, 12*(4), 455–468.

Andrews, D. L. (2000). Posting up: French post-structuralism and the critical analysis of contemporary sporting culture. In J. Coakley & E. Dunning (Eds.), *Handbook of sport studies* (pp. 106–137). Thousand Oaks, CA: Sage.

Arnold, P. J. (1979). *Meaning in movement, sport and physical education*. London, UK: Heinemann.

Atkinson, M., & Kehler, M. (2010). Boys, gyms, locker rooms and heterotopia. In M. Kehler & M. Atkinson (Eds.), *Boys' bodies: Speaking the unspoken* (pp. 73–90). New York: Peter Lang.

Azzarito, L. (2009). The panopticon of physical education: Pretty, active and ideally white. *Physical Education and Sport Pedagogy, 14,* 19–40.

Azzarito, L., & Solomon, M. A. (2005). A reconceptualisation of physical education: The intersection of gender/race/social class. *Sport, Education and Society, 10*(1), 25–47.

Bain, L. (1985). The hidden curriculum re-examined. *Quest, 37,* 145–153.

Bain, L. (1990). A critical analysis of the hidden curriculum in physical education. In D. Kirk & R. Tinning (Eds.), *Physical education, curriculum and culture: Critical issues in contemporary crisis* (pp. 23–42). Basingstoke, UK: Falmer Press.

Barthes, R. (1975). *The pleasure of the text* (R. Miller, Trans.). New York: Noonday Press.

Booth, D. (2009). Politics and pleasure: The philosophy of physical education revisited. *Quest, 61*(2), 133–153.

Bradbury, H. (1989). *The hidden curriculum in physical education.* Dunedin, NZ: Dunedin College of Education.

Burrows, L. (2005). Do the 'right' thing: Chewing the fat in physical education. *Journal of Physical Education New Zealand, 33*(1), 7–16.

Butler, J. (1990). *Gender trouble: Feminism and the subversion of identity.* London and New York: Routledge.

Butler, J. (1993). *Bodies that matter: On the discursive limits of 'sex'.* New York: Routledge.

Butler, J. (2004). *Undoing gender.* New York: Routledge.

Cammarota, J., & Fine, M. (2008). Youth participatory action research: A pedagogy for transformational resistance. In J. Cammarota & M. Fine (Eds.), *Revolutionizing education: Youth participatory action research in motion* (pp. 1–12). New York: Routledge.

Clarke, G. (2006). Sexuality and physical education. In D. Kirk, D. Macdonald, & M. O'Sullivan (Eds.), *The handbook of physical education* (pp. 723–739). London, UK: Routledge.

Coakley, J. (1994). *Sport in society: Issues and controversies.* London, UK: Mosby.

Connell, R. W. (2005). *Masculinities* (2nd ed.). Cambridge, UK: Polity Press.

Davison, K. G. (2000). Boys' bodies in school: Physical education. *The Journal of Men's Studies, 8*(2), 255–266.

Derrida, J. (1976). *Of grammatology* (G. C. Spivak, Trans.). Baltimore, MD: Johns Hopkins University Press.

Derrida, J. (1996). Remarks on deconstruction and pragmatism. In Ch. Mouffe (Ed.), *Deconstruction and pragmatism* (pp. 77–88). New York and London: Routledge.

Drummond, M. (2003). The meaning of boys' bodies in physical education. *The Journal of Men's Studies, 11*(2), 131–143.

Epstein, D., & Johnson, R. (1998). *Schooling sexualities.* Buckingham, UK: Open University Press.

Fernandez-Balboa, J.-M. (1993). Socio-cultural characteristics of the hidden curriculum in physical education. *Quest, 45*(2), 230–254.

Fine, M. (1988). Sexuality, schooling, and adolescent females: The missing discourse of desire. *Harvard Educational Review, 58*(1), 29–54.

Fitzclarence, L., & Hickey, C. (2001). Real footballers don't eat quiche: Old narratives in new times. *Men and Masculinities, 4,* 118–139.

Fitzpatrick, K. (2013). *Critical pedagogy, physical education and urban schooling.* New York: Peter Lang.

Foucault, M. (1972). *The archaeology of knowledge and discourse on language* (1st American ed.). New York: Pantheon Books.

Foucault, M. (1978). *The history of sexuality, volume one.* Harmondsworth, UK: Penguin.

Foucault, M. (1980). *Power/knowledge: Selected interviews and other writings, 1972–1977.* New York: Pantheon.

Foucault, M. (1983). On the genealogy of ethics: An overview of work in progress. In H. L. Dreyfus & P. Rabinow (Eds.), *Michel Foucault: Beyond structuralism and hermeneutics* (2nd ed., pp. 229–252). Chicago, IL: University of Chicago Press.

Foucault, M. (1985). *The use of pleasure: The history of sexuality, volume 2.* London, UK: Penguin Books.

Foucault, M. (1988a). Technologies of the self. In L. H. Martin, H. Gutman, & P. H. Hutton (Eds.), *Technologies of the self: A seminar with Michel Foucault* (pp. 16–49). Amherst, MA: University of Massachusetts Press.

Foucault, M. (1988b). The ethic of care for the self as a practice of freedom: An interview with Michel Foucault on January 20, 1984. In J. Bernauer & D. Rasmussen (Eds.), *The final Foucault* (pp. 1–20). Cambridge, MA: The MIT Press.

Foucault, M. (1995). *Discipline and punish: The birth of the prison.* Westminster, MD: Vintage.

Francis, B. (2010). Re/theorising gender: Female masculinity and male femininity in the classroom? *Gender and Education, 22*(5), 477–490.

Gard, M. (2001). Dancing around the 'problem' of boys and dance. *Discourse: Studies in the Cultural Politics of Education, 22*(2), 213–225.

Gard, M. (2003). Moving and belonging: Dance, sport and sexuality. *Sex Education, 3*(2), 105–118.

Gard, M. (2008). When a boy's gotta dance: New masculinities, old pleasures. *Sport, Education and Society, 13*(2), 181–193.

Gregson, N., & Rose, G. (2000). Taking Butler elsewhere: Performativities, spatialities and subjectivities. *Environment and Planning D: Society and Space, 18,* 422–452.

Grosz, E. (1994). *Volatile bodies: Toward a corporeal feminism.* Bloomington, IN: Indiana University Press.

Hawkins, A. (2008). Pragmatism, purpose, and play: Struggle for the soul of physical education. *Quest, 60,* 345–356.

Hickey, C. (2008). Physical education, sport and hyper-masculinity in schools. *Sport, Education and Society, 13*(2), 147–161.

Jackson, S. (1996). Heterosexuality as a problem for feminist theory. In L. Adkins & V. Merchant (Eds.), *Sexualising the social: Power and the organisation of sexuality* (pp. 15–34). London, UK: Macmillan.

Jamieson, K. (2003). Occupying a middle space: Toward a mestiza sport studies. *Sociology of Sport Journal, 20*(1), 1–16.

Johnson, L. C. (2008). Re-placing gender? Reflections on 15 years of gender, place and culture. *Gender, Place & Culture, 15*(6), 561–574.

Kehily, M. J. (2002). *Sexuality, gender and schooling: Shifting agendas in social learning.* London, UK: Routledge Falmer.

Kirk, D. (2010). *Physical education futures.* London, UK: Routledge.

Knoppers, A., & McDonald, M. (2010). Scholarship on gender and sport in sex roles and beyond. *Sex Roles, 63*(5/6), 311–323.

Lloyd, M. (1996). A feminist mapping of Foucauldian politics. In S. Hekman (Ed.), *Feminist interpretations of Michel Foucault* (pp. 241–264). University Park, PA: Pennsylvania State University Press.

Locke, L. (1996). Dr. Lewin's little liver patties: A parable about encouraging healthy lifestyles. *Quest, 48,* 422–431.

Mac an Ghaill, M. (1994). *The making of men: Masculinities, sexualities and schooling.* Buckingham, UK: Open University Press.

Malson, H. M. (1997). Anorexic bodies and the discursive production of feminine excess. In J. Ussher (Ed.), *Body talk: The material and discursive regulation of sexuality, madness, and reproduction* (pp. 223–245). New York: Routledge.

Markula, P. (2003). The technologies of the self: Sport, feminism, and Foucault. *Sociology of Sport Journal, 20,* 87–107.

Markula, P. (2004). 'Tuning into one's self': Foucault's technologies of the self and mindful fitness. *Sociology of Sport Journal, 21*(3), 302–321.

Markula, P., & Pringle, R. (2006). *Foucault, sport and exercise: Power, knowledge and transforming the self.* New York: Routledge.

Massey, D. (1994). *Space, place and gender.* Cambridge, UK: Polity Press.

McGregor, J. (2004). Spatiality and the place of the material in schools. *Pedagogy, Culture and Society, 12*(3), 347–372.

Morgan, W. (2006). Philosophy and physical education. In D. Kirk, M. O'Sullivan, & D. MacDonald (Eds.), *The handbook of research in sport and physical education* (pp. 97–108). Thousand Oaks, CA: Sage.

O'Donoghue, D. (2007). 'James always hangs out here': Making space for place in studying masculinities at school. *Visual Studies, 22*(1), 62–73.

Parker, A. (1996). The construction of masculinity within boys' physical education. *Gender and Education, 8*(2), 141–158.

Pascoe, C. J. (2007). *Dude, you're a fag: Masculinity and sexuality in High School.* Los Angeles, CA: University of California Press.

Pink, S. (2007). *Doing visual ethnography.* London, UK: Sage.

Piotrowski, S. (2000). The concept of equal opportunities in physical education with reference to gender equality. In S. Capel & S. Piotrowski (Eds.), *Issues in physical education* (pp. 25–46). London, UK: Routledge Falmer.

Price-Chalita, P. (1994). Spatial metaphor and the politics of empowerment: Mapping a place for feminism and postmodernism in geography? *Antipode, 26*(3), 236–254.

Pringle, R. (2003). *Doing the damage? An examination of masculinities and men's rugby experiences of pain, fear and pleasure* (Unpublished PhD thesis). The University of Waikato, Hamilton, NZ.

Pringle, R. (2009). Defamiliarizing heavy-contact sports: A critical examination of rugby, discipline, and pleasure. *Sociology of Sport Journal, 26,* 211–234.

Pringle, R. (2010). Finding pleasure in physical education: A critical examination of the educative value of positive movement affects. *Quest, 62,* 119–134.

Pringle, R., & Hickey, C. (2010). Negotiating masculinities via the moral problematization of sport. *Sociology of Sport Journal, 27*(2), 115–138.

Pringle, R., & Markula, P. (2005). No pain is sane after all: A Foucauldian analysis of masculinities and men's rugby experiences. *Sociology of Sport Journal, 22*(4), 472–497.

Rintala, J. (2009). It's all about the -ing. *Quest, 61*(3), 279–288.

Rose, G. (2007). *Visual methodologies: An introduction to the interpretation of visual materials.* London, UK: Sage.

Skelton, A. (1997). Studying hidden curricula: Developing a perspective in the light of postmodern insights. *Curriculum Studies, 5*(2), 177–195.

Skelton, C., & Francis, B. (2003). *Boys and girls in the primary classroom.* Maidenhead, UK: Open University Press.

Sparkes, A. (1991). Towards understanding, dialogue, and polyvocality in the research community: Extending the boundaries of the paradigm debate. *Journal of Teaching in Physical Education, 10*(2), 103–133.

Stothart, B. (2005). Nine strikes and you're out: New Zealand physical education in crisis? *Journal of Physical Education New Zealand, 38*(1), 95–102.

Stoudt, B. (2006).'You're either in or you're out': School violence, peer discipline, and the (re)production of hegemonic masculinity. *Men and Masculinities, 8,* 273–287.

Thorpe, H. (2008). Foucault, technologies of self, and the media: Discourses of femininity in snowboarding culture. *Journal of Sport and Social Issues, 32*(2), 199–229.

Vernon, M. (2008). *Wellbeing.* Stocksfield, UK: Acumen.

Wellard, I. (2012). Body-reflexive pleasures: Exploring bodily experiences within the context of sport and physical activity. *Sport, Education and Society, 17*(1), 21–33.

Whelen, J. (2011). *Boys and their schooling: The experience of becoming someone else.* New York: Routledge.

Willis, P. E. (1977). *Learning to labour: How working class kids get working class jobs.* Farnborough, UK: Saxon House.

Wright, J. (2004). Post-structural methodologies: The body, schooling and health. In J. Evans, B. Davies, & J. Wright (Eds.), *Body knowledge and control: Studies in the sociology of physical education and health* (pp. 19–31). London, UK: Routledge.

Afterword

It has now been more than five years since I completed my fieldwork at Kea College. Despite some school and PE staffing changes, the underpinning philosophies and beliefs surrounding boys' education continue to hold strong.

The long-standing principal Mr Andersson has now retired and a new principal has been appointed, Mr Adams, who for many years was the deputy principal. Although he is much younger than his predecessor and some of the teachers describe his 'management style' as 'a bit different', according to the new official school prospectus and website, he seems to embody the same values and beliefs as Mr Andersson. Sporting excellence, for instance, holds an even more prominent position in the somewhat revised school prospectus, which now also includes a whole page devoted to the Kea College 'Old Boys' who have gone on to sporting fame in New Zealand and internationally.

Shortly after I left Kea College, Mr Whyte left his role as HoD of PE and worked full time as a teacher of information and communication technology (ICT)/computer programming, something he showed a passion for when I was at Kea College (see chapter four). About two years ago he was recruited by a prestigious school in the south of New Zealand to head their new ICT/computer programming programme. What prompted Mr Whyte to leave Kea College one can only speculate about, but he clearly has a real interest and skill in computer programming. Maybe this was incompatible with his role as the HoD of PE and instrumental person in the First XV rugby team at Kea College. As I am writing this, I am planning on talking to Mr Whyte about this shift in location and career.

The new HoD, Mr Smith, is one of my former PETE students who, when we met for a coffee near the publication of this book, told me that the new principal Mr Adams has emphasized the importance of PE and the school continues to be one of the few in the country that keep PE compulsory through to year 13.

When Mr Smith was appointed to the HoD by the former principal Mr Anderson, he received specific instructions to 'tighten up the practices' of PE, which he thought had become 'a bit too slack'. This included being stricter on wearing of the correct PE uniform, being on time and 'participat-ing fully' in the lesson.

The content and practices of PE are, according to Mr Smith, very similar to the content and practices in 2010, with the year divided into different terms/seasons where different sports and other physical/fitness activities are used to partly accomplish the goals set out in the curriculum. In an effort to involve the students more, Mr Smith says they decide what sports and activities they should be doing as they get older. Drawing on some ideas from Daryl Siedentop's sport education model, the PE classes divide them-selves into different teams and organise tournaments for each sport. They even have a trophy for the winning team at the end of each sporting season.

One new thing they have added, Mr Smith says, is 'ultimate warrior', a game loved by the boys since 'boys love those kind of terms'.

The 10–15 minute warmups/fitness segment at the beginning of each lesson (see chapter five) still also plays an important role, according to Mr Smith. For the older students, the year is also divided into four different terms; students work on one of four fitness components—aerobic, muscu-lar, flexibility and agility—in each term. Knowing and understanding these different components are important to students' recognition of the need for them in their' ongoing lives as physically active and healthy, Mr Smith says.

In addition to this 'core PE', more and more students are electing to have PE as an 'academic subject' that counts toward their final NCEA credits used for university entrance in New Zealand. The school and its new HoD of PE also strongly encourage the boys to do 'PE scholarship', an extra study option that potentially leads to both academic and monetary rewards. The year 12 students who are enrolled in this programme also get their school tuitions waived by the school. Interestingly enough, these kinds of PE scholarships, typically in the form of an academic essay or research project report, need to address both bio-physical and socio-cultural issues related to physical activity and health. At the time of writing, the school has 12 students undertaking PE scholarships, which, according to Mr Smith, is both encouraging and time consuming since he needs to help these students in addition to his normal workload.

Mr Smith himself is also pursuing his passion for education, teaching and leadership by doing masters studies. But due to his extra responsibilities at the school and some time spent overseas, he 'is making slow progress'.

As I am trying to make sense of the broader school culture and PE prac-tices at a school like Kea College, it is clear to me that the notions associated with how best to provide for boys' education remain much the same. Tra-ditional ideas about what boys should be and like doing as they grow into young adult men is perpetuated by school policies, philosophies, spaces, teacher, staff, administrator and is ultimately materialised through boys and their bodies. At the same time, these seemingly traditional and conserva-tive ideas continue to be associated with success, leadership, enjoyment and various forms of (masculine) pleasures that appear to overshadow any concerns for the marginalisation of other possible bodies and identities.

With these tensions in mind, I am more determined than ever to keep researching school cultures, educational policies and PE practices as they connect with boys' (and girls') development of healthy, well-educated and physically active identities that can contribute to equality and social justice in our society.

Index

186–8; and physical education
as socio-cultural construct 9–11;
power/knowledge relations and
20; problematisations of pleasures
and 189–92; social construction of
21–3; spaces of performing 33–40;
stereotypes 29; theoretical framework
16; why study boys PE and 6–9
general politics of truth 121
Gieryn, T. 34
Glasby, T. 163
González-Cutre, D. 42
governmentality 144
Green, J. L. 65
Green, K. 116–17
Gregson, N. 38–9, 184
Griffin, P. 114
Grosz, E. 26, 33, 39
Guba, E. G. 4–5

Hall, S. 121
Harré, R. 20
Harrison, L. 29
Harvey, D. 91
Haywood, C. 68
*Health and Physical Education in the
New Zealand Curriculum* 10
healthism 34, 45
hegemonic masculinity 16, 21–2
heteronormativity 21, 33, 91,
163–4
heterotopia 35
Hickey, C. 21–2, 198
History of Sexuality (Foucault) 42
Holland, J. 80
Howes, A. 66

identities, normalisation of 20–1, 188
inductive analysis 80
instrumental goals 44–6
intervention aspect of PE 8–9
interviews: conducting the 77–9; data
analysis of 79–80; individual 76–7;
probing 66; *see also* ethnography

Jackson, S. 188
Jones, A. 17

Kaplan, I. 66
Kea College as research setting 67–70
Kearney, M. 65–6
Kehler, Michael 7, 26, 32, 34–5
Kirk, D. 8–11, 19, 114, 130, 196

knowledge/power relations 20
Kretchmar, R. S. 45–6, 48, 113, 161

landscape of fear 105
Larsson, H. 30, 32, 111
Lincoln, Y. S. 4–5, 63
Lindisfarne, N. 19
Lloyd, M. 141
Locke, L. 133

Mac an Ghaill, M. 68, 79, 97, 198
Macdonald, D. 29, 37–8
Markula, P. 28–30, 37, 141, 192
masculinising of spaces 34–6, 96–102
masculinity: bodies and 23–33;
examination of pleasurable masculine
bodies and 168–75; hegemonic
16, 21–2; heteronormative 21,
33, 91, 163–4; hypermasculinised
sports in PE and 7; performed in
PE 5, 33; and physical education as
(gendered) socio-cultural construct
9–11, 96–102; privileged 25–6; and
production of masculine (dis)pleasures
through games 134–43; rugby as
"glue" of masculine (dis)pleasures
and 143–50
Massey, D. 92
material body 30–3
materialisation of bodies 30–3, 38,
154
McCaughtry, N. 37–8
McGregor, J. 203
Meyenn, R. 47–8
Michael, S. 80
Millington, B. 22
Mitchell, R. 10
modes of subjectivation 128, 189
Moreno, J. A. 42
Morgan, W. 192
movement pleasures 44–6, 91
multiple and hierarchically ordered
masculinities 21–3

neurotransmitters 42
New Zealand Curriculum 10, 45
*New Zealand Journal of Health, Physical
Education and Recreation* 10
Nietzsche, F. 43
normalisation of identities 20–1, 188

observation, participant 70–2
O'Connor, M. C. 80

For Product Safety Concerns and Information please contact our EU
representative GPSR@taylorandfrancis.com
Taylor & Francis Verlag GmbH, Kaufingerstraße 24, 80331 München, Germany

www.ingramcontent.com/pod-product-compliance
Lightning Source LLC
Chambersburg PA
CBHW050606280326
41932CB00037B/2056